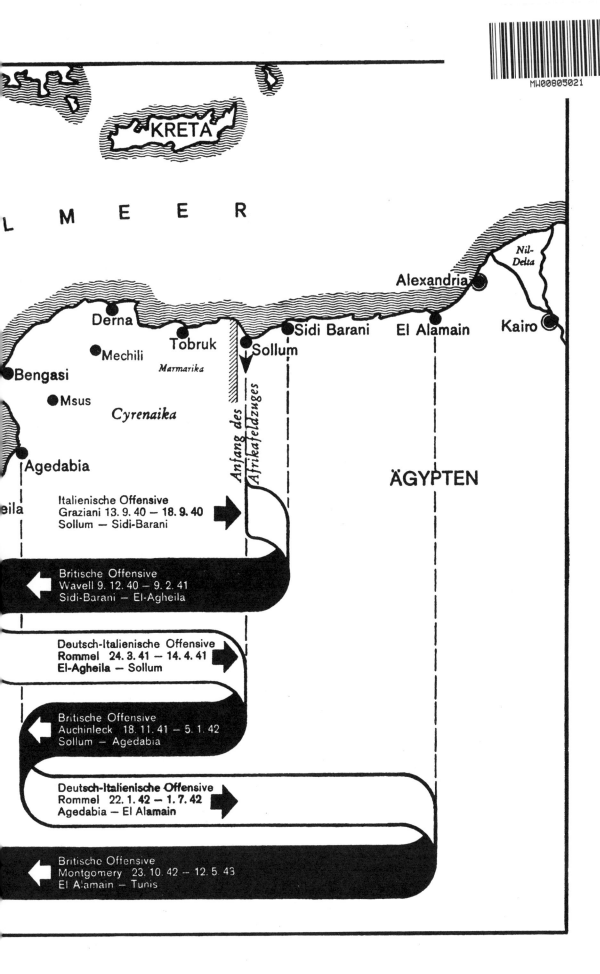

KRETA

L M E E R

Nil-Delta

Alexandria

Derna

Sidi Barani

El Alamain

Kairo

Mechili

Tobruk

Sollum

Bengasi

Marmarika

Msus

Cyrenaika

Agedabia

Anfang des Afrikafeldzuges

ÄGYPTEN

eila

Italienische Offensive
Graziani 13. 9. 40 – 18. 9. 40
Sollum – Sidi-Barani

Britische Offensive
Wavell 9. 12. 40 – 9. 2. 41
Sidi-Barani – El-Agheila

Deutsch-Italienische Offensive
Rommel 24. 3. 41 – 14. 4. 41
El-Agheila – Sollum

Britische Offensive
Auchinleck 18. 11. 41 – 5. 1. 42
Sollum – Agedabia

Deutsch-Italienische Offensive
Rommel 22. 1. 42 – 1. 7. 42
Agedabia – El Alamain

Britische Offensive
Montgomery 23. 10. 42 – 12. 5. 43
El Alamain – Tunis

ROMMEL IN THE DESERT

Volkmar Kühn

ROMMEL

IN THE DESERT

Schiffer
Military
History

Victories & Defeat of the Afrika-Korps 1941-1943

Translated from the German by David Johnston

CONTENTS

Foreword

When the *Afrika-Korps* Society has its first nationwide meeting at Rosenheim, Upper Bavaria, from October 1-4, 1991, it will have four good reasons to celebrate and to reflect.

For the first time it has the privilege of celebrating along with old comrades from the former DDR (East Germany), and to get together again in a free, united Germany.

Forty years have passed since, On July 8, 1951, veterans of the *Afrika-Korps* Society, under the leadership of General of the Panzer Troops Ludwig Crüwell and General of the Cavalry Siegfried Westphal, the painter of African subjects, Wilhelm Wessels, Ernst Drawert and General of the Panzer Troops Hans-Karl Baron von Esebeck, held the founding meeting in Iserlohn.

Two months later the first nationwide meeting took place. On December 1 of this founding year, the old field newspaper of the *Afrika-Korps* - The Oasis — which had been brought to life by Field Marshal Rommel, was published in new form. Its editor was — how could it have been otherwise — an old African veteran: Colonel (retired) Irnfried, Baron von Wechmar, the well-known commander of the legendary Reconnaissance Unit 3, better known by the honorary title of "The Masters of the Forefield."

From this time on, a nationwide meeting or workshop took place every year, at various sites. Very soon our former enemies, but also our comrades in the desert, the Austrians and Italians, also attended. Veterans of the British 8th Army, and particularly the 7th Panzer Division "Desert Rats", wanted to attend, if the "Desert Foxes" would allow. They were followed by Canadians, South Africans and New Zealanders. Foes became friends. Comradeship has a fluidity that people who were not soldiers at the front cannot understand. Shared times of need, dangers endured together, memories of mutual helpfulness, and especially of that help that an enemy gave one, often at risk of his own life, formed stronger bonds than all traditional friend-foe cliches.

General of the Panzer Troops Crüwell, as First Chairman, and Mrs. Lucie-Maria Rommel as honorary member, characterized the society. So too did General of the Cavalry (retired) Westphal, who became the presiding officer of the society in September of 1958. One year later he was named President of the Ring of German Soldier Organizations.

The other honorary members, *Generaloberst* (retired) Jürgen von Arnim, the last commander of the *Armeegruppe Afrika* Field Marshal Albert Kesselring, and General of the Panzer Troops (retired) von Esebeck soon left us. But one thing was clear to every African veteran: These old soldiers did not die. They simply departed from us. They live on in our hearts!

For 24 years Siegfried Westphal, Chief of the General Staff for three field marshals and "Conscience of the Army", directed the society and represented it worthily in the whole world. It was he who took up and carried out the idea of erecting a monument to the German Army, over which the words appear:

TO THE DEAD OF THE GERMAN ARMY - Their Legacy
Peace

The undersigned, who had the honor of editing Rommel's field newspaper for ten years, had the opportunity to speak with all the veterans. True comradeship linked him with General Westphal. General of the Panzer Troops (retired) Walther K. Nehring also shared with him the efforts to present a complete picture of the action and the dedication of the German panzer troops.

When the "Unity of Fate" of the *Afrika-Korps* now meets again in Rosenheim for its 40th anniversary, then its thoughts will turn to its old theater of war, the extent and emptiness of which was an ideal field for tank battles, and also to its deceased comrades, as well as its brave, fair opponents, who have never denied the *Afrika-Korps* their recognition.

50 Years Ago the War in Africa Began

When "only" in the year of 1941 German troops went to Africa to offer help and support to their Italian allies, this had its particular circumstances. In and of itself, the command to transfer the 3rd Panzer Division to Africa was already made on October 14, 1940. But on October 17, *Generalmajor* Thoma arrived from Africa and reported on the situation there — a report which he presented, on the 24th of that month, to the Chief of the General Staff, *Generaloberst* Halder.

Here is an important thought of Thoma's: "In the event that German troops are sent to Africa, it must be a Panzer troop of at least four divisions. Fewer would be senseless, and more would simply be a mistake, because more than four divisions could not be supplied during their march straight across the desert to the Nile Delta."

This remark from his report was to prove bitterly true.

While the British troops' victory march against the Italian forces in Africa went on, wiping out or capturing the entire 10th Italian Army on December 16, 1940, and the Western Desert Force under General Richard O'Connor reached Bardia, the Italian High Command's cry for help reached the Führer's headquarters on December 19.

The first help sent was the X. Flying Corps, part of which — 100 bombers and 20 pursuit planes — was sent to Sicily and prepared there to fly missions to Africa. In the course of the next few weeks, some 300 additional aircraft of all kinds joined them. Among them were 30 Ju 52 planes, which were to take over transport duties.

Only on January 11, 1941 did the Operations Department of the Army High Command give orders to assemble German forces for service in Libya. The meeting between Hitler and Mussolini at Berchtesgaden on January 19, 1941 resulted in Italy's "grateful acceptance of the offer of the 5th Light Division."

Meanwhile a second observer, *Generalmajor* Hans Baron von Funck, returned from Africa on February 1, 1941. He reported that a German barrage unit, such as the 5th Light Division, could not be in a position to prevent a catastrophe in Africa and stop the British advance. Derna had fallen to the British on January 30, Barce and Bardia had been torn away from the Italians.

On February 3, 1941 Hitler declared that he was ready to send a Panzer division to Africa in addition to the 5th Light Division. First, though, the X. Flying Corps had to stop the enemy.

When Field Marshal Keitel announced the final instructions on February 6, it became clear that the German barrage unit was being subordinated to a German general command.

Hitler summoned *Generalmajor* Rommel to the Führer's headquarters. There he was informed by Field Marshal von Brauchitsch that he was to take over an army corps as its commanding general and go to Africa with it.

Rommel in the Desert reports on the ensuing battles in the desert, from the first meeting of the troops of the two sides to May 12, 1943, when the shooting stopped in Tunisia — to the last day of a 27-month struggle that cost great losses on both sides, and left behind neither victors nor vanquished, but only the beaten.

No one knows more about the reality of this last sentence than the participants in that struggle in the desert. They made the sacrifices, they were wounded, died, and were mourned in their homeland. And they know better than anyone else that every war leaves only the beaten behind.

HONOR THEIR MEMORY!

Volkmar Kühn   June 1991

Prelude to the African Campaign

The history of the African Campaign began on June 11, 1940. On that day Italy declared war on England and France. By this time France had already been smashed by the Wehrmacht. Taking advantage of this situation, Mussolini decided to attack his western neighbor in hopes of obtaining a share of the war booty.

The rapid French capitulation upset Mussolini's plans. Hitler was not prepared to accept the demands of his ally, who wanted parts of Nice and Corsica and planned to swallow up all of Tunisia as well as parts of Algeria. Hitler categorically rejected Mussolini's demands on June 18, 1940.

Germany concluded an honorable peace with France. The French Fleet remained under French control and France was allowed to keep her colonies.

Once France had been defeated discussions began in the Armed Forces High Command, as well as in the branches of the armed forces, as to how the war was to be pursued. A plan was submitted by *Generalmajor* Alfred Jodl. In a memorandum dated June 30, 1940 he suggested that there were two possible ways of defeating England. The first was an immediate attack across the channel, the second a series of campaigns at the edges and outer bastions of the British Empire.

Hitler seemed inclined toward Operation "Sea Lion," an invasion of England, but he vacillated. *Generalfeldmarschall* von Brauchitsch doubted that the island could be taken. Therefore, on July 30 he presented a second plan, in which the main effort of the war against England would take place in the Mediterranean region.

As Commander-in-Chief of the Army, *Feldmarschall* von Brauchitsch used the July 31 daily situation briefing to propose sending a German expeditionary force to Africa to support an upcoming Italian operation against Egypt.

Following some discussion, *Generalmajor* Jodl, in his capacity as Chief of the Armed Forces Operations Staff of the OKH, invited the army and air force representatives to a discussion in the Reich Chancellery. He informed those present that Hitler intended to commit strong forces to Africa.

In order to assess the situation in Africa, the Chief of the Army General Staff, *Generaloberst* Halder, sent the commander of the 3rd Panzer Division on a fact-finding mission to North Africa. *Generalmajor* Wilhelm Ritter von Thoma was instructed to find the best way to ship the troops to Africa *and* ascertain where they should be placed to best support the Italian campaign there.

The Italian offensive in Libya began on September 13. Six Italian divisions and eight armored battalions rolled over the weak British frontier defences. The advance reached Sidi Barani where the Italian divisions halted to wait for supplies. The Italian forces had been fighting for three days, and after winning 80 kilometres of ground they went not one meter farther.

When Hitler met Mussolini at the Brenner Pass on October 3, 1940, Mussolini promised to resume the offensive in North Africa by October 15. Hitler promised to send 100 tanks and a large number of vehicles.

On 14 October orders for the 3rd Panzer Division

to move to Africa were ready. Three days later *Generaloberst* Halder received *Generalmajor* von Thoma's report. When von Thoma reported back to Halder on October 24 and gave his verbal report, he concluded with the words:

"In the event that German units were to be sent to Africa, it should be an armored force of at least four divisions. Fewer would be senseless, because a smaller contingent would have no success. More would be equally wrong, because a drive across the desert to the Nile Delta by more than four divisions could not be supplied."

Mussolini had already undertaken another gamble when, on October 28, 1940, he marched into Greece from Albania. He was hoping for a quick success, but the Greeks soon demonstrated their superiority. The Italian troops were driven back into Albania. In consideration of these facts the following plan for Libya was revealed in *Führerbefehl* Number 18 of November 12, 1940:

"Employment of German forces in North Africa will not take place until the Italians have taken Marsa Matruk. The army is directed to hold a panzer division in readiness for North Africa, marine authorities are to equip and hold ready suitable transport ships with which troops and supplies can be shipped to North Africa. The air force is to direct its preparations toward attacks against Alexandria and the Suez Canal."

On December 10 all affected Luftwaffe commands received the plan for special operation *"Mittelmeer"* (Mediterranean). The directions stated:

"The most important target is the British Fleet, especially in the main harbor of Alexandria. An additional objective is sea traffic in the Suez Canal and the Straits of Sicily."

By December 6 the British had concentrated their forces for a counteroffensive. The Seventh Armored Division under Major General O'More Creagh and the Fourth Indian Division under Major General Beresford-Peirse attacked at first light on December 9. They pushed through a gap in the south of the Italian front and then stormed westward in a sweeping enveloping maneuver before turning north toward the coast and closing the sack. Sidi Barani, Nibeiewa and Buq-Bug fell. On 12 December the British Army communiqué stated:

"We have taken 20,000 prisoners with tanks, guns and equipment."

Sollum fell on December 16 and with this city the Halfaya Pass also came into British hands. The next objectives were Capuzzo, Sidi Omar and Musaid. Bardia was surrounded.

By December 16 the Italian Tenth Army had been destroyed and the British Western Desert Force under Major General Richard O'Connor had chased the Italians back to Bardia. On December 19 the Italian High Command sent a call for help to Hitler.

Meanwhile, four Italian divisions were standing ready to defend Bardia. One division was holding Tobruk. Agedabia was the central strongpoint for a further division and four divisions were waiting in Tripoli to meet the expected British offensive.

At the end of December the X. *Fliegerkorps* under *Generalleutnant* Geisler, with 100 He 111 and Ju 88 bombers, as well as Ju 87 dive bombers and 20 fighters, set out for Africa. In total, two-hundred aircraft arrived in Sicily. They were followed later by three-hundred more. The assignment given the *Fliegerkorps* was as follows:

"Attack British convoys in the Mediterranean, British supply traffic in the Suez Canal and hinder the advance of the British Army into Libya." Later was added: "Protect sea transport taking the German *Afrika-Korps* from Italy to Tripoli."

A *Gruppe* of thirty Ju 52 transport aircraft was kept ready to fly important contingents to Africa.

While, on January 4, 1941, a report to the German OKW by Italian General Guzzoni still spoke of Bardia holding out against the enemy for some time, soldiers of the Australian Division had already captured the town. On the following day the British Seventh Armored Division reached El Adem, placing it south of Tobruk.

On January 9, 1941 Hitler ordered all staff officers concerned with the Africa plan to the Reich Chancellery. During the discussion he explained:

"It is important that the Italians not lose Libya. If that happened, the English troops there would be free for employment elsewhere. Moreover, the psychological effects of the loss would weigh much heavier than the loss itself.

Italy must be helped. It is important to send a German armored blocking unit to Libya. This blocking unit must stop the English advance and carry out local counterattacks against the enemy's weak points."

On January 11, 1941 the Operations Section of

the OKH issued instructions for the assembly of German forces for action in Libya. All of the smaller units were to be recruited from the 3rd Panzer Division.

On January 15 an advance staff of the OKH travelled to North Africa. *Generalmajor* Hans Freiherr von Funck, commander of the 3rd Panzer Division, who was to command the newly-formed blocking unit in North Africa, arrived in Tripoli on the same day to explore the situation there for himself. The 3rd PD made available the 5th Panzer-Regiment, the oldest of all panzer regiments. In addition there was First Battalion, 75th Artillery Regiment, the 39th Anti-tank Battalion and the 3rd Reconnaissance Battalion. From these units *Oberstleutnant* Graf von Schwerin formed the 5th Light African Division. General Staff *Oberstleutnant* von dem Borne became the first Chief of Staff of the forming German *Afrika-Korps*.

On January 19, 1941 Hitler and Mussolini again met in Berchtesgaden while Keitel spoke with General Guzzoni. Guzzoni gratefully accepted the offer of the 5th Light Division and declared that transport of the German division across the Mediterranean to the front could begin on February 15.

Tobruk Has Fallen — Libya Is in Danger

On January 20, 1941 aircraft of the Royal Air Force opened the attack on the fortress of Tobruk. The British Fleet joined the bombardment from the sea. By early morning of January 22 the British divisions of the Desert Forces had captured the fortress of Tobruk. 27,000 Italian prisoners went into captivity.

The British units stormed westward in a fast armored advance. Their objective was Derna, over 150 kilometers west of Tobruk. Derna fell on January 30 and on February 1 *Generalmajor* von Funck returned from Africa and reported what he had seen and learned there in front of Hitler, von Brauchitsch, Halder, Jodl and Keitel. Von Funck declared that a German blocking unit would not be in a position to prevent the coming catastrophe. An entire panzer division would be necessary to halt the British advance, even better an entire Army Corps.

At a meeting of all responsible German head-quarters and staff officers on February 3, 1941 at the Berghof, Hitler emphasized that the loss of Libya to the British could not be allowed. He declared that the time had come for the X. *Fliegerkorps* to immediately and effectively strike and halt the enemy with Stuka attacks. The German blocking unit was to be beefed up for an immediate counterattack through the addition of a panzer division.

In the further course of the conference *Feldmarschall* von Brauchitsch advised that a panzer regiment was to be sent to the blocking unit, followed without delay by the remaining elements of a panzer division.

At the close of the conference Hitler ordered the Luftwaffe to immediately examine the possibilities of employing dive-bomber and heavy fighter units in Africa and of subduing Malta from the air.

Meanwhile, in North Africa, Derna had fallen. Cirene fell to the British forces on February 3. Their next objectives were Barce and Benghazi. The shattered Italian forces were in retreat. It was now only a question of time as to when all of Cyrenaica would fall into British hands.

On February 6 Keitel issued the final directive for Operation *"Sonnenblume"* (Sunflower), as the German intervention in North Africa was named. The directive culminated in the announcement that the transport of German forces would begin as quickly as possible *and*, that the force would be placed under the command of a German General.

Rommel Arrives on the Scene

Generalmajor Erwin Rommel, who was on leave at the beginning of February, received word from an adjutant from *Führer* Headquarters that he was to proceed to Berchtesgaden at once.

Rommel arrived in Berchtesgaden on February 6 and reported to the Commander-in-Chief of the Army. *Feldmarschall* von Brauchitsch informed him that he had been appointed commanding general of an army corps which was to consist initially of a blocking unit and a panzer division and was to see action in Africa. It was reckoned that the first German troops would reach Africa in mid-February and that the last elements of the 5th Light Division would arrive in about mid-April. Following them would be the individual units of

*General-
feldmarschall
Erwin Rommel*

the 15th Panzer Division, with the last elements of the division to arrive in the African Theater by the end of May.

In his book *"Krieg ohne Hass"* (War without Hate), Rommel wrote:

"It was planned to put the Italian motorized units in North Africa under my command. I myself was to be under the command of Marshall Graziani."

Generalmajor Rommel reported to Hitler on February 6. Hitler's chief adjutant, *Oberstleutnant* Schmundt, was detailed to escort Rommel while he scouted the terrain in North Africa. On February 7 Rommel also met his Chief-of-Staff, *Oberstleutnant* von der Borne and several officers of his staff. The next day Schmundt, von der Borne, Rommel and several officers of the staff had just assembled to discuss the situation and the decisions which would have to be made when *Feldmarschall* von Brauchitsch arrived and informed Rommel that he had been promoted to *Generalleutnant* by Hitler. Rommel drove to Wiener-Neustadt for a small family gathering. On February 9 he was again in Munich for final discussions with his staff. Following the conference Rommel's staff flew ahead to Rome.

Generalleutnant Rommel, *Oberstleutnent* Schmundt and *Oberstleutnant* von der Borne followed on February 11. That same day they had an interview with Mussolini and General Guzzoni, and in the afternoon they flew to Catania with General Roatta. There Rommel spoke with *Generalleutnant* Geisler, the commanding general of X. *Fliegerkorps.* There Rommel learned that Benghazi had fallen and that the British forces were about to invade Tripolitania. There was nothing there to halt this advance.

Rommel asked Geisler to launch heavy attacks on Benghazi harbor that night and to also attack the British columns at the front at first light on February 12.

The next day Rommel and his party flew to Tripoli. An hour later Rommel was face to face with General Gariboldi, who had taken over command from General Guzzoni, explaining to him that it was his intention to defend Tripolitania at the edge of the Sirte Desert. Rommel and *Oberstleutnant* Schmundt then flew over the battle zone in an He 111. When they returned that evening they found that General Roatta had arrived with orders from the *Duce.* General Gariboldi outlined an advance by the *"Brescia"* and *"Pavia"* Divisions into the Sirte — Buerat area on the following day. The *"Ariete"* Armored Division with its 60 obsolete tanks was to move into the area west of Buerat.

At Rommel's urging the first Italian division was sent in the direction of Sirte on February 14. The first German troops landed in Tripoli Harbor the same day.

Rommel issues orders.

11

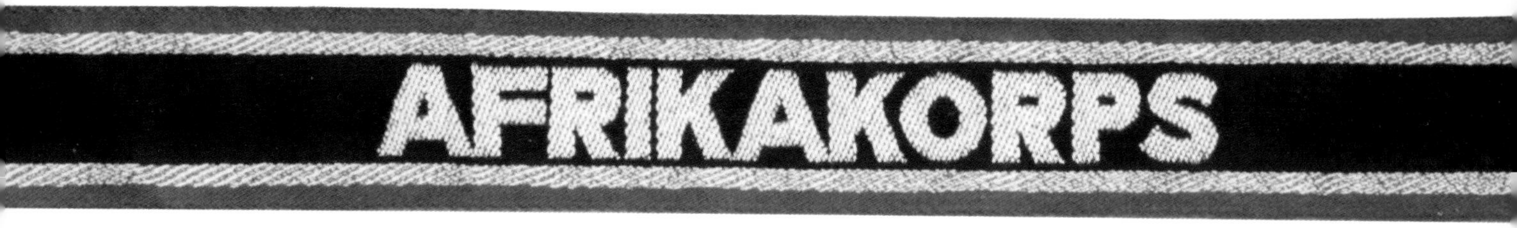
AFRIKAKORPS

The First Battles in Africa

The X. *Fliegerkorps* had been tranferred to Sicily in December 1940. Since attacks against the Suez Canal were of special importance — the majority of British supply traffic for North Africa passed through this waterway — *Major* Harlinghausen, Chief of Staff of X. *Fliegerkorps* and wearer of the Knight's Cross, suggested moving a *Gruppe* of *Kampfgeschwader* 26 to Benghazi. The bombers would use Benghazi as a base for attacks on the canal.

Generalleutnant Geisler agreed, and the 14 available aircraft of II./KG 26 under Knight's Cross wearer *Major* Bertram flew to their new base of operations. Naturally, Harlinghausen went along to Benghazi.

Three machines collided on landing and were lost. The next day three others flew off on reconnaissance missions in the direction of the canal, while the remaining eight stood ready to attack.

A reconnaissance report arrived at noon on January 17 which prompted *Major* Harlinghausen to act at once. The reconnaissance aircraft had sighted a convoy south of the canal sailing on a northward course. *Major* Harlinghausen instructed the eight aircraft commanders:

"While four machines, taking off at half-hour intervals, comb the canal from north to south, the other four will fly in the same manner from south to north. This will guarantee that we locate the convoy."

As the Suez Canal was 1,100 kilometers from Benghazi, fuel economy was of first importance. The most favorable engine speed and best propeller pitch setting were as important as flying at the altitude at which the headwinds were weakest. Harlinghausen personally assumed command of the attack.

A little later the first aircraft took off. At the controls of the lead aircraft was *Hauptmann* Robert Kowalewski. The aircraft carrying the mission commander flew east for four hours before turning a few degrees to the south and arriving over the southern end of the Suez Canal. There it turned north and flew back over the canal. The He 111 passed the Great Bitter Sea, circled it and then flew on after no ships were sighted. The lead aircraft found no targets so it attacked the designated secondary target. All of the other machines were directed to attack secondary targets as no ships had been found.

Harlinghausen had the pilot head south again, although they had scarcely enough fuel. This time they sighted the convoy, which had tied up along shore to avoid passing through the canal by night. They attacked the largest freighter but all bombs missed the target.

The return flight was a test of nerves for the crews of all the aircraft. The meteorologists had advised them to fly at an altitude of 4,000 meters, because the winds were weakest there. However, when the aircraft set course for home at that altitude they encountered strong headwinds. The calculated four hours turned into five. An half-hour later *Hauptmann* Kowalewski began looking for an emergency landing site and finally put the He 111 down on the flat desert in a wheels-up landing. The machine was set on fire and the crew set off on a foot-march towards the north. It was later determined that they were still 280 kilometers

Bf 110

Preparing a reconnaissance aircraft's photographic equipment before a mission.

from Benghazi.

The following day search aircraft spotted the wrecked aircraft. However, it was not until the downed crew had walked three days and nights through the desert that they were found by *Oberleutnant* Wèrner Kaupisch. Kaupisch's machine had been the only one to return safely to Benghazi from the Suez Canal mission. He had noticed the strong headwinds at 4,000 meters and, dropping down to just above the desert, had made it back to base. All of the other aircraft were forced to make emergency landings in the desert.

The first mission in Africa had been less than successful. Two of the He 111 crews forced to land in British territory were taken prisoner. As the front came ever nearer, the few remaining aircraft were forced to fly to airfields farther to the rear. They landed at Castel Benito, Sirte and Arco Philenorum where they were joined at the end of January by the III. *Gruppe* of ZG 26, commanded by *Major* Karl Kaschka. The *Gruppe* flew the twin-engined Bf 110 C heavy fighter.

Arriving at the same time as the heavy fighters were the first Ju 87 dive-bombers of *Stukageschwader* 3. Additional German units arrived and on February 15 the first air combat between German and British aircraft took place, in which a Ju 88 of III./KLG 1 flown by *Leutnant* Grotz was shot down by Flying Officer Saunders.

Three days later 12 Stukas of I./StG 1 attacked British positions near Marsa el Brega. 3 Squadron, RAAF, claimed eight victories; however, most of the Ju 87 dive-bombers escaped with some damage or made forced landings.

The first major air battle over the desert took place a day later. Nine Stukas of II./StG 2 had assembled for an attack on Marsa el Brega when they were discovered by three Hurricanes. One Ju 87 was damaged and was forced to land in the desert, but before the Hurricanes could complete their work several Bf 110s intervened, shooting down two of the British fighters. An He 111 of II./KG 26 was lost over Benghazi.

The Corps Headquarters of the *Deutsche Afrika-Korps* was constituted in mid-February — the German forces in North Africa officially received this designation from *Führer* Headquarters on February 18. Martin Harlinghausen, just promoted to the rank of *Oberstleutnant*, was named X. *Fliegerkorps* liaison officer and operational commander of any units detached from the corps to Africa. Harlinghausen reported to *Generalleutnant* Rommel in Tripoli. A few days later, however, he was recalled for other duties because, on February 20, 1941 the ObdL had created the new position of *"Fliegerführer Afrika."* On the same day *Generalmajor* Stefan Fröhlich was named as the first officer to hold the new position as commander of air forces in Africa. Following *Generalmajor* Fröhlich's arrival in Sirte, *Oberstleutnant* Harlinghausen was named to the position of *Fliegerführer Atlantik."* General Staff *Oberstleutnant* Ernst Knapp became Fröhlich's Ia, *Oberleutnant* Böss was named assistant to the Ia. *Oberleutnant* Ritter von Voigtländer became Ic.

In the meantime, however, the first German troops had landed in North Africa.

A British fighter shot down near Gambut.

With AA 3 in the Desert

The first German units to land in Tripoli were Field Hospital 4/572, Water Columns 800 and 804 and Motor Vehicle Battalion (Workshop) 13. On February 12 *Generalleutnant* Rommel inspected the units in their quarters outside Tripoli. He then flew with his Chief of Staff to Homs, where he inspected an Italian brigade, and subsequently returned to Tripoli, where the first combat units, AA 3 and PzJägAbt. 39, were expected to arrive in the harbor on the evening of 14 February.

AA 3 had been sent to Tripoli aboard the steamer "Saarfeld" as the vanguard of the DAK. The armored reconnaissance unit was at sea for two days and nights. When the ship tied up at the pier in Tripoli Harbor, *Major* Irnfrief von Wechmar, commander of the "Stahnsdorfers," as the unit was known, saw a group of German officers standing there in new tropical uniforms. Only one wore his field-gray tunic. It was a *Generalleutnant* with the *Pour le Mérite* and the Knight's Cross at his throat.

"That's Rommel!" observed *Oberleutnant* Thiel, commander of 1./AA 3, lowering his binoculars. *Major* von Wechmar went ashore and reported to the commanding general. He received the following instructions:

"Wechmar, you must disembark and be ready to march within five hours!"

Work went on without pause throughout the night and, when the sun rose above the horizon on

Shot-down Hawker Hurricane.

February 15, 1941, AA 3 and PzJägAbt. 39 under *Major* Jansa stood in open square formation on the quay, ready to move out. They received their tropical equipment and at 11.00 were bade farewell by *Generalleutnant* Rommel in front of Government House.

With the order "to the vehicles!" the troops mounted up. They rolled past their new commanding general, drove east through the Arab quarter and, following a drive of 26 hours, reached the front lines in Sirte.

The next afternoon, Wechmar and his adjutant, *Oberleutnant* von Fallois, arrived in Sirte. When they jumped down from their vehicle to report to the commander of the *"Pavia"* Division, which was in command there, they were met by *Generalleutnant* Rommel coming out of the lobby of the Desert Hotel.

"Welcome to the desert, Wechmar!" Rommel greeted the battalion commander and, continuing at once, "I have the following assignment for you:
1. Secure the right flank of the *"Pavia"* Division on the hills east of Sirte.
2. Carry out reconnaissance patrols in the direction of Nofilia - el Agheila.
3. Cooperate with the Italian Santa Maria Reconnaissance Battalion, whose commander will be here presently."
In conclusion came one of the rare Rommel compliments:

"Your battalion has marched well. When will it be here?"

"In an hour, *Herr General,*" answered von Wechmar.

"We need a radio call-sign for your battalion, Wechmar. For the time being you're called Tiger!" Rommel smiled briefly and was in position to photograph AA 3 when it arrived. Then he turned to his Chief of Staff.

"The radio message, Borne!"

General Staff *Oberstleutnant* von der Borne had the prepared message sent to the *Führer* Headquarters:

"The first German troops have just reached the front line in Africa!"

AA 3 pitched its tents east of Sirte. Major Marchese Santa Maria, commander of the Italian reconnaissance battalion, arrived and briefed von Wechmar. Both officers understood one another at once.

The next morning *Oberleutnant* von Fallois set out on the first patrol. The objective was Nofilia, 150 kilometers away. The patrol returned without loss after encountering its first African sandstorm — the ghibli.

On the following morning AA 3 with the *Colonna Santa Maria* and the tank hunters under *Major* Jansa set off along the Via Balbia in the direction of Nofilia. En Nofilia was occupied without resistance.

The next patrol sent out by von Wechmar reached the *Arco dei Fileni*, the triumphal arch which spanned the *Via Balbia*. Once again Rommel appeared on the scene:

"Reconnaissance in force toward El Agheila!" he ordered AA 3. Rommel remained with the battalion until lunch time. He had not forgotten to bring a sack of oranges with him. The two reinforced patrols which von Wechmar sent out

The Arco dei Fileni — landmark on the way to the front.

were led by *Oberleutnant* Everth, the commander of the armored reconnaissance company, and *Oberleutnant* Winrich Behr, commander of the motorcycle company.

The first exchange of fire with the enemy took place during the advance, with three British scout cars being destroyed and another damaged. This battle in the morning hours of February 24 was mentioned in the Wehrmacht communiqué of February 26, 1941. It was via this communiqué that the people of Germany first learned of the presence of German troops in the North African Theater:

"In the morning hours of February 24 a German and a British motorized patrol met on the Libyan coast southeast of Agedabia. A number of British vehicles, including several scout cars, were destroyed and several prisoners taken. The German side suffered no losses."

The 5th Light Division and Its Commander

On February 8, 1941 a teletype message from the FHQ reached the 11th Panzer Division in Poland, ordering the commander of the division's PR 15, *Generalmajor* Johannes Streich, to report at once to the Army's Command Group in Wünsdorf for other duties. The message also informed him that he had been awarded the Knight's Cross.

When *Generalmajor* Streich arrived there he was informed by *Generaloberst* Halder of his intended use as commander of the 5th Light Division which was earmarked for Africa.

In the subsequent discussion Halder informed the new division commander that in Africa his division was for the time being only to advance as far as the southernmost point of the Sirte Desert in order to form a barricade there against the British. A further advance would have to wait for the arrival of the 15th Panzer Division which had likewise been ordered to Africa.

On the evening of February 18 *Generalmajor* Streich drove from Berlin to Rome. From there he flew on to Tripoli. On board the aircraft was part of his staff and part of the staff of the Corps Headquarters.

On February 25 Streich arrived in Tripoli, becoming the first division commander of the *Afrika-Korps* to set foot on African soil.

Two days later the 8th Machine-gun Battalion under *Oberstleutnant* Ponath and the rest of the division headquarters arrived in Tripoli by convoy. The soldiers disembarked at 18.30. The ships were unloaded in the early morning hours of February 28 and a short while later the battalion was drawn up for a review by *Generalmajor* Streich and a general of the Italian Army. It was general Gariboldi, successor to Marshal Graziani as Italian commander in the desert.

Afterward the vehicles rolled three abreast over the wide shore road into the camp. There they were loaded and, at 21.00, orders arrived for the advance into the Sirte area.

At 03.00 on March 1 the battalion set off on a path which, for the majority of the men, would

A supply truck burns in the desert.

Knocked-out British tank.

end near Tobruk barely a month and a half later. The drive to Misurata took the troops through Sliten and Homs, past the ruins of Leptis Magna. They reached Sirte and, following a brief rest, continued on toward En Nofilia.

On March 3 the entire unit was moved forward a further 60 kilometers to the *Arco dei Fileni*, which marked the border between Tripolitania and Cyrenaica. Three kilometers farther east the 8th Machine-gun Battalion occupied positions on both sides of the road and to the south of it, facing east and south. The troops now got busy digging in their vehicles and building positions.

On March 1, from his command post at the *Arco dei Fileni*, *Generalmajor* Streich ordered the occupation of the narrow strip of land at Mugtaa. All of the arriving elements of the division established themselves there. The *Colonna Santa Maria* was placed under the command of the 5th Light Division. Other units gradually arrived and the quartermaster of the DAK, *Major* Otto, had to organize supply on small ships along the coast. Because the tanks of PR 5 had not yet arrived, Rommel had the field workshops, which had been set up near Kilometer 5, south of Tripoli, build dummy tanks which were mounted on Volkswagen cars.

Meanwhile, von Wechmar sent patrols to the east and south which pushed far into the forefield, bringing in new reports which helped clarify the situation.

The enemy was standing pat. If Rommel could get the tanks of PR 5 across and assemble them before the next British attack, things wouldn't look too bad. A frontal attack by the enemy could be beaten off easily at the Mugtaa narrows, which had been mined extensively.

Panzer Regiment 5 Arrives!

On March 11 PR 5 disembarked in Tripoli. As a *Major, Generalmajor* Streich had led the regiment's First Battalion in Wünsdorf. With the arrival of the regiment the majority of the 5th Light Division was now on African soil.

On March 15 a mixed German-Italian force led by *Regimentsstab z.b.v.* 200 under *Oberstleutnant* Graf von Schwerin set out on a reconnaissance in force in the direction of Murzuk. Included in the mixed-unit was a platoon from 1./MG 8 and an anti-tank gun platoon from 4./MG 8. Command of this company was assumed by *Oberleutnant* Goedeckemeyer.

At first the force backtracked west along the *Via Balbia* as far as Geddahia. Then it veered south along an old caravan track into the Fezzan desert. Passing through Bug Ngeri, on 16 March the force reached the Hun-Socna area. The patrol stayed two nights in Nun before moving on over the "corrugated steel track" to Sebcha. Finally they reached Murzuk, where the desert track from the north from Misurata intersected the one from the Kufra oasis from the east as well as the southern one from Chad.

After a brief rest the advance continued and, after a 300 kilometer desert drive, El Gatrun was reached. On the following day the patrol turned back. Rommel sent a Ju 88 to meet the desert patrol, landing at the Umm el Araneb oasis, and a short time later a radio message came in from the DAK:

"If the enemy is met, hit him quickly and hard. In any case return with all elements to El Agheila by 1 April."

The patrol had covered more than 2,000 kilometers in the Fezzan desert. It was an unforgettable experience for every man who took part.

On 19 March Rommel flew to *Führer* Headquarters to make his report and receive new instructions. Hitler presented him with the Knight's Cross with Oak Leaves for his actions in France in 1940 while leading the 7th Panzer Division.

From the Commander-in-Chief of the Army Rommel learned that no decisive blow against the English was planned in the foreseeable future. Not until the arrival of the 15th PD was he, Rommel, to attack and destroy the enemy in the Agedabia area. Afterwards, if a favorable opportunity presented itself, Benghazi could be taken.

Rommel replied that the offensive would have to concern more than just Benghazi, rather that all of Cyrenaica would have to be retaken, as the Benghazi area by itself could not be held. In his memoirs he wrote:

"I had little enthusiasm for the intentions of *Feldmarschall* von Brauchitsh and *Generaloberst* Halder to send only limited numbers of troops to Africa and leave the subsequent fate of the theater to chance. We should have taken advantage of the momentary British weakness in the Middle East with all energy to decisively wrest the initiative to our side."

Before Rommel's departure *Generalmajor* Streich had received an order from the commanding general which aimed at the capture of El Agheila.

On March 23 he sent AA 3 on the last patrol to El Agheila and that afternoon came the order to take the town. AA 3 was to capture El Agheila in a surprise attack.

Major von Wechmar called his company commanders together for a conference. He ordered the motorcycle company to advance along the *Via Balbia* as far as it could without being spotted by the British sentries on the wooden tower of the desert fortress. Then it was to veer north and spend the night among the dunes by the sea. At dawn the company was to move toward its objective.

When the morning of March 24, 1941 dawned cold, AA 3 was already advancing towards El Agheila. A radio message from *Oberleutnant* Behr indicated that the motorcyclists were already at the northern edge of the town and were aware of only weak resistance.

"Attack — in you go!" ordered Wechmar by radio.

He himself drove at the head of the main body, while *Oberleutnant* von Fallois moved several tanks forward, and they all charged toward El Agheila. When the battalion reached the town the motorcyclists were already inside and the battalion pennant was waving from the wooden tower.

A little later Rommel, who had returned from Germany on the 21st, appeared. Together with Wechmar and General Staff *Major* Mauser, the Ia of the 5th Light Division, he climbed the tower and issued his next order:

"Our next objective is Marsa el Brega," he said and motioned with a sweeping movement of his hand toward the east, where the desert glistened and flickered in the glare of the midday sun.

AA 3 was not to take part in the attack on Marsa el Brega which Rommel planned for March 30. Since the position lay in a narrows between the sea and an impassable dry salt lake, greater resistance was expected from the British.

Generalmajor Streich drove forward with PR 5 under *Oberst* Olbricht on March 29 and took up position behind a sand hill close to the British blocking position.

The first attack on the morning of March 30 failed to break through. Massed artillery fire smashed into the German advance, inflicting casualties. *Generalmajor* Streich's command post was hit. The attack was halted.

That evening *Generalmajor* Streich called *Major* Voigtsberger, the commander of the 2nd Machine-gun Battalion.

"Voigtsberger, after darkness falls attack with your battalion echeloned to the left directly north of the road from the beach and fall on the enemy's flank."

Major Voigtsberger assembled his battalion. It advanced in wide formation, skirted to the left of the enemy trench system and suddenly found itself in the enemy's flank. All of a sudden the men broke into the enemy positions, led by the wiry *Major* Voigtsberger. Here, for the first time in the desert, the British showed their sensitivity to a threat to their flank. They pulled back from their position and the 5th Light Division succeeded in taking Marsa el Brega in a concerted attack.

Oberst Olbrich's tanks, which had been attacking since the morning of 1 April, met the reconnaissance battalion of the British Second Armored Division in front of the fortress and beat it back. The tanks destroyed 50 armored personnel carriers and a number of trucks. Marsa el Brega was in German hands.

During the night, on his own initiative, *Generalmajor* Streich had the rest of the division rejoin the advance element.

"Hauser," he said to his Ia, "we're continuing the advance toward Agedabia!"

Still on April 1, the division command post was moved forward to the palm grove west of Marsa el Brega. *Oberstleutnant* von Ponath received orders there from the division commander to feel his way forward towards Agedabia with MG 8.

In the early morning hours of April 2 the 8th Machine-gun Battalion had to beat off an attack by armored cars and tankettes. Afterward the artillery opened the advance by *Kampfgruppe* Ponath with a brief, concentrated barrage. By midday the battle group had got to within 4 kilometers of Agedabia. A flanking attack by the enemy was intercepted by 5./MG 8 and 2./Pz JägAbt. 39. In the subsequent pursuit of the enemy 17 armored cars and 6 trucks which had become bogged down were captured. The attack on Agedabia began.

While the 8th Machine-gun Battalion rolled forward on and north of the road, PR 5 was sent to catch up south of the road by *Generalmajor* Streich. When the commanding general arrived at the division at about 10.00 he ordered his forces to regroup. AA 3 was now to be deployed north of the road with the objective of cutting off the enemy's avenue of retreat.

A short while later *Generalmajor* Streich learned from air reconnaissance that the enemy had moved a large number of tanks into well-camouflaged positions behind sand dunes south of the division's route of advance. The tanks were positioned so they could fire their cannon over the dunes.

Streich sent a battalion of his Panzer Regiment forward to attack the enemy tank concentration. At about 15.30 an engagement began between the German panzers and British Mark IV tanks. The battle began and seven British tanks were destroyed from a range of 1,000 meters. The rest pulled back into the desert. German losses were three tanks, but the flanking threat had been eliminated.

Streich ordered AA 3, which was deployed north of the road, to drive past Agedabia and locate the next objective, Benghazi.

With a platoon of the heaviest eight-wheeled scout cars, *Leutnant* Wolf took over the lead of AA 3, which had been assigned to *Kampfgruppe* Ponath as its advance detachment. The cars had just passed the most forward outposts of MG 8

when they ran into British two-man tanks. The tanks opened fire with their heavy machine-guns. The German scout cars replied with fire from their 20mm cannon. Suddenly, however, artillery shells howled in and exploded on the front slope of a rise behind which Irnfried von Wechmar was standing at the scissors telescope. Wechmar, who had meanwhile been promoted to *Oberstleutnant*, spotted an enemy tank which had obviously come forward with an artillery observer and was directing the British fire.

"Pletschner patrol move forward!" he ordered.

As the patrol drove by the *Oberleutnant* ran towards the leading vehicle, his knotty walking stick in his hand.

"Watch out, Pletschner!" he warned the *Feldwebel*. "When you go over the hill ahead the road drops into a wadi. There is a bridge there. Then the Via Balbia climbs again and behind the next line of hills are the Tommies!"

The three scout cars rolled off and soon reached the hill. Pletschner spotted the first British scout car. After two shots it caught fire. However, the artillery fire now shifted to the patrol, and a little later the gunner reported:

"Scout car from the right!"

Pletschner looked to his right and saw the characteristic high antenna array and the eight wheels.

"That can only be *Leutnant* Wolf," he was

heard to say.

It was Wolf, and the scout cars opened fire on the British artillery observer. It took only three shots to turn the enemy vehicle into a burning hulk. Both patrols returned to the battalion without loss.

The actual attack began. In the north AA 3 was driving forward at high speed, because the tanks of PR 5 were now providing flanking cover for the Ponath group. The reconnaissance battalion was under orders to advance as far as possible.

As evening fell AA 3 reached the coast road north of Agedabia and found the area around Solluch free of the enemy. *Leutnant* Wolf, who had gone on ahead, reported enemy tank forces 15 kilometers farther east. The commander was in his tent shaving when *Oberleutnant* von Fallois brought him the report. He had a report sent to the DAK, while a motorcycle messenger was sent to the 8th Machine-gun Battalion.

Twenty minutes later *Oberst* Olbrich appeared at AA 3's command bus. From there he drove forward to observe the enemy tank concentration. Once there he saw that they had been fooled. The supposed tank concentration consisted of knocked out tanks from the previous winter's battle between the Italians and the British.

Oberstleutnant von Wechmar was "sour." *Generalmajor* Streich shook his head and Rommel, who had just arrived to lead the tank battle, observed coolly and secretly somewhat amused:

"The next time I want to see intact English tanks and not shot-up hulks!"

The battle for Agedabia had meanwhile reached its climax. *Generalmajor* Streich had moved forward with his command post to within three kilometers of Agedabia. Two-hundred British soldiers surrendered there on the morning of April 3, the town of Agedabia having already fallen. Rommel arrived in the afternoon and learned that only the fort was still holding out. He immediately weighed the chances of a further attack.

"Streich," he said, touching his chin in a characteristic gesture," we should swing out to the right from the advance road to force the enemy from the coast and into the desert."

Anticipating a similar development, Streich, as luck would have it, had already deployed the Second Battalion of PR 5 as Rommel described and now sent it to the right around Agedabia in order to eject the defenders still holding out in the fort.

Agedabia was taken. The wells in the town were booby-trapped with mines. The parking area in front of the British headquarters had also been literally plastered with mines.

During the afternoon the 5th Light Division pushed 20 kilometers beyond Agedabia and established an all-round defensive position in the open desert.

The 8th Machine-gun Battalion was ordered to form a battle group to carry out "Operation Ponath." The battle group, consisting of a machine-gun company with double the usual complement of weapons, an anti-tank gun company and a platoon from the Pionier company under the command of *Hauptmann* Hundt, was to advance from Agedabia straight across the desert in a northeasterly direction through Giof el Mater, Bir ben Gania and El Mechili directly toward Derna. The objective was to cut off the avenue of retreat of the British forces withdrawing from northern Cyrenaica.

The capture of Derna was also important because there the coast road came down from the highlands of Cyrenaica to the west, snaked through Derna and east of the town again climbed in a serpentine path up the next *djebel*. Any enemy could be held off in the narrows there, with the sea to the north and the deeply eroded Derna Wadi to the south. Also important was the quick capture of the Derna airfield, which lay due east of the serpentine road.

The battle group set off on the morning of April 4. The rest of the battalion was to follow with the divisional units under *Hauptmann* Frank, commander of Second Company.

The operation, which required the troops to cross 450 kilometers of trackless desert in 50 degree Celsius temperatures, was a great adventure. The battle group reached Giof el Mater at the end of the first day. After a few hours rest *Oberstleutnant* Ponath resumed the march, steering by compass. Everyone drove in the tracks of the commander. Another rest stop was made when the commander's vehicle became bogged down in the sand.

At daybreak the battle group moved on. It was able to drive around the areas of quicksand and about midday reached the well at Bir bu Hagara only to find that it had long since dried up. After another six hours the battle group reached the airfield at Bir ben Gania and found — two Junkers Ju 52 transports and with them *Generalleutnant* Rommel.

Rommel intended to sent part of the battle group against El Mechili. The men were to be flown there in the Ju 52s and take the British strongpoint by surprise. This daring plan came to nothing, however, as the reconnaissance aircraft which had been sent over El Mechili returned and reported to Rommel:

"El Mechili is occupied by about 3,000 British troops!" Rommel called off the operation, and following a two-hour halt the battle group resumed its march.

After driving about 30 kilometers several vehicles drove into a minefield, resulting in several dead and wounded. Night fell and the next morning — it was April 6 — a Fieseler *Storch* appeared over the column and landed close by. Out climbed — who else could it have been — Rommel, to order *Oberstleutnant* Ponath to accelerate the advance as much as possible.

The diarist of MG 8 described the journey:

"Once again there began a wild chase across the desert and we were all amazed that our vehicles were able to stand the pace. Finally, at about 06.00, a total of six vehicles with the commander were about 30 kilometers south of Mechili — all the other vehicles had lost contact. A new order came in by radio:

"Bypass Mechili and push on to Derna!"

How could our small force barricade the road with four machine-guns and an anti-tank gun? Our adjutant, *Oberleutnant* Prahl, was left behind here. He was to assemble the trailing bulk of the battle group and follow. We drove off leaving him standing utterly alone in the desert. What if the other groups got lost, or an English patrol appeared? Hopefully we would see Prahl again.

He did, in fact, succeed in assembling the battle group. But *General* Rommel, who was following the advance in his Fieseler *Storch*, gave him a new objective:

"Attack El Mechili!"

While the force was still gathering for the attack the order was cancelled and the previous "on to Derna!" was put back in effect."

The advance by *Kampfgruppe* Ponath continued. The reconnaissance reports were depressing, as 3,000 British troops with heavy weapons were suspected to be in El Mechili and on the El Mechili-Tmimi track was a British screening force consisting of tanks, scout cars and artillery.

At about 16.00 on 6 April *Oberleutnant* Prahl's men came upon the British screening force. Under fire from tanks and artillery the battle group's vehicles rolled through at top speed and reached the El Ezeiat area with their last drops of fuel. The now useless vehicles were camouflaged in a wadi.

The battle group was about to carry on on foot to the road it was supposed to barricade.

Suddenly, the men heard the sound of engines. At once *Oberleutnant* Prahl had the weapons brought into position. A British column appeared. It came nearer and nearer. When the leading car was about ten meters from the men of MG 8, the soldiers sprang up and trained their weapons on the completely surprised enemy. The weak resistance offered was broken. Forty trucks with over 240 men and 4 officers were captured. Now the battle group could refuel and continue on by vehicle.

The advance continued at high speed. The battle group drove throughout the night and on the morning of 7 April reached the track to Derna.

"Onward!" ordered *Oberleutnant* Prahl.

When Ponath's men were still 8 kilometers from Derna they once again came upon a large column of trucks. Leaving the prisoners behind, they drove toward the enemy in a widely spaced formation at high speed and found him — sleeping!

One hundred vehicles were captured and again over 200 prisoners taken. The men left the Tommies to walk and drove on. Three kilometers from Derna they came upon *Oberstleutnant* Ponath, who had taken position in a ravine. With him and his few men were 200 prisoners, including two Generals.

On the evening of April 6 the small advance group of *Kampfgruppe* Ponath had lost contact with the main body and left *Oberleutnant* Prahl behind. That night it encountered an English command vehicle.

"Motorcycles forward and halt!" ordered Ponath.

Two motorcycle crews drove forward, halted and received fire. One man from the first crew was killed. The second motorcycle crew fired a burst of submachine-gun fire into the driver's cab of the truck, killing the driver. The vehicle halted and out climbed British Generals O'Connor and Neame. They had set out to drive from their headquarters in Maraua to Tmimi, but took a wrong turn and ended up heading in the direction of Derna where they were intercepted by the motorcycles.

After *Oberleutnant* Prahl arrived with the main body of the battle group *Oberstleutnant* Ponath returned to his assignment, barricading the road and launching the attack on the town of Derna at 11.00.

Driving at high speed, the motorcycle troops pushed into the northern section of the town and reached the airfield. Six RAF transport aircraft were destroyed there. The men then drove to the south side of the field where they saw a number of Hurricane fighter aircraft. But before they could capture the fighters the enemy counterattacked with scout cars and tankettes. Heavy machine-gun fire forced *Oberstleutnant* Ponath's soldiers to take cover. The British were attempting to eliminate the German threat and save the important airfield. In the close-quarters fighting that followed, the motorcycle troops threw hand-grenades at the British armored vehicles. The British attack did save the fighters, however. They were able to take off at the last second.

Ponath and his men fought their way to the eastern side of the airfield and established an all-round defensive position opposite the fort south of the coast road.

The British attacked again and again, but each time they were thrown back by the concentrated German fire.

In the captured British field hospital both German and British wounded were treated. The entire airfield was still not in Ponath's possession. Therefore at noon on 7 April the motorcycle troops attacked again. The western edge of the airfield was reached. A little later, however, the British counterattacked with Mark II tanks. They forced the Germans back again, and as darkness fell launched another attack, this time with thirty infantry supported by tanks, in an effort to destroy or at least throw out the German force.

Oberstleutnant Ponath was able to repulse the enemy infantry. The tanks, however, could not be stopped. They broke through to the east.

The Germans did manage to hold onto the road. Throughout the night individual vehicles and whole groups tried to break through the barricade, but in vain.

Finally, at about midnight, a single car came in sight. The men around *Oberstleutnant* Ponath let it approach and then stopped it. In the car were two more English Generals.

At dawn the battle group prepared for a renewed attack on Derna. The attack unfolded almost like a training exercise. Prisoners were taken and trucks captured. Following unimaginable hardship and days of action without sleep the men had finally reached Derna. They drove into the town and found that the English had withdrawn.

Derna was in the hands of *Kampfgruppe* Ponath. But what had happened to the 5th Light Division in the meantime?

Attack on Mechili

The entire division was sitting in its all-round defensive position 20 kilometers from Agedabia almost out of fuel. When Rommel arrived on 4 April to discuss the situation with Streich, he ordered all available trucks from the combat train unloaded and sent back with double crews to fetch fuel, ammunition and rations. As a result, the precious contents of the combat train had to be stored on tarpaulins in the open desert.

Until the truck supply column returned, the entire division, with the exception of *Kampfgruppe* Ponath, was immobilized. The trucks sent back to Tripoli had to cover 1,000 kilometers, and as a result it would be several days before the division was combat-ready again.

This was the battle during the first months in Africa. It was marked by a shortage of troops and supplies *and* stamped by Rommel, who refused to give up. Through much improvisation he was able to conduct a war of movement and hold his ground, even win territory.

The following morning Rommel again showed up at the 5th Light. Streich had spent the night in his car.

Rommel now ordered the fuel drained from all of the vehicles and put into the tanks. With the resulting mobile force Streich was to advance that same day through Giof el Mater to Mechili.

"The main body of the division will follow after the return of the truck column sent back the day before!" decided Rommel.

General Zamboon, who had followed up with an Italian division, urgently advised Rommel not to use the road to Giof el Mater, because they — the Italians — had mined the entire road with so-called "thermos-bottle mines" during their retreat.

Rommel insisted that his orders be carried out and so, after the tanks were fuelled, Streich had to carry out the attack. The refuelling was completed as evening fell and, on Rommel's orders, the advance began in darkness without lights. There

was nothing to be seen of the road in the darkness. Each vehicle had to hang onto the one ahead. Streich drove in the middle of the group.

The first mine exploded with a thunderous roar. Then there was an ear-shattering explosion at the head of the column.

"What has happened?" *General* Streich asked his adjutant, *Leutnant* Seidel.

"It must have been one of the Pioniers' (engineers) munitions trucks, *Herr General*," he replied.

"There in front!" called the driver, pointing ahead and to the left. Directly in front of them was a munitions truck, engulfed in flames.

"Pull out to the right and go around!" ordered the division commander. The driver followed the order and drove past the burning vehicle and back onto the road again. "Drive in the tracks of the vehicle ahead!" called the General, as the driver was about to veer off to the left. The driver pulled back into the tracks of his predecessor.

At that moment the column halted and a *Kübelwagen* behind the commander's vehicle tried to drive past on the left. It was barely a few lengths past the General's car when there was a tremendous explosion. The vehicle was shattered and its crew killed.

The lead vehicle had become stuck in the loose sand. When the following wheeled vehicles attempted to free their stuck comrade, they met the same fate.

"Tractors forward! Get those vehicles free," ordered Streich.

It was no use, however. Soon most of the unit's vehicles were stuck in the deep sand at the side of the road.

"All vehicles turn on their headlights!" decided the division commander. "Assemble front and center!"

Streich wanted to at least have the unit together in case the British attacked, which was always a possibility.

Generalmajor Streich ordered the advance to resume at dawn, but only a small portion of his force was able to go on. The tanks, in particular, were getting low on fuel again.

Later, aircraft of the DAK flew back along the route covered during the night and found a few vehicle crews which had become separated and stranded. The aircraft dropped water to the stranded soldiers, saving them from death by thirst.

The division commander was now at the head of the unit in his *Kübelwagen*. At about midday they reached a dry salt lake about 20 kilometers south of Mechili. A halt was ordered. They would have to wait for aircraft to deliver some fuel.

Six wheeled vehicles, which had been sent by the corps and division headquarters, managed to get through to the small advance element. With the division commander on the dry salt lake were two vehicles each with two 20mm twin cannon.

Finally the two Ju 52 transports which had been dispatched landed on the salt lake with fuel. The men had scarcely unloaded the aircraft when English aircraft made a low-level attack. They strafed the Ju 52s with cannon and machine-gun fire; both went up in flames.

Everything was stranded on the dry salt lake. While the men waited idly, *Oberst* Graf von Schwerin, who had been sent ahead to reconnoiter, returned from his observation post. He had observed the movements south of Mechili and was able to report to Rommel, who had also arrived in the meantime:

"Mechili is strongly occupied by the enemy, but an attack is possible."

Rommel flew off to see for himself and returned to the dry salt lake at noon. After the two men had consulted, Rommel said:

"It is now 17.00, Streich. At 18.00 you will advance with the Schwerin Group toward Mechili and take it. I will order the Italian artillery to support you."

Generalmajor Streich now made his way to *Oberst* von Schwerin, who had driven forward again. While searching for von Schwerin he came upon an Italian headquarters, where he was told where to find the Schwerin group. But when he reached the specified location it was no longer there. As it was already getting dark *Generalmajor* Streich headed back. By radio he ordered his group to show a light signal, after which the driver oriented himself and found the way back.

To add to the difficulties Rommel had been unable to locate the Italian artillery. Streich reported his futile search for von Schwerin. Rommel said nothing.

While the movements in front of El Mechili failed to work out, *Kampfgruppe* von Ponath had reached the edge of Derna.

The rest of the 5th Light Division, PR 5 under

Oberst Olbrich, had also not arrived, and on April 7 Rommel set off in his *Storch* to look for the desperately needed unit. He finally found the tanks in the middle of a stony desert in which the tracked vehicles could not move. *Oberst* Olbrich had been forced to backtrack and try and drive around the obstacles and had got farther off course. In these attempts to advance the desert proved to be a hindrance with which soldiers and commanders alike were completely unfamiliar.

In the meantime, *Generalmajor* von Prittwitz, commander of the 15th Panzer Division, which was also to see action in the desert, arrived at *Oberst* Olbrich's armored group. Accompanied by his Ia he had flown ahead of his division to scout the terrain.

There was a bright spot on April 7, however. The Fabris Group, a battalion of *Bersaglieri*, arrived and moved into position southeast of Mechili.

Once again Ju 52 transports landed on the dry salt lake with supplies for the 5th Light Division. Four British fighters attempted a strafing attack. The soldiers fired their rifles at the attackers, and one was shot down by a 20mm flak. That evening eight tanks of I./PR 5 arrived. *Major* Bolbrinker had brought them in safe and sound. Now at least *Generalmajor* Streich had some heavy weapons at his disposal.

"Take Mechili tomorrow morning!" ordered Rommel late that evening.

The next morning *Generalmajor* Streich drove forward toward Mechili with the commanders of his battle groups and units to search for a favorable point to penetrate the British defences. Suddenly, a long column of British trucks appeared in front of them. Streich drove back to his command post.

Major Bolbrinker, who had spotted the thick cloud of dust raised by the trucks, alerted his tanks:

"Everyone after me toward El Mechili!" he ordered.

The seven tank commanders heard the order over their radios and rolled off with their commander. A short time later Bolbrinker saw one group of British vehicles turn toward *Generalmajor* Streich's command post and open fire on it with several machine-guns.

In the command post itself, *Generalmajor* Streich gave the order to open fire. Everyone who could shoulder and fire a weapon opened up. The General, too, fired at the approaching enemy vehicles with a rifle. Suddenly the mass of vehicles veered sharply toward the west.

Go, Rickert! After them with the two 20 millimeters and overtake them on a parallel course!'' shouted Streich, recognizing the opportunity which had been presented.

The adjutant drove off with the two twin-flak and raced after the British. The division commander followed Bolbrinker's eight tanks in his *Kübelwagen*. Just outside Mechili, where the English had dug their infantry trenches, enemy anti-tank guns opened fire. The eight German tanks replied. Four anti-tank guns were knocked out, but three of the German tanks were disabled as well. Their crews, however, managed to escape with their lives.

At that moment a large column of vehicles appeared out of the west heading for Mechili. It was the same trucks that *Leutnant* Rickert had gone after. The *Leutnant* had caught up with the head of the column and opened fire. At that the trucks had turned around and now arrived back at Mechili at this critical moment.

"Fire a few shots at the column!'' shouted Streich to a tank commander who had halted nearby.

The tank swung about. There was a flash as it opened fire with its main gun. The shell howled toward the column and blew up one of the trucks. The next shot was also a direct hit. The long column, which contained most of the Mechili garrison, which had been attempting to withdraw, stopped. The British got down from their vehicles with hands raised. A handful of German troops had captured 2,000 British soldiers and 4 Generals. The 5th Light Division had bagged two battalions of the Second Indian Motorized Brigade and rear echelon units of the British Second Armored Division with the unit headquarters, including the division's commander, Major General Gambier-Parry.

A heavy sandstorm — a *ghibli* — blew up during the final stages of the battle. The storm pinned Rommel down for a few hours. In spite of the whirling clouds of sand a large, black pillar of smoke was visible above Mechili. The English had set alight their fuel dump in the town. This smoke signal subsequently led the way in for the Olbrich group and ΛΛ 3. The two units appeared in Mechili on the afternoon of April 8.

Some British officers asked *Generalmajor* Streich if they might be allowed to search the battlefield for clothing and firewood. They also asked for food for their men. *Generalmajor* Streich placed trucks at their disposal with which they could fetch food from their own supply dumps, as much as they wanted. He allowed the British Generals to spend the night in their own command vehicles.

When the message came in that *Kampfgruppe* Ponath had taken the airfield at Derna and captured 800 prisoners — including the British commander in Cyrenaica, Lieutenant General Neame — there was great jubilation. It looked as if they had snatched victory from a threatening situation.

Rommel acted at once. He recognized a favorable opportunity to advance through Tmimi toward Tobruk and capture this important fortress with its vital harbor.

Tobruk was the key to all of North Africa. As a harbor and supply base the fortress was of incalculable worth. Rommel therefore sent the commander of the 15th Panzer Division, which would not arrive for some time, with a battle group in the direction of Tobruk. The core of the battle group was made up by the 8th Machine-gun Battalion. Also there was AA 3. The command post of the 5th Light Division was set up in Mechili.

While the battle group under *Generalmajor* von Prittwitz stormed forward, *Oberst* Olbrich reported to division that, as a result of the *ghibli*, the turrets of his tanks were unable to turn as they had been jammed by sand. *Generalmajor* Streich suggested removing the turrets at the next halt and cleaning them. Rommel agreed initially. But when the work ran on into the night, a counter-order arrived from Rommel. The tanks were now to drive directly across the desert in the direction of Tmimi.

The work was broken off and the tanks headed off in the direction of Tmimi, arriving there the next morning. *Generalmajor* Streich instructed *Oberst* Olbrich to drive on along the *Via Balbia*. He himself drove forward in his command vehicle to the "white house'' in Acroma, where *Generalleutnant* Rommel was waiting. Streich wanted to obtain directions from the commanding general on the employment of his tanks.

In the meantime, however, Rommel had set off at the head of *Kampfgruppe* Ponath through

Derna as far as the first fortifications of Tobruk. There he sent *Generalmajor* von Prittwitz ahead to reconnoiter. He was to locate a favorable artillery position from which the German guns could lay down effective fire on the harbor and fortress of Tobruk.

The First General Falls

On Monday Thursday, April 10, 1941, elements of the 5th Light Division, primarily *Kampfgruppe* Ponath, as well as the Italian *"Brescia"* Division, were at Kilometer Marker 31 before Tobruk. The commanders had assembled next to Rommel's *Mammuth*, one of the spacious command vehicles which *Generalmajor* Streich had captured from the British. Erwin Rommel personally issued them the order of the day:

"The '*Brescia*' and '*Trento*' Divisions will attack Tobruk from the west and, in doing so, raise a lot of dust. At the same time the 5th Light, swinging out to the south, will go around the city and attack from the southeast. You, Prittwitz, will drive forward at once in your *Kübelwagen* and seek out an artillery position from which the harbor of Tobruk can be fired on. Wechmar, you and AA 3 are to drive through Acroma toward El Adem. The 8th Machine-gun Battalion, whose most forward elements are engaged in heavy offensive fighting near Kilometer 16, will fight its way through."

Generalmajor von Prittwitz drove off at once. With him were his driver and aide. Just as they were leaving the *"Brescia"* Division, which had been ordered forward by *Generalmajor* Kirchheim, reached the battle zone.

"Kirchheim, you're heaven-sent!" called Rommel as the Pour le Mérite wearer of the First World War reported to him. "Drive forward at once along the '*Via Balbia*' and reconnoiter an assembly area for the attack on Tobruk. You can drive as far as Kilometer Marker 13, because the latest reports indicate that Italian security forces are already there."

Kirchheim, who did not belong to the *Afrika-Korps*, but to the special Libyan Headquarters, drove off in his staff car with two of his officers. As the car neared the "White House" near Kilometer 18, which was later to become famous, Kirchheim suddenly saw bursts of machine-gun fire kicking up dirt on the road ahead.

"Aircraft!" shouted the driver. The General had already spotted the three Hurricanes racing toward them at low altitude. Again there was the flash of machine-gun fire and then several hard blows against the car's metal body. At the same time Kirchheim felt a painful blow on his arm and shoulder and a burning pain in his eye. The driver braked sharply. The Hurricanes roared past overhead.

"Those were explosive bullets, *Herr General*. You've been wounded!" shouted one of the staff officers.

Heinrich Kirchheim had his shoulder wound and two upper arm wounds dressed. A small splinter sat just below his eye. Behind them the machine-guns of the British aircraft hammered away at the columns of the *"Brescia"* Division, elements of which were still moving into position.

Standing beside the road, Kirchheim suddenly saw a *Kübelwagen* approaching from the desert. It was *Generalmajor* von Prittwitz' car. The commander of the 15th Panzer Division stopped beside him and said:

"Kirchheim, I congratulate you on the wound which will send you home! If you go to Vienna, will you visit my wife. Say hello to her for me. Tell her that I'm feeling well and that everything's going extremely well here. I have to go on now to reconnoiter an artillery position." "Now, dear Prittwitz, that's fortunate, because I'm to

The White House, 14 kilometers from Tobruk.

reconnoiter the assembly area for the attack on Tobruk. And I wouldn't think of leaving the front because of these few scratches. I'm driving on in a quarter of an hour. Has Rommel told you that there are Italian security forces as far as Kilometer 13?''

"Yes he has," replied von Prittwitz. "Therefore I can drive that far at high speed."

"Fine," said Kirchheim. "But tell the Italians where I can find you."

Fifteen minutes after Prittwitz' departure Kirchheim rolled off in his Mercedes. When he reached Kilometer 14 he spotted his comrade's *Kübelwagen* ahead and seconds later a figure, which came running back along the ditch waving both hands.

"Stop!" shouted the man, and Kirchheim instructed his driver to halt. The *Oberleutnant*, who seconds later came up to Kirchheim out of breath, was von Prittwitz' aide.

"No further!" he blurted out, breathing heavily. "English anti-tank gun ahead. Our car has been hit. Prittwitz was killed by a direct hit. His driver too. They're still in the car."

"Get in!" Kirchheim ordered the *Oberleutnant*. The car backed up and then turned around. Kirchheim drove back two kilometers and reconnoitered the assembly area. He then ordered a medical team forward.

The medics found the *Kübel* and brought back the two dead men. The Battle of Tobruk had begun; one general had been wounded and another killed. On the afternoon of 10 April *Generalmajor* Streich received the order to lead the attack on Tobruk.

Into Battle and the Destruction of the 8th Machine-gun Battalion

After the victory in Derna, *Oberstleutnant* Ponath received orders from Rommel on the spot to drive forward along the coast road to Tmimi as the division's advance detachment.

"There you will cut off the retreat of the British near Mechili, Ponath. You must move out at once, however."

A short time later MG 8 departed and rolled eastward through the falling darkness. In the first morning hours of April 9 the advance element reached Tmimi. The motorcycle troops drove around the town in a wide semi-circle to the east and south and secured there. *Oberstleutnant* Ponath sent motorized patrols to Gazala and toward the edge of the *djebel*, which stretched away to the south of the advance detachment. Near Gazala the men of the patrol came under heavy machine-gun fire and turned back.

AA 3 arrived at about midday on April 9. Once it had been determined that the enemy tanks were wrecks from an earlier battle, the unit had been ordered by Rommel to push through directly in the direction of Benghazi with an attached tank company and an artillery platoon.

The motorcyclists of the Behr Company reached Benghazi at dawn on April 4. They roared through the coastal city which had been abandoned by the British and, by the time the rest of the detachment caught up, *Oberleutnant* Winrich behr was able to report that Benghazi was in German hands. When Rommel arrived in late morning and saw the men sleeping, he said apologetically:

"This won't do, Wechmar! The others are under way straight across the desert. We must move on here as well. But you and your men rest until noon. By then the Flak battery will have also arrived, which is placed under your command until further notice."

Rommel's *Kübelwagen* disappeared in a cloud of dust, heading straight across the desert on his way to visit all of his battle groups and smaller units.

The "Stahnsdorfers" set off again at 12.00. Thick dust clouds wafted high. Men's shirts stuck to their bodies. The next objective, the second Benghazi airfield, was reached. It had already been evacuated by the enemy. The following objective, the hills of Benina and Fort Benina, came into sight. Then a heavy barrage fell on the leading element. The attached tank company rolled forward. There were several explosions as they reached a slope. Three tanks were disabled with damaged tracks. Fortunately, none caught fire, so that all could be repaired.

"Up the hill!" ordered Wechmar. "Motorcycles forward!"

The Third Company dismounted and attacked with rifles, machine-guns and hand grenades. *Oberleutnant* Behr had his three platoons advance left and right of the road. They reached the plateau, on which stood six enemy guns. Moving forward by leaps and bounds, they stormed nests of resistance. Bursts of machine-gun fire whipped about and hand grenades crashed. The enemy was thrown back in close-quarters fighting. The Australian infantry defended desperately. Finally, however, the hill and the enemy forces holding it were overcome. Only Fort Benina remained in British hands.

"We will take the fort at dawn!" decided von Wechmar at an officer's briefing.

When the disappearance of *Leutnant* Langemann and the motorcycle platoon was reported, Wechmar became worried. *Oberleutnant* Behr fired signal flares. But the platoon, which had pushed too far ahead during the attack on the plateau, did not reply. Had it been captured?

The puzzle was not solved until morning, when *Leutnant* Langemann, acting on his own initiative, followed after the withdrawing enemy and occupied Fort Benina with his small force.

The DAK's order was "continue the advance!"

The troops set off again through thick, blowing sand over hills and through valleys, through pebble fields and patches of camel thorn. During a rest stop *Oberleutnant* von Fallois climbed a small stone hill and saw an enemy tank assembly area in front of him. He counted forty tanks.

"Well let the enemy come to us!" decided von Wechmar. "The battalion will assume a defensive position on the hill. The trains will go into cover behind the hill!"

When Rommel's liaison officer arrived at the battalion, Wechmar informed him of his intentions. But the enemy did not come. Not until about noon on the following day did he begin to feel his way forward with a wave of six to seven tanks.

When evening came AA 3 moved on. In the lead were Behr's motorcycle troops. The vehicles rumbled over the uneven terrain. Suddenly the ghostly outline of the enemy tanks appeared before them.

"Volunteer assault squad to me! Armament submachine-guns and light machine-guns!" ordered Winrich Behr.

The *Oberleutnant* led the assault squad toward the first enemy tank. It was — empty! The second and third were empty too. A light burned in the fourth tank. *Oberleutnant* Behr opened the hatch, and brandishing a submachine-gun, ordered the crew to come out. Just then the fifth tank started its engine. A burst of fire from the *Oberleutnant*'s machine-gun silenced it again. It turned out that the tanks had become stranded there through lack of fuel. Behr sent a radio message to battalion and, after the moon rose, set off again with his company.

The advance continued. It was "Rommeling" as the troops had already begun to say. *Ober-*

leutnant Everth had taken over the lead. He drove over a mine. *Oberstleutnant* von Wechmar jumped from his car, which was driving right behind Everth, and ran ahead, falling over a camel-thorn bush in his haste. Luckily he found Evert unhurt. He had "only" driven over a thermos bottle mine.

Feldwebel Schubert and his Pionier platoon went to work. They removed the mines, which had been laid very close together, and placed them in a pile. Suddenly, however, the calm was shattered by a tremendous explosion. The thunder of the detonation tore *Oberstleutnant* von Wechmar away from his map studying. He saw the explosion and knew that something terrible had happened.

A mine had slipped from the hands of one of the Pionier and had fallen onto the pile of live mines at the side which they had been unable to defuse. Six soldiers, including *Oberleutnant* Everth, were seriously wounded. *Feldwebel* Schubert and two of his men were killed. *Feldwebel* Waschke took over the decimated platoon. Three new graves, marked on *Oberfeldwebel* Schlitt's burial map, were left behind in the desert when the advance resumed.

Following the coastal road, at about midnight the battalion reached the pearl of Cyrenaica, Derna, which had been taken by *Kampfgruppe* Ponath. AA 3 had reestablished contact with the DAK. When it reached *Kampfgruppe* Ponath at about midday on April 9, it received new orders from the commanding general which took it out of the ring around Tobruk and again sent it through no-man's-land. Rommel's order was:

"I expect AA 3 to reach Bardia tonight."

The unit bypassed Tobruk to the south and east. With the Mediterranean glittering in front of them they veered back onto the *Via Balbia* and headed east. Their comrades who were to assault Tobruk were left behind. The sand dunes stood ghostly white against the dark horizon. To the right lay the desert. Several *djebels* jutted from the waves of sand.

It was 07.00 when AA 3 reached Bardia. The town, which was situated on a hill above the bay, was searched. No enemy soldiers were to be seen. A lone Hurricane landed on the airfield and was received by *Leutnant* Gustaf, the anti-tank gun commander. The First Company was left behind to occupy the town. The rest of the battalion was assigned to *Kampfgruppe* Herff. *Oberst* von Herff had been named local sector commander. His job was to see to it that enemy forces in the Bardia —Sollum area were contained while the battle for Tobruk was going on.

The 15th Motorcycle Battalion Arrives!

On April 5 the 15th Motorcycle Battalion under *Oberstleutnant* Gustav-Georg Knabe reached Tripoli by ship. That same evening the battalion, whose Fourth and Fifth Companies were still waiting in Italy for transport to Africa, was sent off toward the front. In six days the battalion covered approximately 1,800 kilometers. Hindered repeatedly by African sandstorms, it had to drive day and night with only brief rest stops. This placed great demands on the drivers.

Oberstleutnant Knabe drove ahead of his battalion to Ain el Gazala, where he arrived on 11 April and received the following order from the DAK:

"As 'Advance Detachment Knabe,' the 15th Motorcycle Battalion, with its available companies and the attached Pz.JägAbt. 33, 1./Flak 18 (88mm guns) and 4./Flak 18 (self-propelled 20mm Flak), will advance via the Acroma crossroads to Point 167 south of Acroma — Sidi Azeiz — Capuzzo and occupy Sollum. The reinforced AA 3 has been sent against Bardia."

All of the units which had been placed under the command of K 15 were still in the desert east of Mechili. They had been in action for some time and had insufficient rations and were without water and fuel. On the morning of April 12 they joined up with K 15 at Point 167, about 26 kilometers south of the *Via Balbia*'s Kilometer Marker 30. There they were issued some of the supplies they needed.

During the march K 15 and other the elements of the advance detachment came under air attack several times, which resulted in some dead and wounded.

The Costly Battle of Tobruk - The Verdun of the Desert

On 9 April *Kampfgruppe* von Ponath had driven to within 2 kilometers of the strongly defended line of hills 30 kilometers from Tobruk, when heavy artillery fire forced its soldiers to dismount and dig in. With their naked eyes the men could see three enemy batteries in open field positions. *Oberstleutnant* Ponath sent the vehicles to the rear. The men of MG 8 then moved out and the next morning the attack began. They advanced in widely-spaced skirmishing lines toward the British positions. When no defensive fire followed a trick was suspected. But the enemy had merely abandoned these positions under cover of darkness and pulled back into Tobruk. Immediately the vehicles were sent for, the men climbed aboard and they set off after the enemy. Several times the motorcycle patrol leading the way had to evade enemy scout cars. On the road markers the soldiers read:

"Tobruk — 19 kilometers"

The steep edge of the *djebel* was only 140 meters away to the south. There the plain dropped vertically 10 to 20 meters. The same distance away to the left the terrain climbed in a similar fashion.

As they reached Kilometer 18, heavy artillery fire began to rain down on the men. Vehicles and motorcycles scattered to both sides.

As there was inadequate cover available the men had to run under the artillery fire. They ran in the direction of the bridge that carried the *Via Balbia* over a cleft in the terrain. Before the soldiers could reach it the bridge went up with a tremendous explosion.

Every man from the edge of the *djebel* to the road was a target for the enemy rifle and machine-gun fire. On the left wing the attackers continued to advance until a rapid fire from several machine-guns on the vertical bank and machine-gun positions and foxholes blasted out of the rock forced them to take cover.

Kampfgruppe Ponath was pinned down. Everyone breathed a sigh of relief when the German artillery arrived and opened fire on the enemy positions. Through their binoculars and with their naked eyes *Oberstleutnant* Ponath's men watched as one British gun after another was put out of action. Then they watched as their ambulances drove through the fire, picked up the wounded and roared back toward the rear.

A short while later MG 8 again went to the attack on a 2-kilometer front. Again the men were met by heavy rifle and machine-gun fire. Once

again they had to look for cover. When it was discovered that the enemy had secured his bunker positions with dense barbed-wire obstacles on the floors of the *wadis*, *Oberstleutnant* Ponath called off the attack.

In order to guard both of his open flanks against enemy flanking attempts, Ponath had to extend his battalion over a front of 8 kilometers. It was there, watched by the soldiers of MG 8, that *Generalmajor* von Prittwitz was killed early that afternoon.

On the evening of April 10 an aide delivered orders that MG 8 was to be relieved there by the Italian "*Brescia*" Division and sent to the southern Tobruk sector.

The Italians did not arrive, however. They were found 4 kilometers farther west, but did not move into the positions formerly held by the battalion, which had moved out at dawn.

When the battalion arrived south of Tobruk all of the maps of the area had been given out. However, a little later *Generalmajor* Streich came to see *Oberstleutnant* Ponath and ordered the battalion to attack the fortress from the south.

"You will be supported by the tanks of PR 5," he assured Ponath.

Rommel's plan, to push into the fortress on the heels of the withdrawing enemy, had failed. Now he would have to subdue the fortress with several quick blows. This was easier said than done, however, because General Wavell, the British Commander-in-Chief in the desert, had moved the Ninth Australian Division from Cyrenaica into the fortress. Its commander, Major General Morshead, became fortress commander. He requested and received further reinforcements in troops and aircraft. Seizing the fortress would be a difficult undertaking. On a land front of 40 kilometers the defenders had about 125 defensive positions, which were arranged in two staggered rows. There were also extensive anti-tank ditches and barbed-wire obstacles. The strongpoints each featured an anti-tank gun and two machine-gun positions with barbed wire all around.

The attack on Tobruk was resumed shortly after midday on April 11. PR 5 arrived. After the recent battles and desert marches it had only about 20 tanks left. The German forces advanced in a zone attack, with two companies of MG 8 in the lead, two more farther left, echeloned to the rear, and to their right the 20 tanks. Artillery fire began to fall among the advancing sections. They had covered only 2 kilometers when the soldiers were forced to leave their vehicles. They stormed forward on foot, running under the enemy artillery fire. However, the British artillery shortened its range and shells were soon dropping among the advancing soldiers, who were now also coming under fire from machine-guns and anti-tank guns.

"Take cover!" ordered the company commanders. The soldiers dug in.

The tanks fired on every visible target but, one after another, they were put out of action. Finally, the last tank was forced to withdraw, which meant that the attack had to be called off.

Night fell. *Oberleutnant* Prahl, the battalion adjutant, drove to division at 09.00. When he returned he brought new attack orders with him. As the German artillery could not intervene due to a shortage of ammunition, the attack was again to be supported by all available tanks — several more had arrived from the repair shops.

The tanks arrived at 11.00. They drove at high speed through the artillery fire which had begun to fall again, and passed through MG 8's positions. When the last of the tanks had rolled through, the soldiers, led by *Oberleutnant* Ponath, jumped up and ran after them. The tanks disappeared from sight, but reappeared again a short while later. From the turret of one of the tanks an officer, whom *Oberstleutnant* Ponath recognized as *Oberst* Olbrich, shouted to him:

"We can't get through! There are deep, wide anti-tank ditches 400 meters ahead!"

Once more the machine-gun teams had to dig in and, when the thick dust clouds raised by the tanks had settled, they saw before them broad walls of barbed wire, broken here and there by low stone defensive positions. Farther to the rear were observation posts on tall poles. The British opened fire the instant a German soldier raised his head.

Running through the hostile fire, *Oberleutnant* Prahl rushed back to the division command post. There he received the following order:

"MG 8 will remain where it is. It is to dig in and hold the positions it has reached!" Night fell. With it came the cold, against which the thin tropical uniforms provided little protection. Night passed, the sun appeared and with it the flies. At 11.00 the battalion commander was ordered to the division command post. He returned at 17.00, twice having braved hostile fire. *Oberstleutnant* Ponath had

received orders from Rommel personally to resume the attack that day. At 18.00 six artillery battalions were to lay down a concentrated barrage on the barbed-wire fortifications and destroy the machine-gun positions there. In addition, a battery of 88mm Flak from I./Flak 18 was to drive up into open firing positions and engage any enemy tanks which might appear with direct fire. A light Flak battery was also to drive up to the wire and destroy recognized machine-gun positions with direct fire. MG 8's battle orders were:

"Second and Third Companies, each with an attached anti-tank gun platoon, are to break into the front lines, roll up the enemy positions about 500 meters right and left, and establish a bridgehead for the commander who, with the rest of the battalion, will push ahead to the crossroads.

If the attack proceeds favorably, PR 5 will break in at dawn tomorrow and push through to Tobruk."

The messenger who was to deliver this order to the individual companies was killed.

The Attack Begins

It was precisely 17.50 when the light Flak battery rolled out of its cover and drove toward the barbed wire at high speed. The 88mm battery went into position close behind *Hauptmann* Barsch's 5./MG 8 and seconds later was blanketed by enemy artillery fire. Steel rained down on the light battery, destroying guns. Not a single gun of the light battery escaped. A *Leutnant* and six soldiers were the only survivors from the gun crews.

At 18.00 *Oberstleutnant* Ponath waited for the promised barrage. Beside him *Hauptmann* Bartsch looked at his watch. The German guns remained silent.

"Without covering fire then, *Herr Oberstleutnant!*" said the company commander. Ponath nodded.

"Fifth . . . up . . . advance! . . . advance!!"

The soldiers leapt up and ran toward the objective 300 meters away. The British artillery shifted its fire onto the advancing soldiers. They ran under the artillery fire and then came under fire from anti-tank and machine-guns in the bunkers and trenches.

Elements of the Second and Third Companies

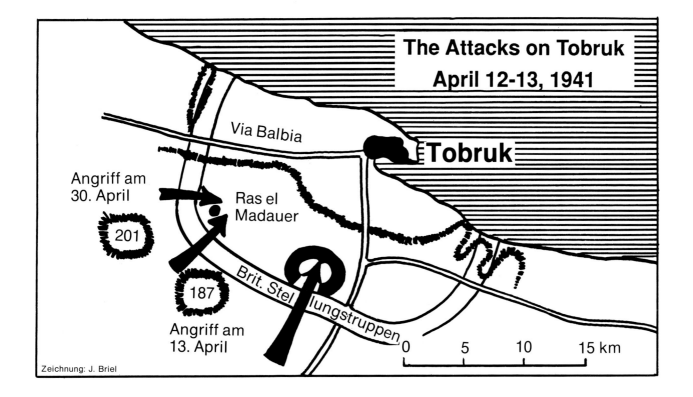

Zeichnung: J. Briel

The Attacks on Tobruk
April 12-13, 1941

Via Balbia

Tobruk

Angriff am
30. April

Ras el
Madauer

201

Brit. Stellungstruppen

187

Angriff am
13. April

0   5   10   15 km

got up and charged at the same time as the Fifth, even though they had not received the attack orders. They reached the anti-tank ditches but were forced back by machine-gun fire.

Oberstleutnant Ponath decided to resume the attack by night. He wanted to make a deep penetration and establish a bridgehead, so that next morning, with the support of **PR 5**, he could move out of the bridgehead and push deep into the fortress. He moved the Seventh Company (anti-tank gun) forward and established his command post in an anti-tank ditch. *Stabsarzt* Dr. Möller also moved the aid station forward to the anti-tank ditch.

During the night the individual sections worked their way forward on a 500 meter front to establish the bridgehead. The men dug in. Australian soldiers moved stealthily toward them. There was a brief battle at close quarters, screams, the rattle of spades — then silence again. Suddenly, an Australian assault squad stormed the boundary between the Fourth and Seventh Companies and killed the gun crews. Then the Australians began to sing: "It's a long way to Tipperary" . . . and charged, giving out loud yells. The left wing of the bridgehead was forced back to the anti-tank ditch.

Hauptmann Frank, commander of 2./MG 8, was seriously wounded and *Leutnant* Hofer of 7./MG 8 was killed in the attack.

A counterattack led by *Hauptmann* Bartsch recovered some of the lost ground. *Leutnant* Dreschler tried to recover the Seventh's lost anti-tank guns. The enemy was thrown back and the guns reached, but just then the heavy artillery fire began again. *Leutnant* Dreschler was badly wounded and many men were killed. *Unteroffizier* Stoldt returned to the anti-tank ditch with five men.

During the night *Oberleutnant* Prahl brought division's order to continue the attack. It promised that the tanks would arrive at 02.00. Twenty-four tanks were fit for action, 24 out of the 120 that PR 5 had brought to Africa.

The night, which had seen such heavy losses, came to an end. Shortly before 03.00 the men heard the sound of approaching tanks. They were led by *Oberst* Olbrich himself. Oddly, the enemy ceased his fire at the appearance of the tanks. The Panzers found the prepared crossing point and drove down through the anti-tank ditch. The leading tank drove over a mine which had not been cleared and ground to a halt. *Oberst* Olbrich's tank stopped beside the battalion commander.

"Have your people climb aboard, Ponath, then we can advance a good distance while it is still dark."

"Good, then I'll have some of the men climb aboard while the rest follow behind the tanks. The Seventh will follow with its anti-tank guns!"

The advance began. It was still dark. The tanks driving ahead on the left and right silenced the machine-gun positions which showed themselves.

When it became light 7./MG 8 was still within firing range of the British strongpoints. *Oberleutnant* Richter-Karge, commander of the company, fell and four of his soldiers were killed in the coverless terrain.

It was 05.00, just as day was breaking, when the advancing soldiers heard the sound of battle from the bridgehead behind them. The British manning the strongpoints bypassed by the assault groups had again opened fire and were shooting at the men of MG 8 who had stayed behind. The anti-tank gunners of 4./MG 8, who had been left behind to secure the bridgehead, suddenly saw heavy Mark II tanks approaching. One anti-tank gun after another was destroyed by direct fire from the British tanks. The tanks reached the anti-tank ditch and fired from the flanks. The aid station was hit several times, until several Australian prisoners got up and made the tanks understand that there were wounded there.

The assault groups, which had continued to advance, suddenly saw a vehicle column not 800 meters ahead. This soon turned out to consist of anti-tank guns, which quickly shed their camouflage and opened fire. The heavy tanks rolled forward, the mediums stayed in the center and the light panzers brought up the rear. The German tanks fired at the anti-tank guns, destroying several. Then the first tank was hit. Soon afterward a second and a third were disabled. The anti-tank guns damaged the tracks of one tank after another. Within seconds a direct hit turned a Panzer II into a blazing hulk on the open plain. Then another caught fire. The members of the crew bailed out, taking the wounded with them. Soon 11 of the 24 German tanks lay burning and immobilized on the battlefield, and it was only a matter of time until the rest, some of which had already been damaged, were also knocked out.

Oberst Olbrich ordered the retreat. When he reached the men of MG 8, he suggested to Ponath that he get aboard so that he could drive back out of the hostile fire. The *Oberstleutnant* declined.

"All you have to do is move forward!" he called to Olbrich. "The English infantry is already pulling out!"

"We would all be knocked out, Ponath!" shouted Olbrich in reply. He was certainly correct, because the turret of his tank had been hit several times and was unable to return the fire of the British anti-aircraft and anti-tank guns.

While the tanks were engaged in their battle, the men of MG 8 penetrated as far as the incomplete English trench system and took up position there. Then the tanks pulled back.

Soon afterward the enemy began to advance. He had meanwhile cleared out the bridgehead to the rear of the German battle group, and was in a position to eliminate Ponath's force. The Australians approached from three sides. At about 10.00 they attacked from the right flank. The attack was beaten off by concentrated fire from the remaining machine guns, using the last of their ammunition. Mortar fire hailed down on the shallow trenches and light tanks attacked. *Obergefreiter* Fichter knocked out one of the tanks with an anti-tank rifle.

Following a brief discussion with *Hauptmann* Bartsch, *Oberstleutnant* Ponath decided to pull back to a hill behind the assault groups. Movement was visible there and Ponath assumed that it was Olbrich's tanks.

"Fifth Company will provide covering fire, we will fall back, set up and cover the Fifth as it withdraws."

The signal was given. While the Fifth Company threw its weapons down on the lip of the trench and pinned down the enemy with a rapid fire, *Oberstleutnant* Ponath and the rest of the soldiers leapt from the trenches and ran back. After twenty meters *Oberstleutnant* Ponath fell dead, shot through the heart. A British tank broke into the trenches held by Third Company, firing at anything that showed itself. Out of ammunition, the company was forced to surrender. More soldiers were killed. *Hauptmann* Bartsch decided, in the face of resistance from several of his subordinates, to cease fighting as further resistance was futile. The remains of MG 8 surrendered. It was 11.30 on April 14, 1941.

The 8th Machine-gun Battalion had lost 700 men in fourteen days. It had ceased to exist.

The commander of the 606th Flak Battalion reports to Rommel.

Self-propelled Flak on the advance!

Attack by self-propelled Flak.

Almost all of the unit's weapons were also lost.

The sacrifices of the tanks, Flak and the men of MG 8 had been in vain. What had been lacking was infantry units and artillery, which could have unhinged the strongly-defended fortress.

On the evening of April 14 those who had survived the three attacks on Tobruk learned that *Oberstleutnant* Ponath had been awarded the Knight's Cross for his breakthrough to Derna.

But what had taken place to the east of Tobruk?

"The 15th Motorcycle Battalion, under *Oberstleutnant* Knabe, received the order to attack Sollum on April 11. On the evening of April 13, following a march of 109 kilometers, it was attacked 60 kilometers west of Sidi Azeiz. The enemy was repulsed with the aid of the anti-tank guns of Pz.JägAbt. 33, which was attached to the battalion. Fort Capuzzo was taken on April 14 in the face of strong opposition. *Oberstleutnant* Knabe ordered an immediate pursuit toward Sollum. Sollum was taken in an enveloping attack. Enemy counter-attacks were beaten off.

Sollum remains firmly in the hands of Advance Detachment Knabe. The taking of Capuzzo and Sollum represents the capture of a strip of terrain which, on account of its commanding position on the coast, with the occupied hills providing an excellent view to the east, will be of decisive importance for future operations."

This was the combat report submitted by *Oberstleutnant* Knabe. Although it is written in concise military language, it reveals something of the drama of those days and hours.

And What Was Happening at Tobruk?

Tobruk continued to hold out in the face of German attempts to conquer the fortress. On April 16 Rommel sent the *"Ariete"* Armored Battalion with a total of 18 tanks against Hill 187 — the Ras el Madauuar. British artillery blasted the tanks, which had driven up the center of the hill where they were without cover.

Finally, on 19 April, Rommel committed the heavy company of PR 15, which had just arrived from Tripoli, against Tobruk. *Major* Schraepler, Rommel's adjutant, led the attack, which Rommel watched from a command panzer. This attempt, too, failed in the face of the British artillery fire.

The next units to arrive at the front were elements of the 115th Rifle Regiment, one of the units of the 15th PD, under the command of *Oberstleutnant* Zintel. *Major* Busch, commander of the regiment's First Battalion, was shown the lay of the land by Rommel. Also arriving were soldiers of the 15th Panzer Division's 33rd Pionier Battalion.

The attack began on 30 April. The infantry and engineers poured through a narrow penetration, and 3./MG 2 under the command of *Oberleutnant* Gottfried Muntau drove toward the fort of Ras el Madauuar and stormed it.

Oberleutnant Willi Cirener, commander of 3./PiBtl. 33, who had already won the Knight's Cross in the French Campaign, led his company as it took several bunkers and bastions of the ring of fortifications. The fort fell late in the evening.

As 1 May dawned the 15th Motorcycle Battalion and the 104th Rifle Regiment, whose First Battalion had just arrived, went to the attack in hopes of expanding the penetration achieved the day before.

SR 104 had entrained in Baumholder in heavy blowing snow on April 19 and had then travelled through the Brenner Pass to Caserta. From there on April 26 First Battalion was moved in the vehicles of Third Battalion to Foggia airport and loaded aboard 120 Ju 52 transport aircraft. The battalion was desperately needed by Rommel for his attack on Tobruk.

After a three-hour flight the battalion arrived in Comiso, near Catania, and next morning took off at 11.00 across the Mediterranean, landing without incident in Benina, near Benghazi.

The battalion was then transported by truck through Derna in the direction of Tobruk. There the men of the battalion came under attack from the air for the first time when the column was strafed by low-flying Spitfires.

They arrived at the "White House" on the afternoon of April 30. There they received Rommel's attack order:

"Attack on the Ras el Madauuar. Attack time 02.00 on May 1."

Hauptmann Faltenbacher, who was leading First Battalion, moved it into its jumping-off positions for the assault during the night.

The battalion launched the attack precisely at 02.00. Extremely heavy machine-gun fire whipped toward the battalion from a dozen machine-gun and anti-tank gun positions. A few hours later the battalion had been largely decimated. *Hauptmann* Faltenbacher, the battalion's commander, received a severe stomach wound and died twenty-four hours later. The commander of First Company was badly wounded. *Oberleutnant* Kampferseck, commander of 3./SR 104, died of head wounds, while the commander of the battalion's Fourth

Company sustained serious wounds. Many soldiers were killed, others captured.

Rommel continued his attempts to bring down the fortress for another three days. The motorcycle troops fought bitterly, but suffered heavy casualties. They had to be pulled out of the line on the night of May 3 and transferred to rest positions near Capuzzo.

The units involved in the attacks on the fortress remained in the Tobruk battle zone until mid-May. Tobruk had proven too hard a nut to crack.

The Luftwaffe in Africa

By mid-March 1941, the *Fliegerführer-Afrika*, *Generalmajor* Stefan Fröhlich, had at his disposal the following units:

A *Staffel* of III. *Gruppe* of ZG 26 in Sirte. (The main body of the *Geschwader* was still stationed in Sicily.)

A *Stukagruppe* each at the airfields at Castel Benito and south of the town of Sirte. With these limited forces Fröhlich was to provide the most effective possible support for Rommel's surprise offensive. The conditions peculiar to the desert placed great demands on the crews. Cockpit temperatures often soared to over 70 degrees Celsius. Movement of aircraft to Africa took place via Italy to Tripoli, and was directed by the Luftwaffe General in Italy, *Generalmajor* Ritter von Pohl. All ground crews and materiel came by sea from Naples. A Luftwaffe loading headquarters was set up in Naples to direct operations. Transport *Gruppen* equipped with Ju 52 aircraft were used for air transport between Sicily and Africa, carrying mainly fuel.

In March *Generalmajor* Fröhlich assembled his air units at the air base in Castel Benito, while moving his own headquarters to Sirte. The verbal instructions given him by the Commander-in-Chief of the Luftwaffe, *Reichsmarshall* Hermann Göring, were:

"As *Fliegerführer-Afrika*, you are to command and deploy the units of the German Luftwaffe which see action in the African Theater — therefore the flying units *and* the Flak artillery — in such a manner as to provide the greatest degree of support possible to the army units engaged in combat there." (see Fröhlich, Stefan: *Fliegerführer Afrika* in manuscript.)

In addition to this general order, in individual cases *Generalmajor* Fröhlich received orders for special objectives, such as the Suez Canal and installations around Cairo.

Stukas and heavy fighters of the *Fliegerführer Afrika* took part in the capture of El Agheila at the end of March. Otherwise, operations at that time consisted mainly of reconnaissance missions.

On April 31, during the advance by the fast units of the DAK, *Generalmajor* Fröhlich received instructions to fly supporting attacks with both *Stukagruppen* and employ the heavy fighter *Staffel* in the close-support role.

Early on the morning of March 31 Fröhlich drove to the new airfield at En Nofilia and personally briefed the crews on their objectives. During the following days the Stukas and Bf 110 heavy fighters, the latter operating in both the fighter and close-support roles, flew increasing numbers of missions in support of the Axis ground forces. A large number of enemy positions were destroyed by dive-bombing attacks. *Staffel*-strength attacks eliminated the assembly areas of enemy patrols and assault groups. Keeping pace with the DAK's advance, the Luftwaffe moved its bases of operations east to Benghazi and Derna. When Derna was reached there was a pause.

When *Generalmajor* Fröhlich visited *General-leutnant* Rommel before Tobruk, he found the commanding general depressed. He was still in shock following the destruction of MG 8 and said to the Luftwaffe officer:

"Fröhlich, from now on we will not be able to advance to the east at the same tempo as before."

At that time the Luftwaffe didn't have a single fighter aircraft in Africa. As a result the British bombers, which had become much more active, could drop their bombs wherever they liked without interference. The only threat they faced was German anti-aircraft fire.

Stefan Fröhlich tried feverishly to obtain fighters for his command. Finally, on April 18, his efforts were rewarded. The first Bf 109 E fighters landed at Gazala airfield. The unit involved was 1. *Staffel* of I./*Jagdgeschwader* 27. The commander of I. *Gruppe* was *Hauptmann* Eduard Neumann. Thirty and later forty machines belonged to the *Gruppe*. The *Staffelkapitäne* were:

1. *Staffel: Oberleutnant* Karl-Heinz Redlich
2. *Staffel: Hauptmann* Erich Gerlitz
3. *Staffel: Oberleutnant* Gerhard Homuth

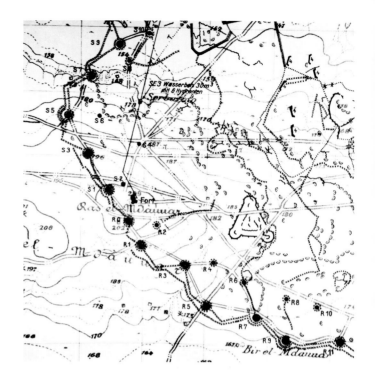

Above: Oberstleutnant Sigl. His Stukas flew missions against Tobruk.
Right: The first German military cemetery outside Tobruk. The sign reads "They gave their lives for the freedom and future of the Reich."

Below: The 5th Light Division's cemetery near Tobruk.
Right: A British rocket launcher captured near Tobruk.

All were successful fighter pilots who had achieved a number of victories in France. *Oberleutnant* Franzisket, the *Gruppe* Adjutant, was the most successful with 14 victories. Also among the initial group of pilots were two *Oberfähnriche*. They were Hans-Arnold Stahlschmidt and Hans-Joachim Marseille.

The enemy made his first acquaintance with the German Messerschmitt fighters on April 19. *Oberleutnant* Redlich shot down two Hurricanes and *Leutnant* Schroer claimed one victory. Finally *Unteroffizier* Sippel shot down a Hurricane over Gazala. In the second air battle of the day *Leutnant* Schroer was shot down by a British fighter. He was able to bring his Messerschmitt down in a forced landing and walked away unhurt.

The battle between German and English fighters had begun, and there was heavy air fighting over Tobruk in the period until April 23. The heaviest fighting occurred on April 22, when 30 Ju 87 dive-bombers attacked the fortress escorted by 12 Bf 109s and 12 Italian G-50 fighters. Several Bf 109s and Stukas as well as 3 G-50s were lost. The enemy air forces suffered losses as well.

On that day the last element of I./JG 27, 3. *Staffel*, arrived in Africa. The next day brought heavy losses for the British, who lost two Blenheims and five Hurricanes. One of the Hurricanes was shot down by *Oberfähnrich* Marseille. It was his first victory in Africa.

Early on the morning of April 25 the last machines of the RAF's 73 Squadron left Tobruk and moved to Sidi Haneish.

On May 1, when Rommel launched his last major blow against Tobruk, eight machines of the 3. *Staffel* of I./JG 27, led by *Oberleutnant* Homuth, took off as fighter cover for a Stuka unit. Again there was an air battle and *Oberfähnrich* Marseille shot down two more Hurricanes.

By mid-May the German fighter pilots had received their baptism of fire in Africa.

*A North African airfield —
summer 1941.*

Bf 110 over a desert fort in Cyrenaica.

Bf 110 over the dunes of the Libyan desert.

Bf 109 fighters in formation.

A Bf 109 of JG 27.

Artist at work at the edge of an airfield.

Left: Hans-Arnold Stahlschmidt
Right: Hans Joachim Marseille

Hell-Fire Pass

In the early morning hours of May 15 units of the British Twenty-second Guards brigade attacked Halfaya Pass, which was held by a company of the 15th Motorcycle Battalion and an Italian battery. The attack took the soldiers holding the pass by surprise and all but twelve were taken prisoner.

The British also succeeded in driving northwest along the Habata escarpment until abeam Sollum and then veered north toward Capuzzo. Sollum and Capuzzo were recaptured and the British forces pushed *Kampfgruppe* Herff farther and farther to the north. Rommel immediately sent a tank battalion of PR 8 (of the 15th PD) and several anti-aircraft guns to assist. But by then the enemy had withdrawn and the German forces were able to occupy their former positions.

The Halfaya Pass, however, remained in enemy hands. As it was a position of the utmost strategic importance and the positions in the pass controlled routes both east and west, Rommel had to retake it.

On May 17 reconnaissance revealed that powerful battle groups with tanks, artillery and anti-tank guns were being sent to the Halfaya Pass. Rommel ordered *Kampfgruppe* Herff to recapture the pass on May 27. The 8th Panzer Regiment under the command of *Oberstleutnant* Hans Kramer was dispatched across the desert from Sollum in a flanking move. Approaching from the east, it was to attack the pass from the rear. Artillery from PzAR. 33, anti-aircraft guns and KB 15 were attached to the regiment in a supporting role. The soldiers of I./SR 104 were to launch a frontal attack under their new commander,

Hauptmann Wilhelm Bach.

The attack began at first light on May 27, 1941. The soldiers around *Hauptmann* Bach jumped up, stormed forward and reached the Wadi Qualala, only to be pinned down there. As soon as the soldiers tried to get over the edge of the *wadi* they were fired on by machine-guns. British field guns fired repeatedly, forcing the German soldiers to stay in cover. *Hauptmann* Bach called the combat messenger to him and sent him to fetch the 37mm anti-tank gun. He had the anti-tank gun go into position and open fire, but the shells fell wide.

The *Hauptmann* then left cover, raised his binoculars and looked across at the enemy positions. He ducked down just in time, and the burst of machine-gun fire meant for him whipped past over the edge of the *wadi*. *Hauptmann* Bach gave instructions to the gun crew and this time the shells were on target, silencing the vital enemy machine-gun position.

"Alright, everyone after me!"

Hauptmann Bach, born in 1892, leapt up and ran forward at the head of his soldiers. As they stormed the pass, Gustav-Georg Knabe's motorcycle troops attacked from the other side and the Cramer's tanks drove into the pass from the east and shattered the enemy positions.

Halfaya Pass was in German hands. The men with *Hauptmann* Bach had done it.

The rest of the day was spent digging in. Positions were blasted into the rock. Soon the fortress had been transformed into a real fortress. The commanding general paid frequent visits to

Pastor Bach to check on the progress of the fortification building. He knew only too well that the enemy would soon attempt a counterattack, perhaps even a counteroffensive, and that this would have to be stopped.

The sector held by I./SR 104 extended from the hill near "Ave Maria" across the "breast" of Halfaya down the pass road to the coast. Mines were laid there by the First Company under the command of *Oberleutnant* Richter.

Also under the battalion's command were 88mm *Flak*, Italian 75mm guns, elements of PzJägAbt. 33 and combat engineers.

A fresh water well was discovered near Lower Sollum which produced about 20 liters of water per hour. From then on a standing force of two men was posted there to collect the water.

At this rather quiet period, when both sides were catching their breath, Rommel wrote:

"Our greatest worry remains the difficult strategic situation in which we find ourselves, because we must lay siege to Tobruk while at the same time being ready to meet a British offensive from Egypt."

At the end of May Rommel summoned the commander of the 5th Light Division, Streich, and informed him that he had requested he be relieved. Streich was to continue to command the division, however, until his replacement arrived. His successor was *Generalmajor* von Ravenstein, who assumed command of the division on June 1, 1941.

Advance in the midst of a ghibli.

Summer Battle near Sollum

English supply problems were solved with the arrival of a major convoy in Alexandria. Operation "Tiger's Brood" saw the delivery of 295 tanks and 50 fighter aircraft aboard five large freighters. The only major loss had been the "Empire Song," which had been sunk by a mine with its cargo of 57 tanks and 10 aircraft. With their supply problems solved, the English command in Cairo began preparing a major offensive against Rommel. Rommel had just received the 15th Panzer Division, and the British intention was to launch an offensive before he did.

General Wavell, the Commander-in-Chief in Cairo, reported his plan to the Empire General Staff on June 10:

"Part of the Fourth Indian Division under General Messervy will advance between the sea and the escarpment. A further Indian battle group will be employed in the center of the attack against the Halfaya — Capuzzo area. The Seventh Armored Division under O'More Creagh will operate freely in the south. It will swing around Sidi Omar and — coming from the north — will drive into the enemy's rear. The Fourth Armored brigade will be separated from the division. Its task will be to support the Twenty-second Guards Brigade in its attack on Fort Capuzzo. Afterward it will rejoin the Seventh Armored Division.

If the movements in the south lead to a confrontation with the enemy's armored forces, they will be smashed."

These attack preparations were uncovered by the German signals intelligence service and *Generalleutnant* Rommel arranged his forces in favorable positions to meet the enemy. The 15th Panzer Division was deployed opposite the line Capuzzo — Sollum. In mid-May *Oberstleutnant* Hans Cramer had set out with 160 tanks on a forced march across the desert to the front. Three-quarters of the tanks broke down along the way. With those that survived the journey Cramer carried out an attack on Capuzzo, which had been reoccupied by the enemy, and won back the fort. Gradually, the rest of the division's tanks arrived at the front and were incorporated into the German defences.

On June 14, with the enemy offensive imminent, the 5th Light Division, which was in the area south of Tobruk, was placed on alert and at 21.00 was moved forward and inserted on the right flank.

The First Oasis Company under *Oberleutnant* Paulewicz went into position on Hill 208, a natural strongpoint which jutted from the desert about 30 kilometers northwest of Capuzzo. Italian engineers had provided numerous foxholes and machine-gun positions in the rocky ground, in which the soldiers were able to take up positions. A platoon of light 37mm anti-tank guns was brought into position and later the Third Battery of I./FlaRgt. 33 under the command of *Oberleutnant* Ziemer was moved forward onto the hill.

On numerous occasions the battery had been assigned from the blocking position east of Bardia to various units to accompany them as a "fire-brigade" during the advance. For example, gun *"Anton"* had been with KB 15 in the Sidi Azeiz area for ten days, engaging English artillery or repelling fast enemy tank advances. The gun also had to defend against approaching enemy bombers.

When *Oberleutnant* Ziemer, who had taken over the battery from *Hauptmann* Fromm after the latter had become battalion commander, inspected the hill, he determined that his four guns would have an outstanding field of fire there. Within 24 hours the four "eighty-eights" were emplaced so that only their barrels protruded from the protective walls. Everything else had disappeared behind stone and sandbags. In particular, *Oberleutnant* Ziemer took great pains to ensure that the battery was invisible from a distance.

It was at this hill that the British tank attack was to be halted.

The Attack

Early on the morning of June 15 the British attacked on a wide front on the desert plain as well as on the high plateau.

In the positions in the Halfaya Pass the alarm was sounded. Engine noises echoed through the stillness. The dull rumbling, which could only be tank engines, swelled. *Hauptmann* Bach hurried forward to the anti-aircraft gun positions. He saw the outline of the first tank appear.

"Let them approach. Don't fire yet!" he ordered, sucking on the inevitable cigar. English heavy tanks appeared. Behind them came equally heavy Matilda II infantry tanks. With a crash the British artillery opened fire.

Shells fell on the pass. The men took cover. Now and then they risked a look and saw that the tanks were followed by trucks. Infantry jumped down from the trucks, formed into companies just like in peacetime and marched along behind the tanks.

Hauptmann Wilhelm Bach raised his arm and then lowered it. This was the signal the gunners had been waiting for. There was a sharp crack as the anti-aircraft guns opened fire. The anti-tank guns joined in, and the dug-in machine-guns added their weight to the barrage.

A British tank was hit and was blown to pieces as its ammunition exploded. "Hit!" roared one of the gunners. The turret was blown off the next Mark II. 20mm Flak joined in and then the Italian battery under Major Pardi opened fire. The tall, dark-haired Major stood erect and assigned targets to his battery.

The tightly-packed assault companies charged, ran into dense defending fire and scattered, taking cover behind rocks and in crevices.

Below, on the floor of the pass, was First Company of the 104th Rifle Regiment. There the British tanks rolled into the minefield which had been laid by the company. Five Mark II tanks went up in flames. Only one of the attacking tanks got through. It drove like a phantom through the mines. He's going to make it, thought the men. But then the tank's commander realized that he was alone. He stopped, selected reverse gear and rolled back into the minefield. A mighty explosion shredded the tank's tracks. The crew bailed out and ran toward the defenders with arms raised.

The enemy also failed to get through SR 104's Third Company, which since the beginning of June had been commanded by the blond, tough *Hauptmann* Voigt from Hannover. The Halfaya Pass held. But what about the English tanks which intended to sneak around to the south through the desert? Had they got through?

Early on the morning of June 16 the fast British forces with the main body of the Seventh Armored Division advanced past Halfaya Pass to the left toward the north. The tanks, about 300 of them, reached Capuzzo and Musaid, taking both positions. One armored group separated from the main body and made a wide swing toward the south as the first act of a bold outflanking operation. THis move was also intended to force the German 5th Light Division back toward the north.

The armored spearhead came upon the most forward positions of the 5th Light. Stronger with its new tanks, the British Seventh Armored Division forced a breakthrough and drove toward Hill 208. But waiting for the British tanks there was a German Flak battery.

The Defence of Hill 208

It was not yet daylight when the sentries on Hill 208 heard tank noises. A powerful tank unit was approaching from the southeast. The alarm call awoke the Flak soldiers and the men of the Oasis Company.

Gefreiter Huebner, gunner of the *"Anton"* gun, sighted a group of 30 tanks following a direct course for Hill 208 and reported to *Oberleutnant* Ziemer.

The enemy's artillery opened fire immediately afterward. The Battle of Sollum had begun.

Oberleutnant Paulewicz, the strongpoint commander, ordered his men to open fire from close range. A little later the tanks were within range, The Flak opened fire. The tanks turned and rolled away at high speed. Once again artillery fire thundered down on the German positions.

The tanks came again at 11.00. There were 70 of them, all the dangerous Mark II variety. The guns held their fire until the range was 1,000 meters. Within a few minutes 11 of the Mark IIs had been knocked out.

The tanks reported behind the hill turned out to be those of PR 5 which was carrying out a relieving attack. That afternoon, however, the enemy rolled toward the hill in two attack groups. The first consisted of 40 tanks, the second 20. The smaller group made a frontal attack and before they had come within range the British artillery again opened up with all guns.

The tank-versus-tank battle now began. There was the flash of striking armor-piercing shot and mighty explosions. Several Mark II tanks were left burning and immobilized, but several continued to approach. From close range, where the sounds of the shot and the impact merged into one, the last of the English tanks were destroyed.

Suddenly the battlefield fell silent. Not a shot was fired. The enemy scattered and fled and two more British tanks were destroyed from long range.

Two of the tanks headed toward the location of the fourth gun. One of them was destroyed. The second rolled through the position and over a gun trail. It escaped despite the shots which the defenders sent after it.

Two men of the gun crew, whose foxholes had been crushed by the tank, were buried alive.

For a while it was quiet. Then ten enemy tanks appeared on the flank. The anti-aircraft guns opened fire from 5,000 meters. Two were hit and the rest turned away.

An hour later the third member of the gun's crew, Huebner, saw 85 enemy tanks assembling for another attack. The tanks advanced in the direction of Hill 208. They probably would have

succeeded this time had the tanks of PR 5 not intervened at the last second. Emerging from a narrow *wadi*, they drove into the enemy's flank. It was tank against tank. But the enemy, weakened and unnerved by the failed attacks on Hill 208, pulled back after a brief exchange of fire. When evening fell the outcome of the summer battle had been decided.

In the British General Staff book *Her Majesty's Stationary Office*, which was released in 1956, the authors had this to say about the English tanks in front of Hill 208 that day:

Operation "Battleax," which had begun so promisingly, failed because it did not succeed in taking the decisive Halfaya Pass *and* bypassing Strongpoint 208. The courage and firepower of the defenders was too great. The German eighty-eight proved a deadly weapon against all British tank types. The combined action of tanks with forward-deployed 88mm batteries was a surprise for the British command and a decisive factor in their defeat.

Rommel's victory was a victory of his command, his superior fighting soldiers *and* his better weapons."

One of the soldiers who had made what appeared impossible possible was *Gefreiter* Arnold Huebner. He received the Iron Cross, First Class from Rommel's hand.

But how did the other units fare on June 16? What, for example, happened at the Halfaya Pass on that second day? What did the two Panzer Regiments achieve?

Left page: An oasis camp.
Left above: Eighty-eight in action.
Left below: Knocked-out British light tank.
Below: Another disabled British tank, in this case a Mark III Valentine.

When the enemy stormed Capuzzo and Sollum and the motorcycle troops received the order to withdraw in order to avoid capture, the 50 tanks of the British Seventh Armored Division drove straight toward Bardia. A single 88mm Flak, which had been brought forward by *Oberleutnant* Tocki of PzJägAbt. 33 halted the British advance by knocking out three of the advancing tanks. The remaining tanks stopped and laid down smoke. This delay was sufficient to allow the tanks of PR 8 to reach the scene. In the lead was *Hauptmann* Johannes Kümmel, commander of 1./PR 8, with two Panzer IVs.

"First Battalion, frontal attack!" ordered *Obersteutnant* Cramer. *Major* Fenski, the battalion commander, acknowledged the order.

"First, Second and Third," he called, "drive in wedge formation. First Company drive through without stopping, Second and Third open fire!"

Hauptmann Kümmel, still standing in his open turret hatch — with hatches closed temperatures inside the tank would reach 60 to 65 degrees — observed the approaching enemy. He heard the hiss of armor-piercing shot whipping past. They drove through the enemy fire until they were within the firing range of their short 75mm guns. Then they made a firing halt. Three 75mm guns

Hauptmann Johannes Kümmel.

opened fire. One of the attacking Mark IIs blew up in a shower of fireworks. The company's Panzer IIIs now arrived on the scene and opened fire.

All around all hell had broken loose. Shells hammered into the ground, throwing up fountains of sand. There was a crash behind Kümmel's tank and soon afterward he heard the voice of *Leutnant* Peters in his headphones:

"Have been hit, must get out. Give us covering fire!"

"Turn, Kruschinski!"

The tank driver swung the Panzer IV around. Two British Mark IIs were already firing at the disabled tank. Kümmel saw the *Leutnant* drag his wounded radio operator from the stricken tank. He ordered his gunner to open fire as soon as he had the enemy tank in his sight.

There was a crash as the Panzer IV fired. The tank shuddered from the recoil. One of the Mark IIs was hit in the flank as it turned. The British tank ground to a halt, but kept on firing at *Unteroffizier* Olsberg's Panzer III. A few seconds later the German tank caught fire. The next shot finished the Mark II.

"Onward!"

The German tanks rolled into the midst of a British anti-tank company and drove over the guns. Through his headset Kümmel heard a call for help from *Oberleutnant* Stiefelmeyer, whose company was in trouble.

"We can't get through!" reported *Major* Fenski. "Request relief attack!"

"Second Battalion come from the left flank!" called *Obersteutnant* Cramer. He himself assumed the lead of II./PR 8 and drove forward at high speed. Farther ahead to the right he could see the tanks of I./PR 8 being knocked out one after another.

He urged the companies onward: "Faster!" The panzers rolled forward in wedge formation. More of their own were hit and left behind, belching black smoke. Though disabled they kept on firing.

All of a sudden Cramer spotted a group of 20 Mark II tanks rolling at high speed toward his regiment's left flank. Apparently these tanks, with their 40mm cannon, were to force a decision.

"Kümmel, veer off and take the tank formation in the flank!" ordered Cramer. The *Hauptmann* turned away. About one half of his tanks, including the two Panzer IVs with their 75mm guns, followed in close formation. The first shots whipped from the short barrels of the Panzer IVs into the enemy's flank. The first enemy tanks were hit and stopped. In a short time Kümmel and his two Panzer IVs destroyed eight Mark IIs, saving the regiment and perhaps more. *Oberstleutnant* Cramer had been given some breathing space. Now he was in a position to decide the battle in his favor. With a hard crash an armor-piercing round struck the ground to the right of his command tank. But before the enemy tank could fire again it was put out of action by *Oberfeldwebel* Krucks' panzer, catching fire after the first shot. The crew bailed out.

"Wheel to the east!" ordered Cramer. Just as his tank turned on one track a hit shook the vehicle. Cramer felt a heavy blow, then a sharp pain in his head and arm. He had been wounded by shell splinters.

A little later the engagement was broken off. The tanks drove back to their assembly area. Half of 1./PR 8's tanks were missing. The other companies had suffered similar losses.

The June 16 attempt on to take Capuzzo in a *coup de main* had failed, but the enemy's advance had been halted.

Rommel realized that the old tactics he had used there would no longer work. He therefore strove to find another solution. In his personal diary he wrote:

"One can often decide a battle merely by shifting a strongpoint, and taking the enemy by surprise."

Rommel had also followed the battle fought by the 5th Light Division. Seeing that the 15th Panzer Division's PR 8 had only 30 of its 80 tanks left, and that the 5th Light Division's PR 5 had gained ground in its attack from the area west of Sidi Azeiz toward Sidi Suleiman, he reached a new decision. He drove to the 5th Light and learned that it would be possible to bring PR 5's battle against the British Seventh Armored Division to a successful conclusion. He urged the division to make a fast, fighting advance into the area northeast of Sidi Omar and from there to continue the attack toward Sidi Suleiman.

This was the battle's decisive turning point.

Rommel immediately ordered the 15th PD to release everything which was motorized and could be let go and send it to the left flank of the 5th Light Division for a joint attack the next morning

to reach Sidi Suleiman and throw back the enemy.

When, during the night of June 16/17, Rommel realized that the enemy intended to stick to his plan, he moved the time of the attack up to 04.30 in order to seize the initiative from the enemy.

At 04.30 *Generalmajor* Neumann-Silkow, the commander of the 15th PD, gave the order to attack. The leading tanks of the 5th Light Division also set off. The German counteroffensive into the enemy's rear began. The first to engage the enemy were the tanks of PR 8. The Fenski Battalion drove into the flank of the British tank unit, resulting in a short, sharp tank battle. A large number of knocked-out enemy tanks were left behind on the battlefield.

At the same time the 5th Light also met the enemy. It, too, fought its way through and at 06.00 reached the area of Sidi Suleiman.

Continuing to advance, the German tanks — Rommel had given the order to drive on to Halfaya on the coast and close the ring around the British — ran into an enemy truck column, which was shot up. Enemy tanks which appeared in the vicinity were blanketed with heavy fire and, at 09.25, General Creagh radioed to the Commander of Desert Forces that he saw no way out, and could General Beresford-Peirse come to Creagh's headquarters to unravel the situation.

When Rommel was shown this intercepted message, he said:

"They don't know where they stand. They won't do anything else now."

A little later the tanks of PR 5 overran the headquarters of Brigadier General Messervy, rendering the British Fourth Armored Brigade leaderless.

While *Hauptmann* Kümmel and his company rolled toward the stone walls of the Halfaya Pass, followed by the rest of the regiment on the left and right, the remains of the British Fourth Armored Brigade began a hasty retreat.

A little later, just after General Wavell and General Beresford-Peirse arrived at the headquarters of the Seventh Armored Division, Peirse gave the order for all remaining units to withdraw. It was General Wavell who initiated the order to retreat in an effort to save what he could of the British forces. Afterward he flew back to cairo and sent the following message to London:

"I regret to have to report that Operation "Battleaxe" has failed."

It was just after 16.00 when the two German divisions reached the Halfaya Pass and attacked northward from the enemy's rear. The British were driven back. Nevertheless, their forces were able to escape through the large gap between Sidi Omar and the Halfaya Pass and escape encirclement at the last second. They beat a hasty retreat and did not halt until they reached Sidi Barani.

Informed of the decisive action taken by *Hauptmann* Kümmel, *Generalmajor* Neumann-Silkow recommended him for the Knight's Cross. In his recommendation he stated:

"The attack by *Hauptmann* Kümmel against the superior enemy tank force west and northwest of Capuzzo was a result of his own initiative. Through the boldness of this decision and the uncompromising execution of the same, he prevented the enemy from advancing farther to the north, where the combat train, which was just departing, would have been caught and destroyed. Without the combat train, which kept PR 8 supplied with vital fuel and ammunition during the three-day battle in the desert, the successful halting and subsequent destruction of considerable enemy tank forces would have been impossible.

It is due to his tough and decisive independent decision that a dangerous enemy breakthrough was prevented."

The enemy had been decisively defeated. The British lost 220 tanks on the battlefield. Many of the German tanks could be repaired and put back into service; only 25 were total losses.

The Halfaya Pass also had to withstand heavy attacks on the 16th and also during the morning of the 17th of June. *Hauptmann* Bach was the backbone of the defences. The Halfaya Pass held. The British had attacked in several waves. The 11th Indian Brigade and the Twenty-second Guards Brigade captured the village of Halfaya. The Fourth Armored Brigade tried desperately to capture the pass on the 16th.

Hauptmann Bach directed the defence. With his ever-present cigar in the corner of his mouth, he scanned the terrain, hurried through enemy fire to the threatened sector and held out against the fierce attacks.

This was the basis of the German victory, for which *Hauptmann* Bach was awarded the Knight's Cross.

Early on the morning of June 16 the battle was on the razor's edge. Rommel sent the following message to the former pastor in "Hellfire Pass," as the British called it:

"Everything depends on whether Halfaya Pass can be held. Hold the pass no matter what!"

The British attacked five times. British and Indian battalions stormed the positions and were wiped out. Then artillery fire rained down on the pass. Finally *Hauptmann* Bach scraped a company together and launched a counterattack, recovering the village of Halfaya.

The German victory was complete. It was achieved through the efficient combined operation of all weapons and the stubbornness of a few units in strategically decisive positions.

"Battleaxe," the largest tank battle in the desert at that time, was a disaster for the enemy.

The front froze. The African summer paralyzed friend and foe. But the first supplies were reaching both sides and both were striving to be ready for action again as soon as possible.

Above right: Rommel (left) present as the Bach Battalion is relieved at the Halfaya Pass. Major Bach (next to Rommel) makes his report. The other two officers are, from left to right, Leutnant Syring and Major Panzenhagen, commander of the relieving III./IR 347.
Middle right: Major Bach leads Major Panzenhagen through the Halfaya Pass positions; far right is Oberleutnant Eichholz.
Below: Rommel at the Halfaya Pass (second from right). A rare photograph of him in short pants.
Bottom right: Lieutenant Lambretto, Oberstleutnant Panzenhagen and interpreter Uffz. Moselli watch a firefight on the Sollum Front.

Winter Battle

Between the Battles

The war had become stalemated around Sollum and Tobruk. The soldiers of the *Deutsches Afrika-Korps*, who had been sent into battle totally unaccustomed to service in the tropics, had learned much. They now knew that one could — and had to — drink salty water, even though it affected their digestion. There was just nothing else available.

The soldiers of the two German divisions also learned how to survive the scorching breath of the *ghibli*; they learned how to find cover in treeless desert and how to dig in vehicles and weapons without becoming buried with them.

The most important thing they had learned, however, was that the enemy could be beaten; that they were at least equal to the experienced British colonial troops *and* were better led. This resulted in an incomparably high level of morale from the beginning, and every man who saw action in Africa was seized by this high morale.

They were regular troops, not a hand-picked elite formation, but in Africa they became the *Afrika-Korps,* bearing the stamp of their commander, Erwin Rommel, and the officers who fought in the front lines with their soldiers. These officers who led from the front were in a much better position to formulate strategy than those whose orders reached the front long after the situation had changed.

The main problem in the desert, as the DAK came to learn, was supply. 1,500 tons of supplies were required daily, including water and rations, which was simply more than could be brought across the Mediterranean by ship. For those supplies that did reach Africa, there was still an endlessly long journey to reach the front lines. It was 2,000 kilometers from Tripoli to the Halfaya Pass.

In the next six months Rommel was able to hold onto the territory he had won in Cyrenaica and the Marmarika against British probing raids, and against attacks on land, sea and in the air. The Sollum — Bardia front was fortified against attack.

Powerful German — Italian forces were tied down in the siege of Tobruk. Tobruk was and remained the thorn in the flesh of the *Afrika-Korps.* If the enemy attacked simultaneously from Egypt *and* Tobruk (the British had poured 30,000 troops into the fortress), the situation would be serious. The danger would then arise that the German forces might be trapped, surrounded and destroyed in the large triangle between the sea, Sollum and the Tobruk front.

What the *Afrika-Korps* needed was fresh divisions, including at least one panzer division.

The summer battle was marked by nightly raids, offensive patrols and air attacks. The Flak once again demonstrated its effectiveness.

The 606th Flak Battalion under its commander Georg Briel had embarked for Africa on March 25, 1941. First Company shipped out aboard the "Ruhr," Second Company on the "Heraklea" and Third Company on the "Adana." The Briel convoy left Naples on 27 March. Initially all went well, but on the afternoon of the 28th "Heraklea" was torpedoed and sank within ten minutes. *Leutnant* Hagl pulled one man after another out

The 606th Flak Battalion embarks in Naples Harbor.

The 606th Flak Battalion in Naples Harbor.

Bottom:
The remains of a shot-down bomber burn in the desert.

Center: Self-propelled Flak advance.
Bottom left: Remains of a British aircraft shot down by 3./Flak 606.
Bottom right: Caserta, May 1941. From left: Hauptmann Kessler, Leutnant Mees, Oberstleutnant Panzenhagen, Oberarzt Dr. Ossenberg.
Top facing page: Generaloberst Rommel inspects III./IR 347. From left: Oberstleutnant Panzenhagen (partially hidden), Generalmajor Veith, Major Kolbeck, Rommel, Leutnant Lang, aide, Major von Mellenthin (important photo).
Center: Bf 110 heavy fighters fly escort for a Mediterranean convoy in the summer of 1942.
Bottom: Bf 110 heavy fighter over the desert, this time flying cover for an air convoy. Note Ju 52 transports behind and below the fighter.

through the hatches. About a third of Second Company was picked up by the escorting destroyers. Two thirds of the company's soldiers died before they reached Africa.

The "Ruhr" was hit by a torpedo at the same time. Despite the large hole in her side she stayed afloat and was towed to Trapani.

The Third Company under *Hauptmann* Reiter reached Tripoli aboard the "Adana" and was immediately thrown into the battle by Rommel, taking part in the advance through Cyrenaica.

The Second Company was reformed in Naples by *Hauptmann* Dr. Ecker and did not reach Africa until some time later. First Company disembarked in Tripoli on 24 April. *Major* Briel now had two of his three companies in Africa.

The 606th Flak Battalion's Third Company suffered heavy casualties in the Battle of Tobruk when the guns drove up to the wire in the open and shot up the machine gun positions which were barring MG 8's way to Tobruk.

When the battalion was finally united in Africa in the summer, Second Company was placed under the direct command of the corps headquarters. Under the command of *Hauptmann* Dr. Ecker it became the "bodyguard" of the *Afrika-Korps* headquarters staff. A platoon accompanied the commanding general on almost every trip to the front. During the Sollum battle First Company was placed under the command of the 5th Light Division. During the summer First and Third Companies combined to form *Kampfgruppe* Briel, which was employed as a fire-brigade wherever trouble broke out.

When peace returned following the summer battle the battalion transferred by platoons to Bardia for "bathing leave" on the coast.

In September 1941 the 612th Flak Battalion arrived in Africa.

The British Side

On June 21, 1941, a few days after the failed offensive, the British Prime Minister, Winston Churchill, wrote to the Commander-in-Chief in Cairo, A.P. Wavell:

"I have decided that the general interest would best be served if General Auchinleck were named commander of the Army in the Near East in your place."

Thus Wavell was sent from the desert into the — desert. The scapegoat system worked on the British side as well.

On July 1 General Auchinleck was named Commander-in-Chief in the desert. Churchill wrote to him:

"You take over this important command at a time of crisis. You should devote your special attention to the situation at Tobruk, the arrival of enemy reinforcements in Libya and the fact that the Germans are now primarily occupied with the invasion of Russia. You will realize, then, how important these problems are."

In the following months Claude Auchinleck came under increasing pressure to begin his offensive. The earlier this took place, the more effective it would be, and would catch the Germans at a time of weakness.

For Rommel and the *Afrika-Korps* it was bad luck that the Russian Campaign began on June 22, 1941. Russia had undisputed priority over all other theaters of war.

Erwin Rommel, promoted to General of Panzer Troops on July 1, 1941, continued to hope for the addition of two more panzer divisions.

General Roatta, who went to Africa to discuss the situation with Rommel, also hoped that Rommel's *Panzerarmee* would be enlarged to four panzer divisions. He himself promised a new *Panzerkorps* with three panzer divisions *and* two or three motorized infantry divisions.

In the meantime the 5th Light Division had been renamed the 21st Panzer Division and *Generalmajor* von Ravenstein had taken over command of the unit.

All of this was known in general to the British and they feared — especially Churchill — a reinforcement of the *Panzerarmee* in North Africa.

It is therefore understandable that Churchill exerted pressure for a new offensive before the German forces in North Africa became any stronger.

During autumn the British Eighth Army received a steady flow of supplies and troops. The newly-formed army possessed four motorized divisions, an armored division, two armored brigades and several independent regiments. Its Commander-in-Chief was General Cunningham. Formed into two corps, the new army was to smash the Axis forces in Marmarica and Cyrenaica, drive them back and recapture Tripoli.

General Cunningham arrived in the desert on September 9. The Thirtieth Corps, consisting of the Seventh Armored Division, the First South African Infantry Division and the Twenty-second Guards Brigade, was commanded by General Vivian Pope. Pope was an armor expert. He was to lead the main attack with this British counterpart to the DAK.

The Thirteenth Corps was made up of infantry units: the New Zealand Division, the Fourth Indian Division and an independent armored brigade.

The British Fourth Armored Brigade, which was equipped with the new Stuart tank from the USA, was under the direct command of the Eighth Army.

On October 5 General Pope and two officers of his staff were killed in a plane crash. His successor was Major General Willoughby Norrie, commander of the First Armored Division, which was en route to North Africa. General Godwin-Austen became the commanding general of Thirteenth Corps.

By the end of October 300 Crusader tanks, 300 Stuart tanks, 170 Matilda infantry tanks, 3,400 trucks, 600 artillery pieces, 80 heavy and 160 light anti-aircraft guns, 200 anti-tank guns and 900 mortars had arrived in North Africa. The British Eighth Army had the best of equipment and was armed to the teeth.

General Cunningham finally approved one of the three plans submitted for the new offensive, which was code-named "Crusader." The plan's success depended on the Thirtieth Corps engaging the *Deutsche Afrika-Korps* in a tank battle and destroying it. Not until this had happened would the garrison of Tobruk dare to attempt to break out. At the same time the Thirteenth Corps was to drive toward Tobruk to catch the besieging units in a trap. Before this took place the Thirteenth Corps was to split the German and Italian forces at the frontier.

The beginning of the offensive, which was planned for November 15, had to be postponed until the 18th because the First South African Division, which had been moved up from Abyssinia, was late receiving its supplies. The division's commander, Major General Brink, refused to attack while his unit was unprepared.

On the British side all was ready for Operation "Crusader," but what of the German side?

Panzergruppe Afrika

General der Panzertruppe Rommel knew very well that the enemy would have recovered sufficiently to launch a new offensive by year's end at the latest. If he was to forestall this blow he would have to attempt to take Tobruk in order to remove the threat posed by this second front. He therefore drew the encircling ring around the fortress tighter and tighter in September and October. By mid-October he had won favorable positions from which to launch a large-scale attack on the fortress.

New units *and* war materiel of all kinds were needed if he was to carry out the attack and be able to defend his own lines against a British assault. This was promised but not entirely delivered.

Instead of a third panzer division *Panzergruppe Afrika* was sent the newly-formed 90th Light African Division under *Generalmajor* Max Sümmermann. The first of the new unit's troops arrived by air in August. The core of the division was formed by the 155th and 200th Rifle Regiments and 361st *"Afrika-Regiment."*

The latter unit was formed by the XVIII Corps Headquarters in Salzburg in June 1941. The soldiers were all former Foreign Legionnaires with as much as 15 years experience fighting with the French Foreign Legion in Indochina and Africa. These troops gave the Germans a unit experienced in warfare in the tropics: the 361st Afrika-Regiment, which was soon to prove itself in action in Africa. The assembly point for the regimental headquarters, the artillery battalion and First Battalion was St. Wendel, that of the Second Battalion was Rheine.

The regiment's officers were as follows: Commander: *Oberst* Grund, Adjutant: *Hauptmann* Kirsten, Commander First Battalion: *Oberstleutnant* Harder, Commander Second Battalion: *Major* Ryll, Adjutant: *Leutnant* Einsfelder, Battalion Medical Officer: *AssArzt* Dr. Popken, Commander Fifth Company: *Leutnant* Ochsenhirt, Commander Sixth Company: *Leutnant* Wipperfürth, Commander Seventh Company: *Hauptmann* Kahl, Commander Eighth Company: *Oberstleutnant* Jörns.

When *Major* Ryll arrived at the Salzburg Corps Headquarters he learned to his surprise that the main body of the 361st Afrika-Regiment consisted of Foreign Legionnaires. He reported that initially it was unclear how the regiment was to be used. In the strength and equipment report, for example, there was the following footnote:

"Camels and pack animals will be supplied following arrival in the Mediterranean Theater."

When the regiment's commander, *Oberst* Grund, flew ahead to visit Rommel to learn how the unit was to be employed, the latter told him:

"What I need, Grund, are not hungry mouths, but full ones. That means: you are to arrive on the scene with a unit fully equipped with automatic weapons."

The first shipment of Foreign legionnaires left for Africa on October 12. The men of the regiment did not arrive in Benghazi until early November, however. They were billeted in the area south of Tobruk in the vicinity of the perimeter road at Trigh Capuzzo. It was intended that the regiment be used as an assault unit in the attack on Tobruk on November 21.

Rommel, who immediately inspected the Legionnaires on their arrival, was greatly impressed by the clever manner in which they dug in and fortified their positions. He gained the impression that this was a unit that would fight like the devil.

The new command structure in Africa was laid down at the end of October. *Generalfeldmarschall* Albert Kesselring became the new *Oberbefehlshaber Süd*. It was his task to achieve German air superiority over the sea between Italy and Africa. X. *Fliegerkorps* under *General* Geisler and the Fifth Italian Air Wing in Libya were placed under his command. Hitler also intended to send Kesselring the II. *Fliegerkorps* from Russia — the reasoning being that, with the beginning of winter, there would be little activity on that front.

The senior Axis commander in Africa was General Bastico. The DAK was under his command as well as its Italian counterpart, the Twentieth Tank Corps under General Gambarra, with the armored divisions *"Atiete"* and *"Trieste."*

Within *Panzergruppe Afrika* was the *Deutsche Afrika-Korps* on the one side under *Generalleutnant* Ludwig Crüwell with the 15th and 21st Panzer Divisions, the 90th Light African Division and the *"Savona"* Division and, on the other, the Twenty-First Italian Army Corps led by Corps General Navarrini, with the *"Trento"*, *"Bologna"*, *"Brescia"* and *"Pavia"* Divisions.

Even though there had been no significant

Top left: Command staff and tank commanders of the 21st Panzer Division; in the center, wearing the jacket, is Generalmajor von Ravenstein.
Center left: General Crüwell, commanding general of the DAK (left), and Generalleutnant von Vaerst. On the far right is Oberst Menny, commander of the 15th Rifle Brigade.
Bottom left: Generalmajor von Bismarck (center) and to his right General Crüwell.
Top right: Tug of war — a popular sport in the desert.
Bottom right: A Bersaglieri

strengthening of his forces, Rommel was planning three different operations. On the one hand he wanted to be ready to meet a British offensive. He had the border fortifications extended and laid giant mine fields which stretched between Sidi Omar and Sollum. Between Tobruk and the left flank on the sea was the *Afrika-Korps*.

In an effort to raise combat readiness *and* at the same time capture a suspected British supply dump, on September 14 Rommel committed the 21st Panzer Division and MG 8, which had been brought back up to full strength.

Three battle groups were formed:

1. Battle Group Panzer Regiment 5 under *Oberst* Stephan.

2. Battle Group *Major* Schütte with MG 8, PzJägAbt. 602, I./AR 33 and a platoon of FlaBtl. 606.

3. Battle Group *Major* Panzenhagen with III./IR 347 (90th Light Division).

The assignment was: the enemy forces on the Hagigag el Agaba plateau in the vicinity of the frontier near Bir el Khireigat are to be attacked and destroyed. The supply dump they are protecting is to be cleared out and brought back. For this purpose each battle group will received a number of trucks; the majority of these will drive with the center battle group, while the battle groups on the flanks protect the center."

All three battle groups set off simultaneously on September 14. An hour later Battle Group PR 5, which was driving in the north, encountered enemy armored forces. A tank-versus-tank battle broke out in which several British tanks were destroyed and the rest forced to retire.

In the meantime the men of MG 8 under *Major* Schütte drove on at high speed and reached Qaret el Ruweibit, where they were fired on by British armored cars. The anti-tank and anti-aircraft guns were moved forward and destroyed two armored cars, leaving them in flames. The enemy force withdrew toward the east into the desert.

Major Schütte, seeing the clouds of dust raised by the tank engagement to the north, was forced to assume that the tanks of PR 5 were unable to advance and called a halt to avoid exposing his flanks. That evening he received orders to pull back to the original area of departure.

The southern battle group under *Major* Panzenhagen advanced farther than either of the two northern groups. Panzenhagen drove ahead of the motorcycle troops in his command car. In the afternoon his force became involved in a minor skirmish with enemy armored cars. Panzenhagen had his forces set up an all-round defensive position for the night, which was just as well, as they were attacked twice by enemy armored cars and infantry. Both attacks were beaten off without loss. The next morning the battle group withdrew to its departure positions as ordered. The attack had achieved nothing.

Everything was ready for the great winter battle, and on October 26 Erwin Rommel decreed that the German offensive was to take place sometime between the 15th and 21st of November. This deadline was subsequently put back to November 23. Rommel reckoned that the British were also preparing for an offensive at this time. The code word for a British attack was *"Hochwasser"* ("High Water").

"Crusader" Begins!

On the evening of November 17, 1941 heavy rain fell on the desert between Tobruk and the Halfaya Pass. It was the first such cloudburst in sixty years. At first the soldiers ran into the open to enjoy the downpour. But then the first streams of water began to fill the formerly dry *wadis*, soon becoming raging torrents which carried off anything standing in their path. A tremendous thunderstorm broke over the desert. Lightning flashed through the darkness. Near Gambut and the Halfaya Pass tents were swept away by the water and soldiers drowned in the desert. Then, through the communications net, rang the code word:

"Hochwasser!" - "Hochwasser!" - "Hochwasser!"

Was this the enemy attack or a warning about the actual high water? No one knew for sure except a few men of AA 33. On patrol, they had seen and reported enemy tank movements in the area of Trigh el Abd.

That night a British armored armada of 1,000 vehicles moved through the desert into its assembly areas under cover of the driving rain. In the south

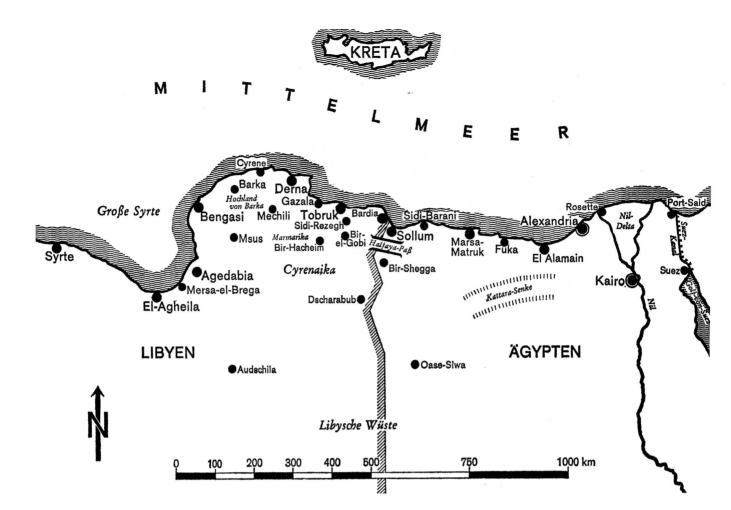

KRETA

M I T T E L M E E R

Große Syrte

Syrte

Cyrene
Barka Derna
Hochland Gazala
von Barka
Bengasi Mechili Tobruk Bardia Sidi-Barani
Sidi-Rezegh
Msus Marmarika Bir- Bir- Sollum
Bir-Hacheim el-Gobi Halfaya-Paß

Alexandria Rosette Nil-Delta Port-Said

Marsa- Fuka El Alamain
Matruk

Suez-Kanal

Cyrenaika Bir-Shegga

Agedabia Kattara-Senke
Mersa-el-Brega
El-Agheila Dscharabub Kairo Suez

LIBYEN ÄGYPTEN Nil

Audschila Oase-Siwa

N

Libysche Wüste

0 100 200 300 400 500 750 1000 km

Map of the North African Theater from, *Ritterkreuzträger des Afrika-Korps*, by Karl Alman.

Flash flood in the desert — men are drowned.

the Thirtieth Corps' Seventh Armored Division, First South African Infantry Division and Twenty-second Armored Brigade rolled out of their assembly areas around Maddalena and drove in a wide arc through the southern desert before veering north abeam Bir el Gobi toward Tobruk.

The Thirteenth Corps sent the Second New Zealand Infantry Division and the Fourth Indian Infantry Division, as well as the British Army's First Armored Brigade, north of the first wave directly toward Sollum, its left wing driving in a wide arc around Bardia toward the sea. Fast units drove into the rear of the Axis forces from the Girabub oasis, their objective being to cut the German-Italian supply lines.

When the first reports of the three widely-separated enemy drives arrived *Generalleutnant* Ludwig Crüwell expressed concern over the development. Rommel's view was that they were merely reconnaissance probes.

But on the evening of November 18, 1941, when the enemy movements continued to develop and *Generalmajor* von Ravenstein reported enemy armored forces from his front, the German armored group command realized that this was the beginning of the British offensive. German reconnaissance units had been pushed back from their line of security between Bir el Gobi and Sidi Omar.

A British staff vehicle was intercepted near Sidi Suleiman and its driver, an NCO, was captured. *Oberstleutnant* Fritz Bayerlein, who had just arrived in Africa as the new Chief of the DAK General Staff, had the NCO brought to headquarters in Bardia for interrogation. The staff NCO told Bayerlein that the British command was in possession of an attack plan which had been signed personally by Rommel. It was the plan for the attack on Tobruk. The NCO described a map he was carrying as British Commander-in-Chief Auchinleck's plan for his strategic build-up.

Immediately after the interrogation Bayerlein contacted Rommel, who had driven to Gambut. His report seemed unbelievable to Rommel.

"The enemy is using this map to lead us astray, Bayerlein," surmised Rommel. Nevertheless, the map was evaluated in the next few days. It proved to be correct.

One thing was certain on the evening of November 18. The British were on the march with 1,000 tanks, 100,000 troops and 1,000 aircraft. The

Officer corps of the 21st Panzer Division before the November 1941 offensive. From left: Major Bach, Oberstleutnant Stephan, Oberstleutnant von Wechmar, Major Schütte, Generalmajor von Ravenstein, guest of the DAK Oberstleutnant Bayerlein, Major Beil, Hauptmann Gierga, Oberstleutnant Knabe.

Generalmajor von Bismarck issues orders to his tank commanders.

striking power of the new Eighth Army was greater than ever before.

The British Attack on November 19, 1941

Continuing its advance from the Maddalena area into the Gabr Saleh area, the Third Royal Tank Regiment, a component of the Seventh Armored Division's Fourth Brigade, encountered elements of AA 3 twenty kilometers east of Gabr Saleh. Under heavy pressure from the British armor, these fell back toward the northwest into the area west of Gasr el Arid. The main body of the Fourth Brigade reached the area of Gabr Saleh without any contact with the enemy, however.

The British Seventh Brigade likewise had no encounters with enemy forces, advancing near to the airfield at Sidi Rezegh. The Sixth Royal Tank Regiment, which was the armored spearhead of the attack, first met resistance east of Sidi Rezegh. It was provided by the Foreign Legionnaires of IR 361, which had just arrived in Africa. The British armored spearhead halted there and assumed a defensive posture while waiting for the main body of the division to catch up.

At noon that day the Twenty-second British Brigade came upon the Italian-defended position of Bir el Gobi. There it was halted. Surrounded in Bir el Gobi, the Italian "Young Fascists" Division defended bravely. Then the *"Ariete"* Tank Division intervened in the fighting, destroying five British tanks.

It was midday on November 19 and still the German command did not have a clear picture of the situation. During the afternoon situation briefing the commander of the 21st PD suggested sending a strong battle group toward Gabr Saleh. Rommel gave his consent.

The German Counterattack

"*Oberst* Stephan will lead the armored battle group of the 21st PD and destroy the suspected enemy reconnaissance forces between Sidi Omar and Gabr Saleh, and on reaching Gabr Saleh will assume a defensive posture.

The 15th PD will move into a waiting area southwest of Gambut, so as to be ready at any time for employment at the focal points." Thus read the DAK's orders.

Kampfgruppe Stephan set off a short while later. The battle group consisted of the 120 serviceable tanks of PR 5, twelve light field guns and four 88mm Flak. The main body of the division followed at a safe distance. It was precisely 15.30 when the battle group came upon enemy forces — the Fourth British Armored Brigade less the Third Royal Tank Regiment — about eight kilometers northeast of Gabr Saleh.

Acting immediately, *Oberst* Stephan sent both panzer battalions forward. The enemy was caught flat-footed. Soon the first enemy tanks were blazing on the desert plain. Trucks and personnel carriers exploded. The enemy gave way and was forced southward by the onrushing German tanks. The retreating British forces passed Trigh el Abd. Stuart tanks attempted to stop the retreat. No less than 23 of these tanks were destroyed. All of the companies of PR 5 took part in the attack. The panzers halted, fired a concentrated volley at the enemy and then drove on. Twenty more enemy tanks were damaged. German losses in the heavy fighting were three tanks destroyed.

Rommel, who had watched over the attack by the battle group, was satisfied with this initial success. The British Fourth Brigade withdrew farther to the south. The British attack at that location had been stopped.

That evening *Generalmajor* von Ravenstein called Crüwell, the commanding general of the DAK, and suggested combining the 15th and 21st Panzer Divisions and then attacking and destroying the enemy forces. The chief of staff, *Oberstleutnant* Bayerlein, presented the idea to Rommel, who gave *Generalleutnant* Crüwell a free hand for the following day and instructed him to destroy the enemy forces in the Bardia-Tobruk-Sidi Omar area before they were in a position to threaten the German forces besieging Tobruk.

On the morning of November 20 the 21st PD rolled into the area of Sidi Azeiz searching for the Third Royal Regiment which had forced back AA 3. *Generalleutnant* Crüwell considered this one of the main thrusts of the enemy offensive and wanted to stop it just as the Fourth Brigade had been stopped. However, the Royal Tank Regiment had already turned around and returned to its brigade southeast of Gabr Saleh.

Thus the 21st PD found no enemy forces. After

reaching Sidi Azeiz it veered south and finally halted in the desert 20 kilometers northwest of Sidi Omar, as it was running low on fuel. Urgent calls went out to the *Panzergruppe* for fuel; however, this did not arrive until late that evening.

At the same time on November 20 the 15th PD set off from the area 13 kilometers southwest of Gasr el Arid to search for and smash the enemy. On reaching the area northeast of Gabr Saleh it ran into the British Fourth Brigade. Once again heavy tank-versus-tank fighting broke out. The tanks exchanged fire until darkness fell. Once again the German method of commanding armor proved superior. Fifty-five of the 123 tanks which the brigade had had on strength that morning were destroyed. Following two engagements the brigade's strength had been reduced to 68 tanks.

The Second New Zealand Division, which was only ten kilometers east of the battlefield and had a large number of tanks available, did not intervene. The commander of the Fourth Brigade rejected the idea with the comment that, according to the battle plan, involving units of the Thirteenth Corps in tank battles was not permissable.

At 21.00 the BBC news service broadcast:

"The Eighth Army has begun an offensive in the western desert with 75,000 well-armed soldiers, which is to destroy the German-Italian forces in Africa." Immediately afterward Rommel sent a message to the DAK, ordering it to combine the two panzer divisions and engage the enemy in a tank battle.

In the meantime, General Cunningham had likewise combined the Fourth and Twenty-second Armored Brigades, massing all of his remaining tank forces.

General Scobie, the commander of Fortress Tobruk, had received orders to break out of the fortress. General Gott ordered Brigadier Campbell to support the breakout with his Seventh Support Group by taking the line of hills near Sidi Rezegh.

Top: Artillery and tanks of the 15th Panzer Division.
Center: II./PR 8 on the march to the front.
Bottom: Command vehicle with Generalmajor von Ravenstein, commander of the 21st Panzer Division.

The Tank Battle near Sidi Rezegh

During the night *General der Panzertruppe* Rommel issued the following order to the *Deutsche Afrika-Korps*:

"On 25. 11. attack the rear of the enemy forces advancing on Tobruk from the area 25 kilometers west of Sidi Omar direction Belhamed."

Five hours later he supplemented the attack order with the following urgent message:

"The situation is serious! Get going as quickly as possible!" At about the same time the British Seventh Armored Brigade made contact with the Seventh Support Group, creating the conditions necessary for the attack on Tobruk, which was to relieve the garrison and support the breakout by the same.

Again the men of the 90th Light fought off an enemy attack near Sidi Rezegh. The critical position was held by *Major* Ryll's II./IR 361. The enemy forces there were smashed. The Legionnaires attacked the tanks with molotov cocktails and destroyed three. The enemy attack was repulsed for the second time.

Generalleutnant Crüwell, who early that morning had assembled the units of the DAK for the new attack, accompanied the DAK's attack into the rear of the enemy's Seventh Armored Division in "Moritz," a captured British Mammoth command vehicle. On that dull, rainy morning the DAK had broken contact with the enemy of the day before. It left behind powerful rearguards, reinforced with anti-tank guns and 88mm Flak, manning a front facing south and southeast, then it set off on a broad front for the new attack, which was aimed at Belhamed and Sidi Rezegh to the northwest. The 21st Panzer Division's objective was Belhamed, while the 15th Panzer Division was to advance via Sidi Muftah toward Sidi Rezegh.

While still en route to their objectives the two divisions were met by about 80 to 100 enemy tanks. The DAK panzers attacked in groups while maintaining a rapid rate of fire and forced the British tanks to withdraw. Driving straight through, by midday the DAK reached the area of the plateau southeast of Sidi Rezegh. It was, however, unable to recapture the airfield at Sidi Rezegh which was held by the British. Anti-tank guns and artillery of the support group fired on the German tanks. At the same time tanks of the British Seventh Armored

Division attacked from the flank, in an attempt to destroy the panzers. The attempt failed. The British paid for this attack with the loss of 30 tanks.

The fighting continued until evening. Then the two panzer divisions broke contact with the enemy, setting up all-round defensive positions for the night, the 15th PD near Sidi Muftah and the 21st PD in the area south of Point 175.

An attempted advance out of the southeastern section of the fortress by weak enemy forces on the morning of the same day had been turned back easily by the besieging forces. During the further course of November 21, however, the British launched another attack from the fortress, this time supported by 50 infantry tanks. This time the attackers broke through the encircling ring, reached the axis road and overran the artillery positions of the "*Bologna*" Division, destroying two battalions and about 35 guns.

Fortunately, AA 3 was in a position to intervene at the last second. Under the command of *Oberstleutnant* von Wechmar, it overpowered the enemy forces and drove them back.

In Bir el Gobi the Italians of the Gambarra Corps also managed to hold out against the steadily growing pressure from the enemy.

In the middle of the night both panzer divisions of the DAK were moved out of their all-round defensive positions. The 15th PD was ordered to drive into the area south of Gambut, while the 21st PD was instructed to reach the area of Zaafran. From there on 22 November they were to carry out a mobile assault against the enemy forces south of Trigh Capuzzo and destroy them.

Unobserved by the enemy, *Generalleutnant* Crüwell regrouped the 15th Panzer Division and sent it east against the enemy's deep flank.

While the 15th PD was changing positions in the area south of Gambut, the 21st PD left the plateau and moved into the area of Belhamed-Zaafran. As a result of this regrouping the supply columns were late reaching both divisions, and it was not until late morning on November 22 that they were able to refuel and rearm.

PR 8 now received orders from *Generalleutnant* Crüwell to encircle the British Fourth Armored Brigade and destroy it, while the 21st PD was committed to attack the enemy forces near Sidi Rezegh. Rommel personally issued the order to 21st PD at noon on November 22.

When Cramer's panzers came upon the enemy, the latter cleverly pulled back.

"After them!" ordered *Oberst* Cramer, and drove forward with Second Battalion.

The deepening twilight and the darkness which soon followed caused the Germans to initially lose contact with the enemy. Nevertheless, Cramer decided to continue the pursuit.

"The commander of First Battalion to me!" he ordered. When *Major* Fenski arrived and reported, Cramer gave him the following orders:

"Fenski, you and your battalion will drive in the lead. As soon as you encounter enemy tanks, report to me and at the same time try to bring the enemy to battle."

A few minutes later the panzers of I./PR 8 drove forward and took over the lead. It was pitch black. Standing in the lead vehicle, Fenski could barely see his hand in front of his face. Nevertheless, he had the battalion — in close formation — drive on at a walking pace. Fortune smiled on him; suddenly they drove right into a dense concentration of tanks. It looked as if they had been abandoned. Fenski peered through his night glasses; there was nothing to be seen!

"Ahead cautiously!" he ordered. "All weapons clear!"

The lead panzer drove into the middle of the British tank laager.

"Surround the tanks!" ordered Fenski.

Oberleutnant Beck, the battalion adjutant, opened "hostilities" by firing a series of white signal flares to indicate the battalion's position to those following.

At first the parked British tanks were as still as stone. They had assumed it was their own tanks moving about, and now they found themselves facing the German tanks which their patrols had reported much farther to the rear.

The first British tank fired up its engine and rolled off. A burst of machine-gun fire and a shot from a panzer's main gun immediately brought it to a halt. Then four British tanks tried to make off from the northern part of the laager. A brief, sharp volley from several tank cannon soon reduced them to blazing hulks. The night was lit by the flickering flames. The guns fell silent again. The remaining British tank commanders resigned themselves to their fate. A ring had closed around the British Fourth Armored Brigade, as well as the supply vehicles of the Eighth Hussars. The prisoners would have to be fetched from their tanks to prevent them from trying something foolish.

"Commanders dismount! Take submachine-guns and take the enemy tank crews prisoner!"

The gunners and loaders remained in the tanks, ready to intervene at once if necessary. Tank headlights were turned on. Several British tank crews prepared to defend themselves. One officer managed to set three tanks on fire before he was taken prisoner. A few minutes later *Major* Fenski reported to his regimental commander, who was approaching at top speed:

"A Brigadier General, 17 officers and 150 men taken prisoner. 35 tanks, a number of guns and several radio trucks captured."

"Thank you, Fenski!" said Hans Cramer, "that will mean the Knight's Cross for you!"

Unfortunately, *Major* Fenski, one of the finest soldiers ever to wear the black panzer uniform, would not live to receive the decoration. He was killed the following day in the battle on *Totensonntag* (Memorial Day). He was awarded a posthumous Knight's Cross on December 31, 1941.

With this surprise stroke the *Deutsches Afrika-Korps* had achieved a great success. The capture of these soldiers and vehicles eliminated a major portion of the Seventh Armored Division. The British Fourth Armored Brigade was no more.

A further success was scored that day by the 21st PD. At midday *General der Panzertruppe* Rommel had personally ordered the division against the enemy near Sidi Rezegh, with orders to destroy his forces there and capture the airfield.

The Panzer Grenadiers of the 21st PD advanced northward with the bulk of AR 155, supported by elements of the 90th Light. At the same time the main body of PR 5 under *Oberst* Stephan drove ahead along the axis road near El Duda, reaching the area west of the airfield and then setting off due east.

Rommel had initiated another pincer attack, which once again took the enemy completely by surprise. In this case, however, trusting in their 180 tanks, the British accepted battle. The battle for the Sidi Rezegh airfield began.

At the decisive briefing *Generalmajor* von Ravenstein had learned from Rommel that the attack by the 21st Panzer Division would be supported by the heavy artillery of Arko 104 under

Generalmajor Böttcher. The 408th Artillery Battalion under *Major* Dr. Böckmann was in a favorable position and opened fire with its 105mm guns. The other batteries soon joined in. II./PzAR 155 rolled forward with the main body, and it was this light battalion which provided the decisive support at the attack's point of main effort. *Major* Beil, the battalion's commander, positioned the unit's weapons so that they all had an excellent field of view along the entire width of SR 104's lane of attack as far as the Sidi Rezegh airfield. Since the ammunition situation was excellent, *Major* Beil was able to support the SR 104's attack with all guns. The enemy's infantry-style defence was smashed, and as a result of this effective fire support, SR 104 was able to cross the glacis-like terrain around the Trigh Capuzzo in its vehicles and advance virtually unhindered as far as the ridge east of Sidi Rezegh, which had formerly been occupied by the enemy. On reaching the ridge the anti-tank gun crews hauled their guns up the slope and opened fire on the enemy tanks remaining there. They were assisted in this effort by the forward artillery observer.

Major Beil and his battalion achieved a great success, much to the advantage of SR 104 and the division.

The panzers under *Oberst* Stephan had meanwhile moved into attack formation. The commander of Fourth Battery, PzAR 155, *Oberleutnant* Hoffmann, accompanied the panzers as they attacked. Observing and providing fire direction, he ensured that II./PzAR 155 was able to provide effective fire support.

The tanks drove right into the flank of the British Twenty-second Armored Brigade, which was moving from south to north against the soldiers of SR 104 which had broken through there. Tank guns roared along a broad front. The first British tank burst into flames. A fully-loaded munitions truck blew up with a tremendous explosion. The German tanks drove forward, constantly changing position then halting by companies and firing. *Oberst* Stephan committed both battalions and directed them toward their objectives.

The rest of the Seventh Armored Brigade and the Seventh Support Group, which had held Sidi Rezegh airfield for three days, was decisively smashed.

When darkness fell the enemy was finished and General Gott, the commander of the Seventh Armored Division, ordered a retreat toward the positions of the South African Division. Of its 79 tanks the Twenty-second Armored Brigade lost 45. The rest were scattered in every direction.

The airfield at Sidi Rezegh was in German hands. The breakout attempt from Tobruk had been foiled.

The only British unit to gain ground was the Thirteenth Corps, which occupied several fortifications on the Sollum Front. All that stood in its

Rommel with Generalmajor von Bismarck.

way was AA 3 along the *Via Balbia* and AA 33 on the Trigh Capuzzo.

AA 33 had been formed early in the year at the Baumholder troop training grounds and came to Africa with the main body of the 15th PD. It saw its first action during the summer before Sollum and in the area of the Halfaya Pass. In his three company commanders *Major* von Nees, the unit's commander, had soldiers who fulfilled any task no matter how difficult. *Hauptmann* Ferry Héraucourt, commander of the reconnaissance company, was always at the fore in the decisive November days. His patrols, under the well-known patrol leaders *Oberfeldwebel* Apsel, *Unteroffizier* Hartmann, *Feldwebel* Lütke and *Oberfeldwebel* Barlesius, always brought back the best reconnaissance results. It was they who had reported the advance by the enemy tanks on November 18.

Early on the morning of November 19 *Oberfeldwebel* Barlesius led a reconnaissance patrol

Major Beil, commander of II./PzAR 155, in May 1942.

deep into enemy territory. He penetrated the enemy's line of security far south of Reghem, and that evening *Oberleutnant* Freiherr von Gienand, the battalion adjutant, was able to report to the DAK that the enemy was advancing in the direction of Tobruk with a powerful screen to the northeast.

Barlesius set out again on the evening of November 22 to search for the enemy and clarify his immediate intentions. When he returned on the morning of November 23 he was met by *Hauptmann* Héraucourt. His report was brief and factual. Héraucourt gave him his hand.

"Thank you, Barlesius. Once again you have done well." The commander of the patrol company decided to make Barlesius an officer for bravery in the face of the enemy. Two days later, however, the outstanding patrol leader was killed.

The Battle on Totensonntag

On the evening of 22 November *Panzergruppe Afrika* reported that in the past four days of fighting it had destroyed 207 British tanks and that the Gambarra Corps had destroyed 50 tanks and about 200 armored vehicles. This report was accurate, as the British command in North Africa reported the loss of 303 tanks by the Seventh Armored Division alone (including armored cars).

According to the reports reaching General Auchinleck, on the evening of November 22 the Seventh Armored Brigade had 10 tanks fit for action and the Twenty-second Brigade 40. The Third Royal Armored Regiment still had a number of tanks.

The units of the DAK were assembled in the darkness, and while the 21st PD formed up on a wide front south of Sidi Rezegh and readied mobile reserves on both wings, the 15th PD reassembled in the area southwest of Sciaf-Sciuf.

In *Panzergruppe* headquarters Rommel's staff officers assembled and reviewed the incoming reports, the most important of which were presented to Rommel. By 22.30 *General* Rommel had a clear picture.

"We haven't time to issue all the orders verbally," he declared. "Therefore we'll have to issue tomorrow's orders by radio."

The six-page radio order, which reached the

Top left: Company officers of AA 33. From left: Leutnant Engelhart, Hauptmann Hèraucourt, Leutnant Bentlage.
Center left: One of AA 33's armored patrols returns with prisoners.
Bottom left: Rommel greets Hauptmann Héraucourt.
Top right: Unteroffizier Luther's armored car near Upper Sollum.
Bottom right: Gefreiter Keller (left) and Unteroffizier Hartmann before the attack on Tobruk.

DAK the following morning, included the following:

"On November 23 the *Panzergruppe* will force the decision in the area south of Tobruk through a concentric attack by the DAK and elements of the Gambarra Corps. To this end the Gambarra Corps will attack at 08.00 from El Gobi toward Gambut with elements of the *"Ariete"* Division.

Concentrating its forces, at 07.00 on November 23 the DAK will attack in the general direction of El Gobi, with the main effort on its left wing, surround the enemy and destroy him.

The axis of the attack, as well as line of attack, is Hill 176 — 6 km southeast of Sidi Rezegh — Bir el Gobi. The line of attack begins near Hill 176 with Number 30.

Recognition signal for the German-Italian forces is two white signal flares. The troops are reminded that the *"Ariete"* Division is using some British vehicles.

The corps supply road is to lead through Sidi Rezegh.

The corps headquarters is located in the vicinity of Belhamed."

When this long radio order, which would take several hours to decode, reached *Generalleutnant* Crüwell in his command post in Gasr el Arid, he decided to attack without waiting for the transcript. Nevertheless, the signals officer received instructions to decode the order as quickly as possible.

"We should attack at once, Herr General!" implored *Oberstleutnant* Bayerlein, chief of staff of the DAK, and following a brief pause Crüwell said:

"Very well, gentlemen, we will not wait for the transcript, rather we will attack at once."

At 05.30 *Generalleutnant* Crüwell, accompanied by his chief of staff and several aides and messengers drove away from his headquarters. Crüwell drove toward the front in his command vehicle "Moritz," which contained his small tactical operations staff, accompanied by two *Kübelwagen.* He was going to personally lead his divisions into this decisive battle.

It was just becoming light half an hour later as the following corps headquarters prepared to drive down the escarpment along the Trigh Capuzzo.

"Gun barrels ahead and to the right!" reported one of the drivers. And while the officers debated

Self-propelled anti-tank gun of the 605th Anti-tank Battalion.

Knocked-out British tank, an M3 General Grant Mark I.

whether or not this was the artillery of the 15th or 21st Panzer Division, the first shells howled in. Rifle and machine-gun fire joined in. It was — the enemy!

"Spread out! Armored cars and Flak open fire!"

The accompanying weapons opened up with a rapid fire, gaining some breathing space for the corps headquarters staff. During a pause in the fighting the vehicles took off again at high speed. However, they had not got thirty meters when the enemy anti-tank and anti-aircraft guns opened fire again. One of the German vehicles exploded.

"Destroy all papers!" ordered the headquarters Ib.

British tanks approached. They belonged to units of the Second New Zealand Division. Had they arrived thirty minutes earlier they would have captured the commanding general as well. But this calamity was bad enough, because *Generalleutnant* Crüwell had lost his entire command apparatus in one blow.

Later, when Crüwell received the news of the loss of his corps headquarters staff, he ordered the DAK to join with the *"Ariete"* Division in Bie el Gobi.

"After joining forces we will launch a concentrated strike at the enemy's rear!" he decided. When the 15th PD set off from the southwest at 07.30 all companies received Crüwell's radio message:

"Today the enemy must be decisively smashed!"

The enemy armored units near Sidi Muftah were attacked first. When *Generalleutnant* Crüwell received reports of further enemy attacks in strength west of Sidi Muftah, he immediately sent his forces ahead for an even more extensive encirclement.

He justified the move to his chief of staff by saying: "We must bag them all, Bayerlein!"

While the 21st PD was engaged in heavy defensive fighting against the tanks of the British Seventh Armored Division near Sidi Rezegh and the Italian *"Pavia"* Division was stopping a breakout attempt by the Tobruk garrison supported by 60 tanks, that afternoon the 15th PD under the command of *Generalmajor* von Ravenstein — with the commanding general present — arrived deep in the enemy's rear in the area south of Hagfed el Haiad. Arriving later were the armored spearheads of the *"Ariete"* Division. The division's 120 light tanks joined those of the

General der Panzertruppe Crüwell on Totensonntag, 23. 11. 1941.

15. PD.

Crüwell massed all of his tanks for a new attack with PR 8 leading the way. On its left were the Italian tanks and on the right flank was PR 5.

A short while later this steel wedge ran into an in-depth anti-tank and artillery front manned by the South Africans. Soon the first Italian and German tanks were burning. The battle between tanks and anti-tank guns began. Increasing numbers of tanks were hit and blew up, but the enemy anti-tank guns and artillery suffered heavy losses. Bitter tank-versus-tank duels broke out in the depths of the battlefield. The enemy forces were squeezed ever tighter by the German pincers and more and more shot-up enemy tanks littered the battlefield. But the battle had not yet been decided. Finally it was PR 8 which tipped the scales. The following are passages from the combat report made by the commander of PR 8:

"The late morning saw successful battles against enemy rear echelon units and the creation of favorable conditions for the afternoon's heavy attack. The victory was bought at a high price: the death of the commander of I./PR 8, *Major* Fenski, who was killed that morning. Advancing deep into the enemy's rear, the regimental commander, *Oberstleutnant* Cramer, alone with his escorting vehicle, drove into the midst of an enemy artillery position. Despite several hits on his tank he managed to make his way back to the First Battalion with valuable intelligence information.

At about midday, as a result of the advance on Bir el Gobi, contact was established with the Italian *"Ariete"* Armored Division. That afternoon the regiment was to see its heaviest fighting of the entire African Campaign.

At 14.30 PR 8 was assembled in the Sidi Muftah area facing north in the following battle order:

Left: Panzer-Regiment 8, right: the attached PR 5 with 40 tanks.

The two regiments were arranged in echelon.

First Echelon: I./PR 8 with regimental headquarters, behind 3./Flak 33

Second Echelon: II./PR 8

On orders from division, SR 115 was to follow close behind II./PR 8 which, as the supporting tank battalion, was to make possible the breakthrough by the infantry.

SR 115 was unable to reach the assembly area and link up with PR 8 as it became bogged down in marshy terrain near Sidi Muftah and came under fire from enemy artillery from the north and east. SR 200 was assembled behind PR 5 for the attack.

At 14.45 the division issued the order to advance. The objective was the destruction of the South African Division and its supporting armor in the area of Sghifet-Adeimat.

General der Panzertruppe Rommel and the Ia of Panzergruppe Afrika, Oberstleutnant Westphal, in November 1941 near Gazala.

The British artillery fire, which had interfered with the assembling of the attack force, increased in intensity. The German artillery was unable to silence the British guns as they were awaiting the attack in prepared positions which had been reinforced considerably during the course of the day.

The tank attack rolled forward under the covering fire of its own artillery. The regimental commander immediately recognized that the attack could succeed only if the reinforced regiment maintained the direction specified in the attack order and drove straight into the center of the enemy position without regard to threats to its flanks. He personally led the regiment in that direction, correcting any deviation from the proper course with a brief radio message.

By 15.30 the First Battalion of PR 8 under the command of *Hauptmann* Kümmel had broken into the enemy positions and destroyed numerous defensive weapons. This penetration paralyzed the enemy. The defenders gave up wherever there were German tanks. The anti-tank fire from in front and the flanks stopped for several minutes. The artillery fire falling on Second Battalion and the rear elements continued unabated, however. *Hauptmann* Kümmel urgently requested that the infantry follow up to mop up the battlefield and round up the prisoners.

Finally SR 115 came forward in its vehicles to I./PR 8's point of penetration. The reinforced panzer regiment had meanwhile moved on. The regiment's commander had decided to continue the attack without waiting for the infantry.

At 16.00 the reinforced PR 8 was deep in enemy territory. First Battalion was attacking northward through the enemy's deep defensive zone. Second Battalion veered slightly to the northwest to create some breathing room for the infantry, which had been left behind, and nip in the bud a counterattack against the division's left flank by about 20 enemy tanks.

In the meantime the main body of PR 5 had turned east to evade the heavy artillery fire. Only a few of its tanks managed to join *Hauptmann* Kümmel and take part in the attack. This evasive move was contrary to *Oberstleutnant* Cramer's orders and threatened to disrupt and weaken the attack. From that time PR 5 was also out of radio communications.

As II./PR 8 was unable to follow the rapidly-advancing First Battalion as a result of beating off the British tank attack and waiting for the following infantry, the enemy's defensive fire once more came to life. Nevertheless Second Battalion, under the command of *Hauptmann* Wahl, who had taken command after *Oberstleutnant* Ramsauer, continued to move northward. It fought its way through the enemy's deep zone with the objective of destroying the enemy artillery, which was making things so difficult for the infantry. The infantry followed at a pace which, for the tank commanders, was endlessly slow, suffering heavy losses to the heavy artillery fire and enemy anti-tank and anti-aircraft guns in their unarmored vehicles. Many of the infantry's vehicles were already burning.

At 16.30 the picture facing the regimental commander, who was with the tanks of Second Battalion, was as follows:

His First Battalion had successfully broken through the enemy's deep zone to the north with the objective of destroying the enemy artillery which was still firing. His Second Battalion was echeloned to the left rear, deep in the midst of the enemy and holding on to allow the infantry to approach. The battalion's fire had eliminated enemy resistance within a narrow radius and destroyed a large number of enemy tanks. The attached PR 5, which had strayed far to the right, was out of the picture completely.

Without a moment's hesitation the regimental commander ordered the commander of Second battalion, *Hauptmann* Wahl: "Second Battalion turn back in the midst of the enemy and bring the infantry forward under all circumstances!"

This maneuver was carried out under fire in an exemplary manner, although the three company commanders (*Oberleutnant* Wuth, *Leutnant* Adam and *Oberleutnant* Körner) were killed and a large number of tanks lost. The attached Flak battery (3./Flak 33), under the command of the Battalion CO, *Hauptmann* Fromm, provided outstanding support for the tanks as they disengaged from the enemy. This maneuver enabled the infantry to advance several hundred meters, but very soon afterward II./PR 8 was again alone in the midst of the enemy.

The enemy continued to mount a determined and resolutely-led defence. Artillery fire continued to fall among the tanks with undiminished intensity. The regiment's commander now threw

his last reserves — regimental Pionier in personnel carriers and the remaining escort tanks of the regimental haedquarters — together with what was left of Second Battalion into the battle in an effort to carry the day without the infantry. The operation was an example of bravery and self-sacrifice. The regimental Pionier overran the artillery and anti-tanks and flushed the gun crews from their holes.

In the meantime radio communications with I./PR 8 were lost when the battalion commander's radio equipment was destroyed by a shell from an anti-tank gun. Driving at the head of his battalion, standing erect in his tank with the command pennant in his right hand, *Hauptmann* Kümmel continued to lead his forces and carried out his assignment. At 16.55 he reported to the commander:

'First Battalion has broken through to Sidi Rezegh airfield, contact established with the 21. PD attacking from the north!'

The regimental commander's intention, to have First Battalion wheel about and drive toward the Wahl Battalion, was no longer necessary.

At 17.00 an enemy force of trucks and armored vehicles attempted to break through to the south and southeast. Minor elements succeeded in getting through, but the British were too weak for a counterattack.

The battle was decided before nightfall. The in-depth enemy defence had been shaken by I./PR 8's breakthrough and broken on the iron front of Second Battalion.

A shining example of soldierly conduct was provided in this battle by the division commander, *Generalmajor* Neumann-Silkow, who followed closely the attack by his panzer regiments. His unshakeable calm and confidence in victory contributed greatly to the fact that, despite the heavy losses, at no time during the battle was there any loss of will to attack.

A not insignificant number of tanks and guns were left on the battlefield. More than 1,000 prisoners were taken before darkness fell.

After it had become dark the regiment assembled on Sidi Rezegh airfield. In doing so the regiment's commander drove with Second Battalion past the scene of First Battalion's battle, which showed the scars of heavy fighting. Both battalions had had to fight their way through a powerful enemy defence that day. Second Battalion's task had been some-

Top and center: II./PR 8 on the move.

Enemy artillery ranges in.

what more difficult and it had therefore been accompanied by the regimental commander. Both battalions discharged their responsibilities in a masterful fashion and despite heavy losses decided the battle *without* the participation of the infantry."

This ends the combat report. Now back to the other units, beginning with the 21st Panzer Division.

The 21st Panzer Division

Early on the morning of November 23 the 21st Panzer Division —less PR 5 which had been sent to take part in the 15th PD's attack — was given the assignment of repelling any attack by the enemy in the direction of Tobruk in conjunction with infantry and artillery forces. Fighting without tanks, the 21st PD held the northern front of the battle near Sidi Rezegh firmly in its hands, repelling attacks by the enemy and pouring heavy fire on enemy forces attempting to break out of Tobruk or drive into the fortress. It prevented the British Thirtieth Corps from linking up with the garrison of Tobruk. The motorcycle troops fought dismounted. They carried the weight of the defence and held firm against the pressure exerted by the enemy.

In the confusion of battle the commanding general's "Moritz" was surrounded by British tanks. The British tankers probably saw the Balkan Cross painted on the side, but they also saw that it was a British command vehicle. As a result they were uncertain.

Several Tommies got down from their tank and approached the command vehicle on foot. Crouching inside were *Generalleutnant* Crüwell with his chief of staff and tactical operations staff. One of the British soldiers rapped on the vehicle's steel side with an iron rod. *Generalleutnant* Crüwell opened the hatch. For a few heartbeats the enemies stared at each other. Then the German commanding general closed the hatch again.

Volleys from a quick-firing cannon suddenly whipped across the terrain. A German 20mm Flak had opened fire on the British tankers and forced them to flee. Once again *Generalleutnant* Crüwell had narrowly avoided being captured.

As darkness fell the battlefield was littered with burning combat vehicles, British and German.

The battle had not yet been decided and was far from over. At several locations the British and South Africans had managed to escape from the pocket. Not until after midnight did the gunfire began to ebb. The fighting on *Totensonntag* had ended.

Generalleutnant Crüwell's scheme had frustrated all of the enemy's attack plans.

The battle had cost the British 70 to 100 tanks and many guns, some self-propelled. The number of motor vehicles lost went into the hundreds.

The Fifth South African brigade had been scattered, the Twenty-second Armored Brigade smashed and many other units of the British Army badly battered.

Late that evening General Cunningham realized that his heavy losses in tanks could have dangerous effects on the entire situation. He therefore requested a meeting with Sir Claude Auchinleck. That evening Auchinleck, accompanied by Air Marshal Tedder, arrived at Cunningham's headquarters and instructed him to continue the offensive.

On the German side it was not until after midnight that they were able to obtain a clear picture of the situation. The units were sorted out and the day's losses were counted. PR 8 alone had lost 14 Panzer IIs, 30 Panzer IIIs and 9 Panzer IVs, although not all where total losses. Two thirds could be repaired. Nevertheless, the unit's operational strength was down to 61 battle tanks and 4 command tanks.

The most significant result of the battle, however, was the removal of the immediate threat to the siege ring around Tobruk. What was more, a large part of the enemy's tank forces had been destroyed. The effect on the enemy's morale was great. His far-reaching plans were not going to materialize. At least that is what Rommel and his commanders thought.

Rommel was still out of communication with *Generalleutnant* Cruwell that night when the results of the battle were in front of him. But he knew that he would be able to depend on the commanding general. He therefore sent the following communication to Berlin at midnight:

Intentions for 24. 11. 1941:
(a) Complete the destruction of the enemy's Seventh Armored Division,
(b) advance with elements of my forces against

Sidi Omar with the intention of attacking the enemy on the Sollum Front.

Early on the morning of November 24 Rommel, already under way with his escort, came upon the commander of the 15th Panzer Division and ordered *Generalmajor* Neumann-Silkow to prepare to attack.

Two hours later, at 06.00, he came upon *Generalleutnant* Crüwell's "Moritz" command vehicle on the axis road. Crüwell reported to Rommel:

"The enemy near Sidi Rezegh has been destroyed and only minor elements have escaped, Herr General!"

This report strengthened Rommel's decision to launch a tank raid to the southeast deep into the enemy's rear. He said to Crüwell:

"The Tobruk attack force has largely been destroyed. Now we'll fall on the enemy on the eastern front and destroy the New Zealanders and Indians before they can rejoin the remains of the battered main force and carry out a joint advance toward Tobruk. At the same time we'll take Habata and Maddalena, and so cut the enemy's supply lines.

Speed is of the essence! We must take advantage of the shock effect of the enemy's defeat and advance at once with all elements at the hardest pace toward Sidi Omar."

In order to carry out this daring plan Rommel had to gather up all of his mobile forces and leave the less-mobile elements behind in the siege ring around Tobruk under *Major* Böttcher, the Arko 104. Böttcher was to employ his heavy batteries to counter any relief or breakout attempts by the enemy. This decision by Rommel was strongly criticized by the OKH and OKW. In the opinion of many officers who had never seen the African Theater the plan was *too* daring. However, Alan Moorehead, a historian of the African War, wrote:

"While the tanks were still in the midst of this most bloody of all desert battles, Rommel had decided on a scheme which was at the same time brilliant and daring."

Oberstleutnant Siegfried Westphal, the Ia of *Panzergruppe Afrika*, warned the General that the available forces of the DAK were too weak to carry out this plan and that they would be lost for Tobruk. Rommel ignored the warning. He wanted to advance, destroy the enemy and drive to the gates of Egypt.

"I'm driving to Sidi Omar, Westphal, and I'm going to lead the 21st PD against the Halfaya Pass myself!"

With these words Rommel took leave of his staff officer and set off with his Chief of Staff, *Generalmajor* Gause, to join the *Afrika-Korps*.

The die had been cast. While the 15th PD prepared to attack the enemy near Sidi Omar and a thrown-together battle group set out to capture the Maddalena supply dump, Rommel drove from Bir Seferzen, where he had issued his orders, to the 21st PD and personally launched it against the Halfaya Pass.

On the way back to Sidi Omar his command vehicle broke down with engine trouble. Luckily, with darkness falling, *Generalleutnant* Crüwell's command vehicle "Moritz" came along. Rommel and Gause left "Max" behind, climbed into "Moritz" and drove toward the barbed wire that formed the border with Egypt.

They found no way through the wire, and as things were taking too long for Rommel, he relieved the junior officer and took over the role of navigator himself. This time, however, his sense of direction failed him completely. They very nearly drove into a British sentry position and enemy staff cars and motorcycles were flitting past the command vehicle. Fortunately for Rommel it was a captured British vehicle and the British paid it no notice.

Generalmajor Walter Neumann-Silkow.

British vehicles, including tanks, drove past the command vehicle all night. Finally, when it became light, they found a way back. Meanwhile in El Adem *Oberstleutnant* Westphal, *Panzergruppe Afrika*'s Ia, was out of communication with Rommel and was to remain so for the next four days and so was forced to command the Tobruk front on his own.

On November 24 Rommel issued orders for the divisions of the DAK to attack and destroy the enemy near Sidi Omar and Sollum on the 25th. He was convinced that the retreating enemy forces would have to withdraw to the southeast and east. He wanted to exploit this withdrawal, directing his two divisions into a wide intercept position extending from an area 10 kilometers south of the Halfaya Pass as far as the Trigh el Abd, about 30 kilometers west of Sidi Omar. Also at Rommel's disposal was the Italian *"Ariete"* Armored Division.

He positioned the 21st PD the farthest to the east and had the *"Ariete"* move into the western end of his position. In the center, leading the 15th PD

himself, he intended to attack the enemy wherever he found him in order to make the demoralization complete. At the same time, however, he also wanted to recapture Sidi Omar. He had the 21st PD send PR 5 to support the attack by 15. PD.

Rommel had ordered *Generalmajor* von Ravenstein to wait with his 21st Panzer Division — less PR 5 — southwest of the Halfaya Pass until he received orders to attack or until the enemy tried to break out to the east from Sidi Omar or Capuzzo.

The two panzer regiments set out separately for the attack on Sidi Omar. PR 5 soon became engaged in combat with the Seventh Indian Brigade, which had reached the area just ahead of *Oberstleutnant* Stephan's panzers. A large number of German tanks was lost in the heavy fighting that followed. The panzers also scored successes. They eliminated a wide, fan-shaped anti-tank barrier, but their strength was broken. The regiment's commander was killed on the battlefield when his command vehicle was struck by a direct hit. The field artillery of the Fourth Indian

Rommel's disastrous foray following the battle on Totensonntag.

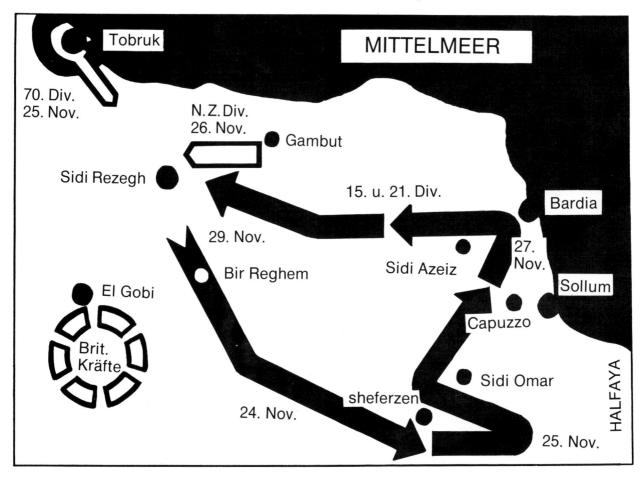

78

Division knocked out a series of German tanks. *Major* Mildebrath took over the command of PR 5.

At the same time PR 8 ran into a powerful British armored force. It was able to gain the upper hand but won little ground.

AA 33 attempted to storm the British supply base at Habata and cut the enemy's supply lines, but was soon spotted by RAF aircraft. The aircraft strafed the fast column, inflicting heavy losses. This stroke of Rommel's had also failed.

Rommel, driving from one unit to another, now attempted to commit the 15st PD to an enveloping maneuver. Sent westward in an open formation, the fast elements of the division rolled west around Sidi Omar. In this situation about twenty British tanks, mostly Mark IIs, attacked. Sixteen of the attacking tanks were knocked out in the subsequent action. The British tanks belonged to elements of the Seventh Armored Brigade and they inflicted significant losses on PR 8.

British fighters and bombers swirled about over the battlefield. Due to the loss of Gambut airfield the Luftwaffe fighters were unable to intervene, so that the Royal Air Force was able to locate its targets and bomb and strafe them without danger to itself.

When evening fell on November 25, Rommel had failed to reach his objective. The DAK had reached the Trigh Capuzzo west of Sidi Azeiz and won a sector of terrain of about 30 kilometers, but the enemy had not yet been surrounded. Subsequent attacks by PR 5 on Sidi Omar also failed to get through. A radio message sent from there to *Panzergruppe* headquarters at 20.00 said:

"Still heavy fighting, now 8 km southwest of Fort Sidi Omar. PR 5 has 12 tanks left, only two of which are serviceable. Regimental commander killed. Battalion commander missing. Request orders!"

It was obvious that PR 5 was almost destroyed. PR 8, which reported in a short while later, still had 53 operational tanks.

The *"Ariete"* Division was stopped and pressed hard all day by the First South African Division and the British Fourth Brigade.

The 21st PD was unable to set out for the Halfaya Pass that day because its supply vehicles were unable to locate the division. *Generalmajor* von Ravenstein was unable to start out until the early morning of November 26. On the evening of

November 25, a day which for Rommel had been very unsatisfactory, *Oberstleutnant* Westphal sent a radio message to the DAK's Commanding General:

"From Panzergruppe Afrika Ia   25. 11. 41
to: General Crüwell   22.57 hours
Has the situation map been discarded? — Tobruk quiet.

Böttcher repelled attack by two tank battalions of a reinforced New Zealand division at elevation 55 left 2 to 6. Enemy southeast of Bir el Gobi — 2 brigades, elements of an armored brigade — apparently — in retreat to southeast. Elements of retreating units south 72 right 2 to 6. — Elements of Second South African Division set out to the southwest via Sidi Barani 25. 11. 07.00. — Pavia former area, de Mio 57/6. Trieste without regiment near Böttcher 50. — Request situation Sollum Front and intentions of commander-in-chief. Until now all messages had to be sent blind. If necessary, in which direction should Böttcher and Trieste pursue tomorrow? Suggestion: direction east. Panzergruppe Ia."This message revealed that *Oberstleutnant* Westphal had no contact with his Commander-in-Chief, and that he had little hope of receiving an answer to the message, which was in fact the case. A number of the Commander-in-Chief's radio stations had already been knocked out of action in these battles.

Generalmajor von Ravenstein, who on November 25 was involved in heavy fighting in the Sidi Rezegh area, received an alarm call from the supply dumps and columns of the DAK which were strung out along 20 kilometers of the *Via Balbia*. He summoned *Hauptmann* Briel and gave him the following instructions:

"Drive at once to the supply base and restore order. You have full authority to act as you see fit!"

Briel, commander of the 606th Flak Battalion, requested written authority, and it was well that he did. A short time later he drove at full speed across the Sidi Rezegh battlefield, and as he reached the *Via Balbia* he saw a New Zealand unit coming from the direction of Bardia heading in the direction of Tobruk along the edge of the escarpment which ran parallel to the *Via Balbia*.

At that moment the leading element of the New Zealand unit drove down the escarpment and headed toward the rear echelon units of Briel's battalion. In position there, however, was *Oberleutnant* Franz with several 20mm cannon and machine-guns. Franz opened fire and the New Zealanders retired back up the escarpment and drove on to the next path down the slope near Gambut.

Georg Briel, who knew this area well, pressed ahead to meet the enemy there. On the way he was joined by the rear echelon personnel and, much to Briel's joy, eight tanks and eventually a 210mm howitzer under *Wachtmeister* Wolf.

"With these weapons," Briel later recounted, "I established a defensive position around the white house in Gambut. All weapons were trained on the path which led down the escarpment. The enemy came as expected.

On this decisive November 26, 1941 the Second New Zealand Division attempted to descend the escarpment so that it could drive along the coast and link up with the Tobruk garrison or possibly support a breakout attempt from the fortress.

The battle group drove the enemy back and the New Zealanders moved on along the escarpment in the direction of Tobruk." The supply trains had been saved.

On the evening of November 25 Rommel ordered the 21st Panzer Division, which he assumed had already taken the Halfaya Pass, to "advance farther to the south and attack beyond Halfaya, past Sollum toward Bardia."

Generalmajor von Ravenstein set off with his division.

Critical Situation at the Siege Ring around Tobruk

In their positions on both sides of Belhamed and south of the *Via Balbia*, the soldiers of *Kampfgruppe* Böttcher remained under constant attack throughout November 25. Supported by tanks, the infantry brigades of the Second New Zealand Infantry Division were attempting to achieve a breakthrough there. But Böttcher, the Arko 104, had SR 155 and the 361st Afrika-Regiment at his disposal. In addition the defenders were effectively supported by the artillery which ringed Tobruk. The attacks were beaten off.

It was clear to *Oberstleutnant* Westphal, however, that the situation at the siege ring around Tobruk was worsening by the hour and that the danger of a breakout and breakthrough from the fortress was growing steadily. Once this happened the situation would become critical. The enemy would have achieved the objective of his offensive and the long siege of Tobruk would have been meaningless.

The New Zealanders continued their attacks after darkness fell. In his daily report Westphal indicated that the enemy was steadily building up his forces south of Tobruk and that the danger of a breakthrough there was growing.

This report reached Rommel on the morning of November 26. It strengthened his resolve to smash the enemy in the areas of Sidi Oamr and Capuzzo quickly in order to have a free hand for Tobruk.

Captured British troops near Sidi Azeiz.

Just how bad the situation was at Tobruk, however, Rommel did not know.

During the night of November 25/26 the New Zealanders launched a concentrated attack with tank support and took Belhamed. That morning at 06.30 the garrison of Tobruk, supported by 50 heavy tanks, began a drive out of the fortress. The tanks rolled over the German positions and led the following infantry to El Duda.

Supported by a successful counterattack by the Bersaglieri Regiment of the *"Trieste"* Division, *Kampfgruppe* Böttcher was able to hold on to the positions in the north.

However, on the afternoon of that decisive November 26 another attack force, which included thirty tanks, was able to break out of Tobruk and establish contact with the British forces near Belhamed.

The riflemen and infantry of the German-Italian siege forces fought all day in an effort to close the narrow corridor out of the fortress. They destroyed 26 enemy tanks and following heavy fighting restored the situation. The main body of the enemy force finally withdrew back into the fortress.

The bitter battles lasted throughout November 26 and finally the badly battered *Kampfgruppe* Böttcher was forced to give up the narrow corridor once more. It withdrew and occupied a blocking position to the south behind the *"Trieste"* Division. The New Zealanders had established contact with Fortress Tobruk.

On the morning of November 26 Siegfried Westphal tried feverishly to contact Rommel and report the new critical situation at Tobruk. No less than five Fieseler *Storch* aircraft, which were employed as courier aircraft to the DAK and Rommel, were shot down by the RAF. Thus this decisive day was spent trying to contact the Commander-in-Chief and the Commanding General.

Oberstleutnant Westphal had a hard time of it in this situation, because the commanding generals of the Italian Tenth, Twentieth and Twenty-first Corps with seven divisions had to put themselves under his command as well as the *Division Afrika z.b.V.* and *Kampfgruppe* Böttcher.

Finally, when all efforts to contact Rommel failed, Westphal took action on his own. He had to recall the *Afrika-Korps* no matter what it cost. He therefore sent a radio message to the corps headquarters of the DAK, which said:

"The Afrika-Korps is to immediately march at maximum speed toward Tobruk. All conflicting orders are cancelled.

Headquarters Panzergruppe Afrika Ia."

The radio message reached the 21st PD, and when *Major* Freiherr von Süsskind, the Division Ia, handed it to his commanding officer, the latter signed the release, read the message and said dryly:

"So, it's back to Tobruk!"

The division, which had reached the Bardia area, turned and set off along the *Via Balbia*. In the

The battle near Gambut. Two of the tanks attached to Kampfgruppe Briel engage armored cars of a New Zealand unit.

*Wachtmeister Wolf (left) and Hauptmann Briel watch the
road down from the djebel near Gambut.*

British parachute flares near Gambut.

face of stiffening resistance from New Zealand troops the division reached Gambut. There resistance stiffened even more, but the division fought its way through. When von Ravenstein finally stood before Rommel and reported, the latter said in amazement:

"What is the meaning of this? What are you doing here?"

Now it was von Ravenstein's turn to be aghast. He reported the radio message to Rommel, who exploded:

"That's a barefaced swindle! The English must have our codes. The order is a trick and comes from them!"

That evening when Rommel appeared at the headquarters in El Adem he greeted no one. He climbed into his command bus, looked at the map and studied the reports and radio messages his Ia had tried to get through to him.

Westphal then made his report. Afterward Rommel realized that the decisions made by his Ia, the "operational conscience of the army," had been correct. Rommel recommended *Oberstleutnant* Westphal for the Knight's Cross of the Iron Cross for his decisive action.

The situation at Tobruk had made the decision necessary. According to Churchill, at the time Westphal's message arrived, *Generalmajor* von Ravenstein's forces were only a few miles from a giant British supply dump. Perhaps the capture of this supply dump would have altered the outcome, but a continuation of the attack to the east might also have meant the end of the entire DAK.

British Decisions

The move to the east by the DAK with its two cadre divisions had given the new Commander-in-Chief of the British Eighth Army, Major General Ritchie, a chance to regroup and reinforce his divisions around Tobruk. Powerful tank reserves moved forward from Egypt. The Fourth and Twenty-second Armored Brigades were brought back to almost full strength. On November 27 Ritchie wrote to General Auchinleck, who had returned to Cairo:

"The way I see it, from our standpoint the overall situation in Cyrenaica is very favorable; everything suggests that it is becoming ever more unfavorable for the enemy."

On the morning of November 27 the 15th Panzer Division under *Generalmajor* Neumann-Silkow, which was to have attacked Sollum, was instead driving straight toward Tobruk. All of a sudden the division came upon the headquarters of the Fifth New Zealand Brigade near Sidi Azeiz. *Oberst* Hans Cramer immediately led PR 8 at high speed to Sidi Azeiz. The regiment overran enemy anti-tank guns and artillery and shot up the enemy positions. The fast-moving panzers overran the infantry trenches and machine-gun positions and smashed the brigade. About 700 New Zealanders were captured. Hans Cramer reported:

"After we broke into the New Zealanders' lines a large number of unarmed prisoners streamed toward us. What were we to do with prisoners when our own infantry had no vehicles? We couldn't just send them to the rear, because in the desert war the "rear" was an uncertain concept. If we left them to themselves they would have picked up their weapons again as soon as we left and found transport somewhere. While the first prisoners assembled I stood with my adjutant in the open on my command tank and received the enemy commanders who were brought over by several panzer crewmen. More and more New Zealanders gathered around my command tank.

As was usual in Africa when someone had suffered a misfortune, I spoke a few friendly words to the officers and emphasized that their people had fought bravely.

At that moment my lookout shouted: "Two enemy tanks, Matilda type, coming toward us!"

I turned quickly. Through my field glasses I saw that the two tanks were wearing German markings and just then I remembered that our *Panzerpionier-Kompanie* 33 was to have employed these tanks at Capuzzo. It was the Pionier, and subsequently our infantry from the 115th arrived and led the prisoners to the rear."

The 21st PD was to use November 28 to attack the enemy near Point 175 and Zaafran and establish a blocking position to the east. At the same time the division was to seek contact to the north where the *Afrika Division* — which was soon to be renamed the 90th Light — was in defensive positions.

Advancing to the left of the 21st PD, the 15th Panzer Division attacked the escarpment south of Sidi Rezegh and threw the enemy tanks there back to the south. When it became evening Rommel breathed a little easier, because he was again in a good position to encircle and destroy a part of the Eighth Army on the battlefield around Sidi Rezegh.

November 29 went badly. Late on the evening of the 28th *Generalmajor* von Ravenstein had been to the headquarters of the DAK and reported the approach of his 21st Panzer Division to *General-leutnant* Crüwell. Crüwell once again had two panzer divisions at his disposal. For the next morning he ordered an attack by the 15th and 21st Panzer Divisions on the enemy forces assembled near Sidi Rezegh. Von Ravenstein had to stop off at the 15th PD on his way back to his division to receive his orders from Rommel. When he and his escort arrived at the agreed location early in the morning they were suddenly greeted by machine-gun fire. The staff car caught fire and von Ravenstein's driver was wounded. Everyone jumped out and took cover, but it was too late. They had driven into the midst of a well-camouflaged New Zealand position.

General Freyberg, the commander of the New Zealand division, was just having breakfast when he received the news that the commanding officer of the 21. PD had been taken prisoner.

November 29 was the decisive day. *Generalmajor* Böttcher, who had taken command of the 21st PD in place of von Ravenstein, closed the pocket to the east, but at the same time was forced to meet an attack against his southern front by the British Seventh Armored Division and the First South African Infantry Division.

The 15th Panzer Division rolled north through Bir Bu Creimisa and that evening occupied the important ridge near El Duda. At the same time the 90th Light advanced from the north toward Belhamed. It did not, however, succeed in establishing contact with the spearheads of the 15th PD advancing from the south.

The "Ariete" Division, which was fighting south of the 15th PD, was moved north to shore up the siege ring around Tobruk. Since the Germans had been unable to completely seal off the west side of the pocket surrounding the Second New Zealand Division, relief attacks from Tobruk were a possibility.

The German tanks pulled back from the hill near El Duda to refuel and rearm. A half-hour before midnight the enemy launched an attack which penetrated the thin lines held by the infantry, which numbered only about 150 men. El Duda was lost to the British in the battle. A total of twenty British tanks were destroyed that day.

In fact the Second New Zealand Division and elements of the Seventh Armored Division were surrounded. The corridor to Fortress Tobruk was closed in the morning hours of November 30. The tank attacks from the south had been beaten off. The *Panzergruppe* command decided to finish off the Second New Zealand Division once and for all. At the same time it was decided to evacuate the supply bases between Bardia and Tobruk and relocate them west of the line El Adem — Bir el Gobi.

November 30 saw the continuation of the concentric German attack on the surrounded New Zealanders.

The Germans failed to gain any ground during the morning fighting. Later in the afternoon the 15th Panzer Division drove north and then veered east toward the hill west of Sidi Rezegh for an attack on that defensive bastion, resulting in renewed heavy fighting.

It was there that *Kampfgruppe* Mickl, which consisted of SR 155 and the former *Kampfgruppe* Böttcher, which Mickl had taken over when *Generalmajor* Böttcher left to take command of the 21st PD, struck the decisive blow. Together with the 2nd Machine-gun Battalion, and supported by an assault group from PR 8, the battle group stormed toward Sidi Rezegh. Advancing from three sides, the German attack force threw back the enemy in close-quarters fighting and recaptured Sidi Rezegh. El Duda, however, remained in the hands of the British.

Oberst Johann Mickl, who had been captured on November 28, managed to escape and flee. As a result he was available for Rommel to call upon to lead the difficult attack. Mickl was awarded the Knight's Cross for his exploits on December 12, 1941.

On the evening of November 30, 1941 Rommel discussed the *Panzergruppe*'s supply situation with General Bastico. Both sent urgent demands to Italy for weapons and ammunition, especially for tanks. At the same time they knew that there was little chance of receiving the requested weapons.

That day the 21st PD had available fifteen medium and six light tanks. The 15th PD's situation was somewhat better, with twenty-eight medium and eleven light tanks.

The British Seventh Armored Division, on the other hand, had more than 120 tanks of all types. December 1, 1941, a day which brought fog to the area of Sidi Rezegh, saw the 15th PD once more on the attack, receiving all the support available. Two battalions of PzAR 33, a 210mm howitzer battery from Arko 104, the 200th Special Purpose Regiment and the 2nd Machine-gun Battalion, as well as K 15 were assigned to support PR 8. The enemy near Belhamed was to be driven back.

Initially the attack got nowhere. Northeast of Sidi Rezegh *Kampfgruppe* Mickl became involved in heavy fighting with the British Fourth Brigade, which had launched a relief attack. The attack was beaten off. The corridor to the British forces outside the fortress was sealed off again. By the evening of that day the pocket had been cleared. 1,500 New Zealanders were taken prisoner and 26 guns captured, but the *Afrika-Korps'* strength was exhausted. Fortunately, so was that of the Eighth Army.

The British offensive "Crusader" — one of the largest battles in Africa — was over. German units were surrounded at the Halfaya Pass and in the Bardia and Sollum areas. Rommel tried to hang on. On December 3 there were only 34 tanks reported operational in the whole *Afrika-Korps.* That was exactly thirteen percent of its authorized strength. 167 German tanks and scout cars had been destroyed, and over twenty percent were in need of repairs.

The Eighth Army reported to Cairo the loss of 814 tanks of all types. It still had 100 operational tanks left. The following assessment of the recent events is contained in *Panzergruppe Afrika's* war diary:

"At the beginning of the offensive the British Eighth Army had a superiority over the German-Italian forces of about 75 percent in tanks, 750 percent in armored cars and 180 percent in light guns. Only in infantry battalions and heavy artillery was the superiority somewhat less, at 30 percent.

The British air force had been enlarged to a size never attained before. In fighters it possessed a superiority of about 200 percent and in bombers and reconnaissance aircraft about 50 percent.

Command of operations by the *Panzergruppe* was marked by attempts to employ our own numerically inferior forces at decisive locations and in an offensive fashion wherever possible. These attempts were limited to a certain degree by the fact that the war was being fought with our ally. But it became ever more apparent that due to our numerically inferiority only an offensive conduct of the war could lead to success. Therefore, even when it was necessary to go over to the defensive, this was conducted as a mobile defence. It was only by following this principle that the command was able to strike and possibly destroy the enemy. The occupation of terrain or the conquest of territory played no role in this. Likewise the temporary occupation of Cyrenaica or Marmarica by the enemy had no effect on the outcome of the operation. Rather it was decisive to preserve our forces in order to be able to launch a counterattack at a suitable time. The recapture of territory which had formerly been lost was the inevitable result of a successful counterattack."

AFRIKAKORPS

Retreat

On December 2, 1941 Erwin Rommel sent the following radio message to *Führer* Headquarters in Rastenburg:

"In the uninterrupted heavy fighting from 18. 11. to 1. 12. 814 of the enemy's tanks and armored cars were destroyed and 127 aircraft shot down. A great booty in weapons, munitions and vehicles was also taken. The number of prisoners has exceeded 9,000, including three Generals."

No decision was reached in the fighting of the following days. German forces did succeed in attacking and smashing a concentration of enemy forces in the area of Bir el Gobi before it became fully operational. On the night of December 4/5 the DAK rolled west through the three-mile-wide corridor between El Duda and Sidi Rezegh and arrived at the assembly area near El Adem, from where it was to set out toward Bir el Gobi with the two divisions of the motorized Italian Twentieth Corps under General Gambarra. The Italians, however, did not arrive. The "Young Fascists" Division, which had put up such a heroic defence of Bir el Gobi, now made its way to join the DAK.

The first enemy met was the British Guards Brigade. Soon afterwards the British Seventh Armored Division also came out to face the DAK. The DAK fought its way through this barrier and by evening had reached an area 15 kilometers northwest of Bir el Gobi.

During the same period the British Seventieth Infantry Division sortied from Tobruk, reaching and occupying the line of hills between El Duda and Belhamed. The *Panzergruppe* simply no longer had sufficient strength to achieve victory.

Rommel wrote in his diary on the evening of December 5:

"The advance by the DAK has not destroyed the enemy near Bir el Gobi, especially since the Italian motorized corps did not show up. It must therefore be anticipated that the enemy in the Gobi area will be reinforced with fresh troops and with his superior forces very soon go to the attack himself.

Nevertheless, it still appears possible that a concentrated attack by the rest of the German and Italian mobile divisions in the area around Gobi could lead to a favorable conclusion. If we do not succeed in destroying significant elements of the enemy forces, then, on account of our high losses in men and materiel, the decision will have to be considered to break off the battle and withdraw to the Gazala position, and later abandon Cyrenaica."

Following this realization, on December 6, 1941 Rommel tried once again. The DAK launched the last attack. The remaining tanks of the 15th and 21st Panzer Divisions rolled into battle. The heavy exchanges of fire with the British forces led them to veer off toward Bir el Gobi. Had the *"Ariete"* and *"Trieste"* Divisions arrived the battle would have been won. *Generalleutnant* Crüwell, who recognized this last chance, sent message after message to Rommel and also to commanding General Gambarra. The message was always the same:

"Where are Gambarra and his divisions?" Finally the message was even sent uncoded in clear text. But the two divisions did not come. The commanding General of the Italian Twentieth

Corps reported to General Bastico:

"My troops are exhausted and no longer fit for action."

On December 7 the battle raged on. One after another the German tanks were put out of action: knocked out, bogged down in the sand, destroyed by enemy artillery or aircraft. *Generalmajor* Neumann-Silkow was caught in an artillery barrage as he tried to get his tanks moving. Standing in the turret hatch of his tank, he was killed by a direct hit.

Oberst Erwin Menny temporarily took over command of the decimated division. Later, on December 9, *Generalleutnant* Gustav von Vaerst became the division's new commanding officer.

Generalleutnant Crüwell, who the day before had pleaded with Rommel to order a withdrawal, spoke with him once again the next day. Crüwell convinced Rommel to give the order to retreat. The order probably saved the DAK from total destruction as it was already in danger of being outflanked on both sides.

The DAK's View of the Retreat

While the defences of the Tobruk western front continued to hold, during the night of December 7-8 the DAK and the Italian motorized corps withdrew. Elements of the less mobile Twenty-first Italian Corps and the German 90th Light Division had pulled out first and were now reaching the Gazala position. Since the main danger to the retiring DAK and the entire *Panzergruppe* was the danger of a enveloping move by the enemy from the south, the task fell to the DAK of providing flanking cover to the south. The units pulled back in stages. The 15th Motorcycle Battalion provided the rearguard. The battalion suffered heavy losses, but it saved the DAK several times. By December 12 the *Panzergruppe* had reached the Gazala line. That day General Bastico, the Axis Commander-in-Chief in Africa, arrived at Rommel's headquarters in Ain el Gazala. Rommel described the meeting in his diary:

"His Excellency Bastico visited me in a rocky gorge southeast of Ain el Gazala and was very displeased with the course of the battle. Above all he was worried about the Agedabia area and wanted to send an Italian division there as quickly as possible. This resulted in a very sharp disagreement during which, among other things, I informed Bastico that I would not stand for him taking any of the Italian units. Otherwise there would be nothing left for me to do but make the retreat through Cyrenaica alone with the German units and leave the Italian units to their fate. I told him I was convinced that we could fight our way through, something the Italians could not do without our help. In brief: I would not allow a single Italian soldier to be removed from my command. Afterward Excellency Bastico changed his tune."

This interlude demonstrated Rommel's iron hardness, which caused him to stand up to superiors and even put a gun to their heads if necessary.

On the following day the reinforced British Guards Brigade managed to break through the positions of the Italian Twentieth Army Corps, and advanced reconnaissance elements reached Bir Temrad, about 20 kilometers behind the front. This placed the British beyond the flanking positions of the DAK, and there was now a danger that these armored forces might reach the crossroads at Mechili before the German units and cut off their source of supply.

The result of such a move by the British might possibly be to cut off the retreat of the entire *Panzergruppe Afrika* through Cyrenaica. At this point the Twentieth Italian Army Corps attacked the enemy force with everything it had and destroyed a large part of the Guards Brigade. 800 prisoners were taken, including the brigade commander. Numerous guns and twenty tanks were destroyed.

An advance by 150 tanks and armored cars against the rear of the DAK was likewise beaten off. On December 15 Rommel reported to the OKW:

"Following four weeks of uninterrupted and costly battles the fighting strength of the units is showing a decline in spite of outstanding individual efforts, especially since supplies of weapons and munitions have been totally absent. The army therefore intends to hold the area around Gazala on 16. 12. However, by the eve of 17. 12. at the latest a retreat through el Mechili — Derna will be unavoidable in order to prevent being encircled and destroyed by the enemy."

Rommel shocked the Italian command. On December 17 General Cavallero, chief of the Italian High Command, arrived at Rommel's headquarters. Several situation briefings resulted in harsh controversy. At 23.00 that day General Cavallero reappeared at Rommel's headquarters, this time accompanied by *Feldmarschall* Kesselring, General Bastico and General Gambarra. Cavallero demanded that Rommel withdraw the order to retreat. He was not in favor of this retreat and "he feared the political consequences for the Duce if Cyrenaica were lost." (See Rommel: *Krieg*

ohne Haß)

Feldmarschall Kesselring supported General Cavallero, saying that under no circumstances could the airfield at Derna be given up. None of this changed Rommel's intention to act as *he* saw fit. He declared to the generals and the Field Marshal:

"My decision cannot be changed. The orders have been given and are already being carried out. If I am not to permit the destruction of my Panzergruppe, then all that is left to me is to break through the enemy during the night" — Nothing could change his mind.

"I am now," he continued, "faced with the question of staying where I am and sacrificing the Panzergruppe and afterward losing Cyrenaica and Tripolitania, or breaking through and beginning the withdrawal tonight and reaching the area of Agedabia, in order to be able to at least defend Tripolitania."

Placed together under the command of *General-leutnant* Crüwell, on the evening of December 17 the DAK and the Italian Twentieth Corps withdrew across the southern edge of the Cyrenaican mountains toward El Abiar, while the Italian foot soldiers marched through Cyrenaica.

This was the overall story of the retreat. The effects of the retreat on the individual units is illustrated by the experiences of the 15th Motorcycle Battalion.

The Destruction of a Battalion

At the outset of the retreat the 15th Motorcycle Battalion, led by *Major* Curt Ehle, had a combat strength of almost 500 men. On December 15 in the Gazala position *Major* Kriebel, Division Ia of the 15th Panzer Division, found that it had a strength of 5 officers, 14 NCOs and 58 men. It had left three self-propelled gun carriages, ten trucks, five *Kübelwagen* and six motorcycles, as counted that day by *Leutnant* Kordel that day. *Major* Kriebel delivered the wish of the division commander that K 15 was no longer to be employed as rearguard. However, *Oberstleutnant* Ballerstedt, commander of the battle group to which the battalion was attached, advised him:

"We'll have to use them again today, Kriebel, there's no way around it."

Rearguards in action December 1941. Staff of the 15th Motorcycle Battalion with Major Ehle, Oberleutnant Kordel, Leutnant Servas and driver Thiel.

Leutnant Servas, K 15's "tank buster."

"Again!" said *Leutnant* Servas, a student of political economics and a young father figure to his comrades.

The men of the battalion were in positions near Solluch, which was to be held for the night to allow the other units to retire in an orderly fashion. *Leutnant* Kordel, *Leutnant* Dreyer and *Leutnant* Servas were the only officers among the small group. With his platoon of anti-tank guns on self-propelled carriages *Leutnant* Servas took command during the march to Solluch. The experienced patrol leader *Gefreiter* Raugs, who had been sent on ahead, returned with the news that Solluch was free of the enemy and that 11./IR 361 had already established itself there in defensive positions.

On arriving in Solluch the motorcycle unit received orders to secure the two tracks that led across the hill which extended back into the desert. It was almost dark when *Leutnant* Servas reached the first track. He found 10./IR 361 there. The commander of the company reported no enemy forces there and Servas drove ahead to scout the second track.

Just as Servas and his men reached the edge of the hill they ran into an British patrol with several armored cars which was coming directly toward them. *Leutnant* Servas fired first. The leading armored car was set on fire. By the time the second British scout car opened fire Servas already had it in his sights. His first shot destroyed the vehicle. Turning quickly he knocked out a third. At that moment another armored car unit was sighted on the first track.

"Back to the junction of the tracks in the valley!" ordered Servas.

When they reached the junction Servas positioned his anti-tank guns in the most favorable locations. Everyone else dug in behind them and waited for the approaching enemy. Nothing happened all night. Not until daybreak did they hear the sound of engines. The forward sentries reported:

"The Tommies are coming!"

Slowly, the armored cars appeared on the upper edge of the hill and rolled down the slope toward the *wadi*. When they had come near enough *Leutnant* Servas gave the order to open fire.

Three shots cracked as one. Three hits! There were fires and explosions among the enemy. Once more three shots, and three direct hits! Once again there were explosions, flames and fleeing British soldiers, who were caught by the machine-guns of the heavy MG platoon.

British guns opened fire. The small German force suffered casualties, dead and wounded. The cries of the wounded mixed with shouts for medics. These ran from hole to hole, tending to

Servas with captured British 40mm anti-tank gun.

Italian M13/40 tank.

Knocked-out British Crusader tank.

their wounded comrades.

"One more salvo and then withdraw!" ordered Servas.

Once again the three guns crashed, and everyone who had a weapon opened fire. Then the motorcycle troops climbed into their vehicles and drove off.

A mass of vehicles and armored cars roared toward the Germans from the right. Once again Servas' three anti-tank guns opened fire. British trucks burst into flames. Ammunition exploded, and Servas covered the battalion's withdrawal with his three anti-tank guns. Then they, too, turned and caught up with the battalion. Driving along on its flanks, they fired on the British armored cars and trucks passing to the left and right. They drove on until they came to an Italian airfield, where just then Arabs were firing at the parked aircraft.

Italians were standing in front of the airfield buildings with arms raised. They took the men of K 15 for British soldiers. When they saw Servas and his three anti-tank guns turn and open fire on the pursuing enemy, they ran to the anti-aircraft guns and four tanks which they had abandoned. A total of two complete companies of Italian soldiers appeared from every direction and joined in the defence of the airfield.

A little later the Italians climbed aboard their vehicles and roared off to the west with the battalion commander, *Major* Ehle. The three fighters at the airfield also took off and headed west.

A short time later when Curt Ehle reported the completion of his rearguard assignment to *Oberstleutnant* Bayerlein, the Chief of Staff gave the *Major* his hand.

"You've been lucky once again, Ehle!" he said, appreciation showing in his voice.

On February 21, 1942 *Leutnant* Servas was awarded the German Cross in Gold for these exploits and previous actions.

Rommel meets an Italian officer at the edge of a desert track.

Rommel receives the Italian Service Cross.

Interval

Back to Marsa el Brega

As planned by Rommel the retreat went quickly and Agedabia was reached on December 25. The enemy had not been able to outflank or encircle the DAK or elements of *Panzergruppe Afrika*.

The improvised defensive positions built by the rear echelon units on either side of Agedabia were occupied by the foot soldiers of the *Panzergruppe*, while the motorized German-Italian divisions were assembled in the Agedabia area for a mobile defence. It was there at the crisis point of Agedabia that the Eighth Army could have finished the *Afrika-Korps*, but it had gambled away its chance. More and more the British felt the disadvantages of long supply lines, while *Panzergruppe Afrika* was drawing nearer to Tripoli, its main supply port.

The situation for the Axis forces was relieved when, on December 19, ships arrived in Tripoli and Benghazi carrying two panzer companies, several batteries of artillery and supply goods. This was the first shipment of weapons that Rommel had received since mid-November.

Still, the situation for the German-Italian units near Agedabia was not a rosy one. Rommel decided to withdraw even farther and, while fighting a delaying action, direct the troops into the Marsa el Brega position. With the Ia of the DAK, *Oberstleutnant* Westphal, he overflew the new 60-kilometer-wide defensive position between Marada and Marsa el Brega in his Fieseler *Storch* to personally assess its defensive potential. The situation appeared favorable. There, near Marsa el Brega, they could defend Tripolitania.

Rommel was able to convince the *Comando Supremo* that the enemy could be halted near Marsa el Brega. At present, however, that was not yet the case.

Tank Battle near Agedabia

A day after the German-Italian forces arrived in Agedabia the British Reuters correspondent in Cairo reported for the London Gazette:

"The remains of the German Africa Corps and the Italian Army are flooding back along the Sirte on the roads leading to Tripoli. The main objective of the Eighth Army, the destruction of the enemy forces in the western desert, has been achieved. The German tank forces have been smashed. There are only a handful of German tanks left and these are attempting to escape in panic to Tripoli."

In London there was an outbreak of relieved jubilation. Rommel, the magician in the desert, had been beaten! This was a report that was worth its weight in gold to the British, but it was not entirely accurate.

In the Agedabia area the Eighth Army launched a frontal attack with the First and Seventh Armored Divisions and the Guards Brigade, while the Twenty-second Armored Brigade tried to outflank the German positions.

Once again *Kampfgruppe* Ballerstedt, with the main body of K 15 and a company each of Pionier and anti-tank guns, a platoon of light Flak and a battery from II./AA 33, was in action in the rearguard role. *Major* Ehle's motorcycle troops and their fast "home-made" tank destroyers were once more in action, engaging and destroying the pursuing enemy.

The battle which was to become known as the "Tank Battle near Agedabia" began on December 27. The rested British Twenty-second Armored Brigade advanced at high speed through el Haseiat, while the main body of the Eighth Army began a frontal assault. The tank battle lasted three days. Rommel forced the enemy to fight on changing fronts. On December 28 the 60 tanks of the 15th and 21st Panzer Divisions met 90 tanks of the British Twenty-second Armored Brigade. The result was an extended tank-versus-tank duel. Once again the German commanders demonstrated their superior skill in handling large armored units.

One British tank after another was knocked out of action. When the battle was over, 37 British tanks lay burning on the battlefield. The two divisions of the DAK lost a total of seven tanks.

At the front the British tanks came up against German anti-aircraft guns. In position there were the "eighty-eights" of the 135th Flak Regiment, commanded by *Major* Hecht. Hecht's gunners engaged the enemy tanks from a range of two kilometers, knocking out large numbers of them. For this defensive success *Major* Hecht was awarded the Knight's Cross on February 4, 1942.

A total of 136 knocked-out enemy tanks were counted in front of the German positions. The remaining tanks of the Twenty-second Armored Brigade escaped into the desert, pursued by four Panzer IVs. In Rommel's opinion, only the low fuel state of the German tanks prevented the total destruction of the British brigade.

The British divisions engaged in the frontal attack also withdrew to the northeast. By the evening of December 29 the danger to the Agedabia position was gone.

Rommel used the following quiet period to assemble his troops and pull back step by step into the Marsa el Brega position. Prior to this, however, the positions around Agedabia witnessed one more fireworks display. This time it consisted mostly of star shells, flares, and bursts of tracer. It took place at 24.00 on December 31 as the troops welcomed 1942.

Terrified, the Italian headquarters called the *Panzergruppe* command post and asked *Oberstleutnant* Bayerlein what was going on. Bayerlein soon calmed the Italians. Then the troops in the desert began singing the German national anthem, the *Deutschlandlied*. One position after another took up the song until the entire front was singing. The radio station of the British Twenty-second Armored Brigade radioed Cairo:

"Last night the German Africa Corps sang the German national anthem in its positions. Rommel's units may not have any tanks left, but it would be premature to speak of a shattered army. We should not fool ourselves into thinking that these soldiers, led by an unbroken General, will be inclined to give up the struggle. They will fight on like the devil."

The officers of this British armored brigade, which had come within a hair of being completely destroyed by this shattered army, knew better! They placed a higher estimate on the fighting morale of the DAK then their strategists in Cairo and the brash agents of the press.

On January 2, 1942 the Axis forces began an orderly withdrawal to Marsa el Brega. The Italian foot units withdrew first. They were followed by the German foot units and then the fast units. By January 12, 1942 all of *Panzergruppe Afrika* was in the Marsa el Brega position. The withdrawal had been a success. But what had happened to the garrisons of the encircled cities of Bardia and Sollum and of the Halfaya Pass?

Bardia - Sollum - Halfaya Pass

On December 30 elements of the Eighth Army launched an attack on Bardia, which was holding out even though it was 700 kilometers beyond the front held by *Panzergruppe Afrika*. Powerful artillery and air forces, supported by heavy shipboard guns, poured fire into Bardia.

Then the British launched their assault, supported by powerful armored forces. They made a deep penetration in the defences directly toward the supply and munitions depots. Bardia fell a short time later when the city commandant —with the approval of the army — surrendered the city. All of this took place on January 2, 1942.

In Sollum, which had been in German hands since November 21, were located the Tenth Oasis

Company, the remains of Twelfth Company and the headquarters of 300th Special Purpose Oasis Battalion under *Hauptmann* Enneccerus. There, south of Bardia, close to the sea and at the western foot of the Halfaya Pass, about 70 German soldiers held out until January 12, 1942. They received their last rations on January 10. This consisted of 20 grams of bread, a handful of rice, a spoonful of raisins and some wine.

On January 11 the enemy attacked and achieved a penetration between the main strongpoint and the battalion's command post bunker. The soldiers of the battalion headquarters launched a counterattack and threw out the enemy.

The British tried again. They assembled every available artillery battery and mortar, and on the morning of January 12 opened up with a mighty barrage on Sollum. To *Stabsgefreiter* Herrmann it seemed as if they wanted to "blast the place completely to bits!" Then came the assault troops. They were turned back with the last of the ammunition.

Half an hour later the Tommies attacked again. All that was left in the bunkers was tracing ammunition and flares. When the last signal cartridge was fire into the ranks of the perplexed enemy, *Hauptmann* Enneccerus sent out one of his prisoners with a white flag. Then he instructed the three remaining strongpoints:

"Cease firing! — Destroy all weapons! — Prepare to surrender!"

After 56 days of fighting against far superior forces the men of the Oasis Battalion stepped into the open. *Hauptmann* Enneccerus spoke only a single word:

"Comrades . . ." Then he turned away. The Battle of Sollum was over.

The Halfaya Pass was still holding out. Defending there was *Major* Wilhelm Bach, who had won the Knight's Cross for capturing the pass. But there, too, rations were getting short and, with the capture of Lower Sollum by the British, the last source of drinking water was cut off.

Oberleutnant Eichholz, commander of Second Company, 104th Rifle Regiment, was instructed to lead an assault squad to recapture the well and hold it until sufficient water had been sent to the pass. The attack was a success. A full water truck ensured the continued existence of the battle group holding the pass.

It was Christmas, and *Panzergruppe Afrika* had reached Agedabia. To celebrate the holiday the soldiers holding the pass were given a wonderful present: an extra cup of water!

Erwin Rommel attempted to supply the defenders of the pass with Ju 52 transport aircraft from Crete. These flights were discovered the second night, however, and the Ju 52s were shot down by British night fighters.

In mid-January the remnants of the Italian "Savona" Division under the command of Division general Giorgi came up the pass. They had withdrawn here from positions farther west with Rommel's approval.

A short time later Wilhelm Bach sent his senior company commander, *Hauptmann* Voigt, as a parlementaire to the South Africans. The former pastor Wilhelm Bach said of this:

"In a situation where the holding of a position no longer makes sense and it can only be held a few days longer through the loss of further soldiers and finally the whole unit, a commander must take the bitter path and save what can be saved."

After *Hauptmann* Voigt completed the preliminary negotiations the commander and the leader of the Pionier platoon, *Leutnant* Schmidt, drove down to surrender their forces.

They were greeted correctly by the South Africans, and when *Major* Bach had formally concluded the surrender he set in motion the secret arrangement he had made with the *Leutnant*. Schmidt nodded to the driver of the staff car, who without a word moved the white flag from the right to the left side of the car. This was the signal to the men in the pass that the surrender had been concluded. A forward German sentry reported the signal by radio to those above, following which all vehicles, weapons and equipment were blown up.

On the morning of January 17, 1942 the defenders of the Halfaya Pass fell in for the last time. Just as they were ready to march into captivity they were startled by a sudden outburst of gunfire from the South Africans. The shells fell close by First Company. *Oberleutnant* Dr. Gehring shouted a warning and everyone ran for cover, including the South Africans who were to escort them into captivity. Only *Major* Bach and the South African Lieutenant in charge of transferring the prisoners to the rear remained standing, staring speechless at one another.

When the fire abated the Lieutenant sent off a messenger. He came back a few minutes later and reported to the Lieutenant in a low voice. The Lieutenant called for the interpreter and said, turning to *Major* Bach:

"I knew that this could not have been done by any of our troops. It was Free French forces who fired on your people contrary to orders. I feel shame and contempt for this act and I beg that you believe me."

Major Bach did not reply. He saluted, but the salute was for the soldiers who had died in this senseless and underhanded act following the termination of hostilities.

The last Axis bastion east of Marsa el Brega had fallen.

Unloading German tanks in Naples.

The Luftwaffe in Summer and Winter

Established in his new headquarters in Derna, *Generalmajor* Fröhlich had been able to welcome several additional small air units since May 1941. I./JG 27 and I./JG 53 both arrived in Africa, followed later by a *Gruppe* of JG 77. Finally, in autumn, all of JG 53 was assembled in Africa. Also available for long-range reconnaissance tasks if needed was a *Gruppe* of Ju 88s.

The program for the German air units included attacks on enemy positions and bunkers, the destruction of supply columns and attacks on enemy transport ships bound for Tobruk. Rommel's headquarters also made frequent requests for air support for an attack or a defensive effort.

German dive-bomber units were escorted by German fighters. The Italian fighter units and the dive-bomber units were directed to cooperate with the *Fliegerführer Afrika*.

The German fighters carried tactical reconnaissance missions as well as offensive fighter sweeps, usually in *Staffel* strength. Several "aces" were already making their presence felt in Africa. *Staffelkapitän Oberleutnant* Rödel was awarded the Knight's Cross on June 22, 1941. *Oberleutnant* Ludwig Franzisket received the same decoration on July 23. Most of the victories by German fighters were achieved during Stuka escort missions over Tobruk.

Bf 110s over the Sicilian coast; returning from a mission over Africa.

Hans-Arnold Stahlschmidt beside his aircraft. Note 48 victory bars on rudder.

During the Battle of Sollum the Luftwaffe flew close-support missions in support of the DAK.

One Stuka pilot who rose to prominence in the missions over Tobruk was *Hauptmann* Helmut Mahlke. He was awarded the Knight's Cross on July 16, 1941.

The crews of the heavy fighters, the Bf 110s, also played an important role in the efforts by the Luftwaffe. The morale among the crews of these fighters was demonstrated in late summer 1941 when a Bf 110 was forced to come down in the desert while on a patrol. Another Bf 110 landed beside the first machine, took the crew on board and took off again.

The situation for *Generalmajor* Fröhlich became difficult with the beginning of the November battles as the enemy had significantly strengthened his air forces. Following the war the former *Fliegerführer Afrika* said:

"During the turbulent events at that time the task of air reconnaissance over the battle zone fell to the heavy fighters. Target selection for the Stukas was based on the information they brought back. Fighters flew cover over the target area and at the same time conducted battlefield reconnaissance. The available Gruppe of Ju 88s was also brought in for short-range missions."

Three times during the retreat by *Panzergruppe Afrika* in December, units of Fröhlich's command just managed to take off at the last minute in the face of the approaching enemy.

Major Kaschka, commander of the heavy fighter *Gruppe*, distinguished himself during the retreat. On his last mission he destroyed an enemy column, including two scout cars, before he was shot down by anti-aircraft fire.

In mid-december the Axis forces reached el Agheila. On January 1, 1942 Stephan Fröhlich was promoted to *Generalleutnant*. His air units had pulled back to Marsa el Brega.

It was during this phase of the battle that two German fighter pilots, *Oberfähnriche* Stahlschmidt and Marseille, first gave rise to comment.

Christmas celebrations took place near Agedabia. During the year of 1941 the men of JG 27 under "Edu" Neumann had proved their skill and readiness for action.

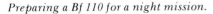

Preparing a Bf 110 for a night mission.

The German Navy in the Mediterranean

Overall View

As early as September 1940 *Grossadmiral* Raeder, the Commander-in-Chief of the *Kriegsmarine*, addressed several memoranda to Hitler advocating the shifting of the focus of the war to the Mediterranean. The objective would be to place the lands of the Near East in the hands of the Axis military forces. In this way the German Army and Air Force, together with the Italian armed forces, could play their part in the battle against the main enemy, Britain.

What Raeder could not offer was the participation of the *Kriegsmarine* in this effort with U-boats. As far as the Grand Admiral was concerned, the task of the German naval forces was to pursue the campaign against merchant shipping in the Atlantic.

Following the startling successes of the British forces in Africa in the winter of 1940-41 the Italian forces were in danger of being forced completely out of North Africa. It was then, as previously recounted, that Mussolini accepted German offers of assistance. The *Afrika-Korps* was sent to Africa.

Questions were already being raised as to how the navy was to protect German troop transports across the Mediterranean *and* how German underwater forces could inflict the maximum possible damage on the enemy. Initially, however, there was no large-scale commitment of submarines to the Mediterranean, although a small U-Boat group did operate off Gibraltar.

The British Admiralty sent the following radio message to Malta on January 10, 1941:

"Stop all supply transports from Italy to Tripoli!"

The order was addressed to Captain G.W.G. Simpson who, on January 10, had taken over the position of commander of the British Tenth Submarine Flotilla in Malta. At that time "Shrimp" Simpson did not have a single submarine in his command. Not until later did the promised submarines begin to arrive. Once there, however, they immediately set about their task: the sinking of German and Italian transports.

The first success was achieved by the "Upright," under Lieutenant E.D. Norman, which sunk the Italian cruiser "Diaz" on February 25, 1941. The Italian warship had been escorting a large Naples to Tripoli convoy. Soon the Malta flotilla numbered twenty submarines. In the period April 25 — May 1 the "Upholder," commanded by the most successful British submarine captain, Lieutenant Commander M.D. Wanklyn, sank three ships totalling 15,410 gross tons from German-Italian convoys near the island of Kerkennah. The blows fell in quick succession. The high point of the submarine offensive was an attack by the "Unique," commanded by Ensign Collett, and the "Upholder" on a convoy which sailed for Tripoli on September 18, 1941. The convoy consisted of the "Marco Polo" (12,172 tons), "Esperia" (11,398 tons), "Neptunia" (19,475 tons) and "Oceania" (19,507 tons). The convoy was escorted by four destroyers and a torpedo boat, which were joined on September 19 by four more destroyers. The steamships "Neptunia," "Oceania" and "Esperia" were sunk. The destroyers were able to prevent the sinking of the "Marco Polo."

The cost to the Africa Corps was enormous. It lost seventy percent of its supplies and this loss threatened the very existence of the DAK. Rommel urgently requested the employment of German submarines in the Mediterranean. They were to seal off Tobruk from the sea and neutralize the fortress.

The first six Atlantic U-Boats passed unhindered through the Straits of Gibraltar into the Mediterranean at the end of September 1941. The 23rd U-Boat Flotilla was established in Salamis. The first commander of the flotilla was *Kapitän-leutnant* Frauenheim. The 29th U-Boat Flotilla was formed in La Spezia and Pola at the end of October. *Korvettenkapitän* Becker was named its commander. At the beginning of November *Korvettenkapitän* Viktor Oern, the first commander of U-Boats in the Mediterranean in charge of protecting commercial shipping, arrived at the German command center in Rome: the *Marinekommando Italien*.

The U-Boats very quickly achieved their first successes against commercial vessels and small warships. The first major blow in the Mediterranean was struck on November 13. U 81 under *Kapitänleutnant* Guggenberger sank the aircraft carrier "Ark Royal" and torpedoed the battleship "Malaya" which was towed, heavily damaged, to Gibraltar. The battleship did not see action again.

Later, on November 25, 1941, the submarine U 331, commanded by *Oberleutnant zur See* von Tiesenhausen out of Salamis, torpedoed the battleship "Barham." The 31,000-ton giant sank in barely four minutes. 862 British seamen went down with the battleship.

The cruiser "Galathea" was sunk on December 14. On the night of December 18/19 Italian frogmen sank the British battleships "Queen Elizabeth" and "Valiant" in Alexandria harbor.

Three more waves of U-Boats had been sent to the Mediterranean by November 20, 1941. At the end of November, 14 of a total of 16 boats sent to the Mediterranean were in action. Two submarines — U 433 and U 95 — had been lost.

The strategic effects of the U-Boat's successes in the Mediterranean were tremendous. The balance had swung toward the Axis naval forces, ensuring marine superiority in both parts of the Mediterranean for at least six months.

The Axis naval successes had beneficial effects on the DAK and the newly-formed *Panzergruppe Afrika*. Supplies again flowed to Africa and a reinvigorated Rommel was able to strike at the British Eighth Army in January 1942, negating its earlier successes.

Seen from this point of view the employment of German U-Boats had been a great success and a decisive help to the *Deutsches Afrika-Korps*.

The New Offensive

Preparations for the Attack

A German-Italian convoy arrived in Tripoli on January 5, 1942, delivering a whole range of vitally-needed supplies to the DAK, in addition to 50 tanks, 20 armored cars and a large number of anti-tank guns. Rommel and *Oberstleutnant* Westphal had overflown the front numerous times, on several occasions barely escaping disaster at the hands of enemy fighter aircraft. Rommel was once again formulating an offensive strategy. When he revealed his intentions to Westphal, the latter said:

"We must steal a march on the enemy, *Herr General*. The British have not yet reorganized their units and have not yet brought up supplies. If we catch them now, they will not be prepared for a new concentrated attack. We have to take advantage of this period of weakness."

On January 13, 1942 Rommel's mind was made up. He told his staff:

"We are going to attack!"

This disclosure, which Rommel made to his staff officers at the morning briefing on January 13, was a bombshell, because the last thing any of them expected was a new attack.

"If we leave the Eighth Army in peace until February it will have so grown in strength and moved such a large quantity of supplies to the west that nothing will be able to stop it. Therefore we cannot wait. We *must* put the enemy off his plan."

It was also thanks to the efforts of *Luftflotte* 2 that the Malta submarines were now not so active as before. As a result more and more supplies were getting through and Rommel was becoming more optimistic day by day that he could pull it off.

The objective of the German attack was to disrupt the enemy build-up and prevent a British offensive. In order to attain this objective Rommel, as he had done before and would do again, sought a new strategy.

Rommel made sure that the password for the imminent further withdrawal was issued to every billet and headquarters. As a result the rumor reached Rome and finally, in the form of a report by British agents, lay on the desks of the senior British commanders in Cairo:

"Rommel is planning to withdraw all the way to Tripoli!"

General Auchinleck, however, smelled a rat and ordered intensified reconnaissance.

Further transports reached Africa on January 19. At that time Rommel had 111 tanks at the front and a further 28 in his rear areas. The Italian Twentieth Motorized Corps had 90 tanks.

Rommel's plan proceeded to action.

Sheds and other buildings were burning in Marsa el Brega on the evening of January 20, 1942. In the harbor ships were being blown up. British agents were already sending their reports to Cairo, clearly and unmistakeably indicating that Rommel was "packing his tent" and blowing up the ships behind him. Rommel had made all the preparations for a withdrawal — or so it seemed — and that evening even General Auchinleck was convinced that the last act of the battle in North Africa had begun.

On the morning of January 21, 1942, however, this retreat looked quite different. On that morning the following was posted in front of the quarters of every soldier of *Panzergruppe Afrika*:

The Commander-in-Chief   H.Q., 21. 1. 1942
Panzergruppe Afrika

Army Order of the Day

German and Italian soldiers!
You have heavy battles against far superior enemy forces behind you. But your fighting spirit is unbroken.
At this time we are numerically superior to the enemy facing our front. Today our army will set out to destroy this enemy.
I expect that every soldier will to his utmost in these decisive days.
Long live Italy! — Long live the Greater German Reich! Long live the Führer!

The Commander-in-Chief
Rommel
General der Panzertruppe

A tank rolls back to the front from the repair shop.

Those soldiers who saw their General Rommel on the morning of the new attack noticed that he had received the Swords to the Knight's Cross. The day before he had become the sixth German soldier to be awarded the decoration. A few days later, as had been announced beforehand, Rommel was promoted to *Generaloberst*.

The German offensive got under way. Intended merely as a spoiling attack against a British offensive, it was all of a sudden to become a drive towards the East.

Rommel's Drive through Cyrenaica

At six o'clock on the morning of January 21, 1942, a typical cold desert winter morning, Rommel and his tactical advisors left his headquarters. They drove directly to *Kampfgruppe* Marcks. *Oberstleutnant* Werner Marcks, commander of the 90th Light Division's 155th Rifle Regiment, had been sent some Pionier, as well as anti-tank guns and a few tanks from the *"Ariete"* Division. He also had some troops from the 21st Panzer Division. His battle group was to drive along the *Via Balbia*, make a frontal attack against the positions of the British Guards Brigade, overrun them and drive on through the gap toward Agedabia.

Generalmajor Werner Marcks (also an Oberstleutnant and Oberst during his service in Africa).

As this was the initial blow of the planned attack Rommel wanted to be on hand to command it in person. An half-hour earlier he had received notification from *Führer* Headquarters in Rastenburg that effective immediately the *Panzergruppe* was to be called *Panzerarmee Afrika*.

The entire 90th Light Division, which since *Generalmajor* Sümmermann's death on December 10 had been commanded by *Generalmajor* Veith, who had come from the Russian Front, was to follow up through the gap created by *Kampfgruppe* Marcks. The Italian Twentieth Army Corps was to fight its way through as well.

While *Kampfgruppe* Marcks was roaring off in armored personnel carriers, trucks and motorcycles, the DAK was going to drive in a wide arc through the desert to the south in an attempt to catch the British by surprise. Moving along the Wadi Faregh, it was to turn northeast and fall upon the rear of the forces which *Kampfgruppe* Marcks, the 90th Light Division and the Italian Twentieth Corps were attacking frontally and destroy them.

Generaloberst Rommel drove to *Kampfgruppe* Marcks in his *Mammut*. When he arrived there Marcks informed him that everything was ready to begin the advance.

"Then get going, Marcks! Your objective is Agedabia!" replied Rommel.

Werner Marcks stood up in his command car and gave the hand signal. Engines roared to life. The battle group began to move and then drove away.

"Rommel's on the move again!" offered one of

the motorcycle troops.

"Rommel!" had become a magic word in the western desert.

Leading the way were the light armored cars; behind them were several heavy tanks which had been given the task of eliminating machine-gun nests and anti-tank barriers.

The first enemy tanks soon appeared in front of a British blocking position. They were eliminated in a tank-versus-tank duel. Afterward the battle group reached the British positions, which pouring heavy anti-tank gun fire at the tanks and armored cars. The tanks engaged the anti-tank guns and put them out of action. West of Giofia a British howitzer battery was overrun, the crews captured and sent to the rear with several German wounded.

"Forward! — Everyone after me!" ordered the battle group's commander.

It was 11.00 and they had already broken through the enemy's defensive positions.

Rommel now ordered the Italian Twentieth Army Corps forward. Under its new commanding general, Corps General Zinghales, it drove through the gap that had been smashed in the British defensive line. Zinghales was the Italian tank expert and those who knew him called him the Italian Guderian.

Kampfgruppe Marcks drove straight on toward Agedabia, overrunning and shooting up British patrols and strongpoints along the way. Agedabia was reached the following morning. The battle for possession of the town lasted exactly one hour. The tanks drove into Agedabia in wedge formation. They were followed by the mounted motorcycle troops and infantry, then the Pionier and anti-tank guns. Following a brief, sharp battle the town was in the battle group's hands.

When Rommel received the encouraging report that Agedabia had been taken he ordered: "Drive on toward Antelat!"

Antelat meant a further march of sixty kilometers. The wiry *Oberstleutnant* led the way toward the objective in his fast command car. He sent out a reconnaissance patrol to scout along the *Via Balbia* to the coast. Marcks himself drove toward Antelat on the battle group's forward left flank.

Some of the vehicles became bogged down in the sand and had to be dug out. Individual British units which approached or were holding out in

camouflaged positions were overcome. At Rommel's forward command post near Saunnu, Werner Marcks received orders to drive southeast from Saunnu toward Abd el Grara and from there toward Giof el Mater. This wide arc would place the battle group in the southeast flank of the British First Armored Division, which was holding position between Agedabia and Giof el Mater. Werner Marcks had been given the task of closing the ring which was forming around the enemy forces.

In those first two days Rommel, through the clever employment of his battle groups, split the enemy forces into several groups and was able to attack and destroy them individually. Of this Alan Moorehead wrote in *African Trilogy*:

"Cooperation between our units was missing from the very start. The surprise paralyzed our operations staff. The infantry in the front lines got no help. The reserves either stood idly in the rear or, if they tried to move forward, found the way blocked by the onrushing enemy. Then the Germans streamed in three large columns into the British lines. They deployed and the old game began: individual British units were destroyed one after the other. Within two days the British offensive strength was broken."

How this happened is illustrated by the experiences of the German battle groups.

Kampfgruppe Warrelmann

Next to *Kampfgruppe* Marcks, *Kampfgruppe* Warrelmann, which had also been committed toward Agedabia, was Rommel's second iron in the fire. *Major* (later *Generalmajor*) Hinrich Warrelmann, commander of the 2nd Machine-gun Battalion, wrote in his combat report:

"We had orders to be ready by January 20, 1942. On that day we commanders were ordered to a conference with Rommel. The result of the conference was a clear attack order for the retaking of Cyrenaica, with the ultimate objective of capturing Tobruk.

Agedabia was to be taken first in a *coup de main* in order to open the way to Cyrenaica. My battalion was to set out at 05.00 on January 21, 1942. Things happened quite differently, however, because elements of the 90th Light (*Kampfgruppe*

Marcks) broke through ahead of us and took Agedabia. All we could do was follow through the hole it had punched in the British lines. Great quantities of fuel and rations fell into our hands.

As I was refuelling my vehicles there — in addition to my battalion II./PzArtAbt. 33 under *Hauptmann* Meyer and a company of the 15th Motorcycle Battalion had been placed under my command — General Rommel suddenly roared up:

'What are you doing here?' he asked, and I replied:

'I'm refuelling!'

'You're not supposed to refuel. You're supposed to attack!' he said, and then began to instruct me on our next objective. 'You will set out east along the track and after about a 40 kilometer drive will reach the desert fort of Antelat. You are to take and hold it. A major battle will develop east of Agedabia.'' (Both *Kampfgruppen* Marcks and Warrelmann were deployed against Antelat.)

"It was already getting dark when I set out. I soon noticed that I was alone with my battle group. After about two hours we reached the desert fort and assembled there with our artillery in the center. In the morning twilight of January 22 we moved into an all-round defensive position. When it became light we saw an amazing sight. British combat and supply units were moving past and around us in every direction, some in the direction from which we had come. In the distance we could hear artillery. We were wide awake and, surrounded by British troops, did not feel particularly well.

All of a sudden two British aircraft approached to land beside us. Both were shot down by machine-gun fire. Nine British fliers were taken prisoner.

At that point I received a report that 800 meters away was a British airfield with several aircraft. I immediately sent a mounted company to attack and capture the aircraft. As a result of the shooting-down of the two aircraft the British had become aware of the presence of their unwelcome visitors and immediately deployed a company of armored cars to the airfield. As a result we were unfortunately forced to destroy the eight machines there. In the meantime we established radio contact with the DAK.

At my question, what was going on, came the answer:

'Hold Antelat at all costs!' The next message from the DAK said, 'Rich booty at Antelat!'

At about midday the enemy attacked with tanks. I ordered the anti-tank company not to open fire until the range was 100 meters. The effect was extraordinary. After eight of their tanks had been set afire the British withdrew.

Following this defensive success I asked the DAK for freedom of action for attacks on the enemy columns. No further orders came, however. The sound of battle moved farther away from us.'' (The noise of battle they heard was caused by *Kampfgruppe* Marcks.)

"On the afternoon of January 22 I gave the commander of II./AR 33 a motorcycle company for security and named him commander of Antelat. With my Fourth Company I drove into the flank of a large British column, cut it off in the center and returned with seven armored cars and many prisoners and vehicles.

"On January 23 and 24 I undertook two more such flanking raids, which were successful, and when evening fell on January 24 my battle group had taken about 1,800 prisoners and assembled a considerable motor pool on my hill.

An order from the DAK arrived late on the evening of January 24. It read:

'*Kampfgruppe* Warrelmann will depart at about 05.00 on 25. 1. to attack the Msus desert fort and link up there with the *Deutsche Afrika-Korps!'*

Protected by patrols, on the 25th we drove in the direction of Msus, 60 kilometers away. We made good progress. After a march of 20 kilometers a report came from the advance guard:

'A group of tanks from the right. Unable to tell if they are German or British!'

The tanks came nearer. They were flying pennants, therefore they were British. We counted 42 tanks. We hastily formed a defensive front. My 12 anti-tank guns went into position. Behind them was Meyer's artillery.

The battle began with the crash of gunfire. From close range the artillery was very effective. After several tanks were set on fire the British group turned away in the direction of Msus. Without tanks of our own we set off after the British tanks. However, they were faster than we were. A short time later we saw giant clouds of smoke rising in the direction of Msus and, barely visible behind them, troop movements.

We increased our tempo and were soon met by a

battalion of British self-propelled guns. When I deployed my artillery battalion the British pulled back. We pushed on and reached Msus without further contact with the enemy. However, the DAK was not to be found.

We had hardly reached the Msus hills, when a British battalion with 12 tanks and many vehicles approached us from behind. As we had not yet occupied positions I had my artillery turn around and open fire at once.

The British turned away to the east. Immediately afterward I received a report from my patrol that about six kilometers away there was a tank unit whose crews had abandoned their tanks and climbed into trucks. I immediately deployed a company to investigate the situation and, if the opportunity arose, take immediate action. More than 30 tanks fell into our hands. We later learned that the tank battalion was to have refuelled in Msus, but could not get through us and therefore had to abandon its vehicles.

We captured 12 aircraft on the Msus airfield. We also took over a large supply dump with foodstuffs and band instruments, including a piano. Unfortunately, the fuel dump was already burning.

We had just set up defensive positions when another small group of vehicles, three tanks and two armored cars, appeared following in our tracks.

This time it was not the enemy, but *General-oberst* Rommel, who was trying to establish with me the personal contact he maintained with all of the units and battle groups of *Panzerarmee Afrika* during those decisive days. He listened to my report and then corrected me:

'It was not 24, but 26 tanks which were knocked out by you, Warrelmann!'

He had observed the scene of engagement closely, as was Rommel's style.''

Like *Kampfgruppe* Warrelmann, which knew nothing of the deployment of *Kampfgruppe* Marcks and fancied itself alone on a broad stage, all of the other battle groups had been given special assignments and acted accordingly. It was the large number of German units which puzzled the enemy and finally caused him to panic.

Kampfgruppe Geissler

The first days of the battle were described by the commander of the 21st Panzer Division's 115th Rifle Regiment in a combat report entitled, ''Rommel Strikes Back.'' The following is his description of events:

''When we set out early on the morning of January 21, 1942, with the rising sun in our eyes and the infantry sitting in their vehicles, we came upon a completely surprised enemy who merely replied with weak artillery fire and in general fled in panic. We repeatedly came upon clusters of abandoned vehicles. In many cases the engines had been rendered useless by rifle bullets and all of the gas tanks were empty. Unfavorable terrain limited the chances of a flanking movement by our panzers and allowed the enemy to withdraw toward Agedabia.

The town was taken on January 22. Elements of the DAK drove on as far as Saunnau-Antelat and at that point had already advanced over 100 kilometers to the northeast. As a result of this advance a battle group of the British First Armored Division with 117 tanks and armored cars, 33 guns, many vehicles and over 1,000 men had been surrounded and forced to surrender.

On January 23, after breaking the resistance of the British covering group, the DAK drove on as far as Msus, the junction of several desert tracks. Travelling at maximum speed our units rolled

*Hauptmann
Josef Hissmann.*

106

northward in a wide deployment — past many abandoned enemy combat and other vehicles, past a working enemy tank repair shop and an airfield with a whole squadron of enemy fighters. It was a wild drive. A breathtaking race with the withdrawing enemy. Through the dust we could see British columns driving in the same direction with clusters of soldiers hanging onto trucks in an effort to escape. The supply center of Saunnau had fallen into German hands.

While the main British force was withdrawing toward El Mechili, a strong enemy group was still holding out in the Benghazi area. From there it posed a threat to our lines of communication to the rear as the pursuit to the northeast went on. The army headquarters therefore decided to first take Benghazi and clear Cyrenaica. Two mixed battle groups were formed for this purpose. One was the existing *Kampfgruppe* Marcks, which was sent toward Benghazi, and the other a mixed battle group under my command. The latter combined the headquarters of the 15th Rifle Brigade, three rifle battalions, an anti-tank company, a battery of artillery and a Pionier company.

We received orders to advance northward toward Maraua, block the roads leading through Cyrenaica and intercept the enemy forces withdrawing from the Benghazi area.

Near Maraua the battle group encountered the first determined resistance, which the previously-used tactic of a quick rush was unable to break. The high ground on both sides of Maraua along the *Via Balbia* was heavily occupied. Directed fire from several enemy batteries made any approach difficult. I decided to attack with all of my forces after brief preparations.

The attack, which had to be carried out across undulating, but open terrain, began late in the afternoon of January 28 and slowly gained ground in the face of heavy defensive fire. The news that the spearhead of the attack had run into a minefield several hundred meters in front of the enemy positions — I myself drove over a mine in my half-track, which tore away the vehicle's forward chassis — as well as the quickly-approaching darkness led me to call off the attack until it became light.

During the night the Pionier company assigned to me removed 360 mines from our lane of attack. Early on the morning of January 29 Maraua and the enemy positions on the *Via Balbia* were stormed and taken. During the night the enemy had very cleverly withdrawn part of his forces, including his artillery.

During the course of the morning *Generaloberst* Rommel himself appeared near Maraua. He informed me of his intention to exploit the enemy's growing uncertainty and recapture Cyrenaica with just *Kampfgruppen* Marcks and Geissler. He ordered us to set out to the east together as soon as *Kampfgruppe* Marcks, which he had personally sent from Behghazi (since taken) along the *Via Balbia*, arrived.

We remained under the direct command of *Armee* headquarters. The enemy put up a determined defence, skilfully utilizing barricades and mines and supported by strafing attacks from the air.

By February 6, 1942 the broad region of Cyrenaica had been cleared of the enemy. We secured our success in a loose, strongpoint-style disposition on the western edge of the Mamarica between el Mechili and Tmimi."

Because of the dry, factual style of this report by *Oberst* Geissler it fails to mention many of the dramatic moments faced by his battle group and all of the other attacking units.

The attack on the main body of the British First Armored Division, for example, deserves to be told in more detail. The attack began early on the morning of January 24. Tanks of this British division tried to break through the blocking position which had been established by *Kampfgruppe* Marcks to the east and southeast. They were engaged and destroyed by anti-tank and anti-aircraft guns. The British infantry was halted and pushed back into the pocket. Wherever the action flared up *Oberstleutnant* Marcks was there, throwing his reserves into the battle.

When darkness fell on January 24 the battle was over. The British First Armored Division had been shattered. *Kampfgruppe* Marcks received a new assignment:

The battle group was now to set out to the west toward Msus as part of an enveloping attack, while the DAK and the Italian Twentieth Motorized Corps moved in from the west. The move was designed to eliminate the remnants of the British First Armored Division which had escaped to Msus.

Early on the morning of January 25 the African sky was a dull grey. *Oberstleutnant* Marcks gave the signal to move out. Tank engines roared to life, accompanied by the noise of motorcycles and half-tracks starting up.

Suddenly, *Generaloberst* Rommel appeared on the scene. He shared *his* watchword with the *Oberstleutnant*:

"Exploit, Marcks! Exploit!"

Two hours later some enemy tanks which stood in the battle group's way were eliminated. The 2nd Machine-gun Battalion, which had been assigned to *Kampfgruppe* Marcks, engaged British infantry which tried to hold up the attack.

All of a sudden British artillery fire from Msus began to fall on the battle group and the whole DAK. At that point Rommel appeared again.

"Listen, Marcks," instructed the Commander-in-Chief curtly, "we're going to assemble all the anti-tank and anti-aircraft guns in the rear of your battle group. Then you will drive straight toward Msus with your fast elements in order to draw the enemy tanks toward our defensive ring."

It was a typical Rommel assignment. Moments later the battle group rolled off toward Msus. The British guns shifted their fire onto the approaching groups of vehicles. A shell burst near the commander's vehicle, showering the men inside with sand and steel splinters. About 15 meters away a scout car took a direct hit and exploded in a ball of flame. The driver of the command car steered around the burning vehicle.

When near enough to Msus *Oberstleutnant* Marcks gave the order to turn around. The battle group swung west in a wide arc. Marcks could see the enemy's reaction through his field glasses. The British fell for the ruse. They believed the enemy was on the run and sent their tanks to finish him off. The German vehicles rolled through the positions of the "eighty-eight" anti-aircraft guns of the 135th Flak Regiment, and then the massed anti-tank and anti-aircraft guns opened fire on the pursuing tanks.

After three volleys seven enemy tanks had been destroyed. The rest turned and fled back to Msus at high speed.

"Now attack!" ordered Rommel.

The attackers raced forward through the British field positions, over barbed wire obstacles and past abandoned trenches as well as those from which the enemy was still firing. They reached Msus.

Suddenly there were explosions and thick columns of smoke. The British were blowing up their supply depots. Flames leapt from the fuel dump. *Kampfgruppe* Marcks had taken Msus.

The soldiers set to work extinguishing the fires. Tremendous amounts of equipment fell into the hands of *Panzerarmee Afrika*. More than 600 vehicles of all kinds were captured, as well as 127 guns. In the tank repair shop the Germans found 50 serviceable British tanks.

Kampfgruppe Marcks received new orders and set off again as the spearhead unit. This time its thrust was aimed through El Rhegima and Benina directly toward Benghazi. Marcks received orders from Rommel to capture Benghazi, and when Rommel subsequently asked the tough *Oberstleutnant* if he could carry out further combat assignments afterward, Marcks replied:

"The battle group will carry out every task given to it!"

Rommel placed AA 33 at Marcks' disposal and made sure that *Kampfgruppe* Geissler would attack in support. Then, in conclusion, he said to the *Oberstleutnant*:

"Save a place for me and my section, Marcks!"

Signals intelligence gathering and Arab spies had revealed that the Benghazi garrison consisted of three Indian brigades. Part of the force was in the city itself, but the main body was deployed due east of Benghazi.

On the evening of January 26 *Kampfgruppe* Marcks began to move in a northerly direction, while *Kampfgruppe* Geissler (as recounted previously) had been committed toward Maraua and El Mechili.

An hour after departure a heavy desert sandstorm, or *ghibli*, began. The storm raged. *Generaloberst* Rommel, who was accompanying the battle group, assumed the lead in order to — as so often before — assume the role of navigator. Finally it began to rain. The motorcycles and trucks became stuck in a broad *wadi*. In vain Werner Marcks tried to get his battle group moving. Not until the ground had hardened again was movement restored.

On the morning of January 28 the leading element reached Ridotta Rhegima. By 16.00 Benina had been reached and the Benghazi airfield taken. Elements of the battle group also occupied the eastern edge of Benghazi, where they were met by defensive fire from the Indians.

Without hesitating *Oberstleutnant* Marcks sent his Grenadiers to the attack. One detachment was sent to Coefia. During the battle Marcks' command car was shot up. He climbed into an armored car. In Benghazi the enemy was already blowing up his stores. A little later Benghazi was in German hands.

The Indian Brigade surrounded between Benghazi and Coefia now attempted to break through to the east. Marcks' forces attacked at once. Some of the Indians were taken prisoner.

The words of an American radio announcer typified the surprise and amazement which followed this coup by Rommel:

"General Rommel, the rascal among modern generals, has once again pulled a new rabbit out of his hat."

In the days that followed, *Kampfgruppe* Marcks, always in the lead and far ahead of the main body of *Panzerarmee Afrika*, forged onward. On January 30 it captured Barce and Tocra. Maraua was captured in cooperation with *Kampfgruppe* Geissler.

In a further advance Werner Marcks and his Grenadiers drove into Cirene. Giovanni St.Berta was the next objective. This was reached and captured.

The Fifth Indian Brigade made a stand near Martuba. It was smashed in a three-hour battle. When the enemy began to run, Marcks decided on his own initiative to give chase. He bypassed Er-Rzem and attacked Tmimi. There, too, the enemy was battered and put to flight.

All of Cyrenaica had again been cleared of enemy forces. *Generaloberst* Rommel had recaptured the entire territory in 17 days.

The DAK, which supposedly had been dead, had roared through the desert like a gale wind. The planned British attack on Tripoli had been ruined even before it began.

On February 5 Werner Marcks received the Knight's Cross of the Iron Cross from the hand of *Generaloberst* Rommel. He later said of the decoration:

"Such a symbol involved blood, tears and destruction. But at the same time it also represented bravery, loyalty and the selfless readiness for action of many brave men."

In Battle with the 8th Machine-gun Battalion

By January 13, 1942 *Leutnant* Möcker had scouted the terrain in front of MG 8 for a new advance. Patrols had revealed that it and the DAK were facing the following units: elements of the First Armored Division, the Fourth Indian Division, the Second Armored brigade, the Seventh Infantry Brigade and the Twenty-second Guards Brigade. All of these units were well known to the machine-gun battalion.

On January 22, a day after the beginning of the attack, the battalion left its assembly area north of Maaten Belcleibat and closed up with PR 5. During the march east and northeast it formed up on the right of the tanks, its objective being to reach Bleidet el Taraut. Within a few kilometers, however, the battalion became bogged down and was unable to move forward or backward in the sand dunes.

Major Schütte, the new battalion commander, who had previously led MG 8 in the winter battle, sent a patrol to scout a southern route around the sand dunes. At a level area, through which the units of the 15th Panzer Division had already passed, prime movers were able to tow the battalion's vehicles through.

Remaining close to PR 5, on January 23 the battalion reached the area 70 km east of El Agheila, and following a three hour pause in the march it received instructions to advance along the *Via Balbia* as far as Agedabia. When it reached the city at 22.00 it was already free of the enemy.

Once again the men were sent forward, and following a strenuous night drive they reached the new target area of Hseir el Aunami, 15 kilometers west of Saunnu, on the morning of January 24.

All of a sudden 2./MG 8, which was leading the advance, sighted British vehicles to the left and right of the road. The column was surrounded. One hundred prisoners were taken and 48 trucks captured. The column was part of the supply train of the First Armored Division.

Afterward MG 8 occupied the designated positions. 3./MG 8, supported by two platoons of the 39th Anti-tank Battalion, was sent ahead to a hill which lay 800 meters farther on. It had just moved into position when 20 British tanks attacked. Five of the tanks were destroyed by the anti-tank guns. The rest turned away and disappeared.

A short time later orders arrived for MG 8 to support an attack by PR 5 on Saunnu. The entire 5th Panzer Regiment consisted of 25 tanks and two attached 88mm Flak. Shortly before reaching

Saunnu PR 5 encountered an enemy unit with a strength of about 100 tanks which was moving north.

The regiment immediately joined battle. In a bitter fight, which was directed personally by *Generalmajor* von Bismarck, the new division commander, three enemy attacks were beaten off and a number of British tanks destroyed. The British continued to attack under cover of smoke, but were beaten back.

On orders from the commanding general of the DAK, *Generalleutnant* Crüwell, MG 8 covered PR 5's flank. Employing all of its weapons the battalion prevented several flanking attempts by the enemy.

Generaloberst Rommel appeared at 13.45 and ordered a continuation of the attack to the northeast in order to engage and destroy a British tank unit which was heading west.

The advance went on. Driving on MG 8's right was the rest of PR 5. The advance continued over undulating terrain toward the deep valley in which lay the Saunnu watering place. On reaching the crest of the ridge the soldiers of the spearhead were presented with a breathtaking sight. Before them were 50 tanks and two batteries of field guns in the process of assembling, as well as a number of trucks close by the water hole.

While MG 8 went into position, the tanks rolled west around the valley so as to sandwich the entire British unit.

Ten enemy tanks managed to reach the ridge and attacked the flank of MG 8. Anti-tank guns of the 39th Anti-tank Battalion's Second Company destroyed three of them and the rest turned and drove back into the valley.

Once again the enemy laid down smoke, and under cover of the thick, purple swaths several tanks drove directly toward the position of the anti-tank guns. They rolled over three guns and shot up the gun tractors.

The battle was soon over, however, because PR 5 had meanwhile destroyed 32 of the British tanks and both batteries. Seven knocked-out enemy tanks lay before the positions of MG 8.

The German units assembled in the valley and the next morning, January 25, 1942, a British column approaching to fetch water was caught in a pincer attack. After a brief exchange of fire 5 trucks had been set on fire and another 12 captured.

3./MG 8 remained behind to guard the watering place, while the main body of the battalion joined up with PR 5 which drove on in the direction of Maaten el Grara. This flanking move by the panzer regiment was intended to bring relief to *Kampfgruppe* Marcks.

The next day the 21st Panzer Division advanced farther in the direction of Msus in order to carry out Rommel's order to "raise dust near Bir el Gerrari" on January 27 and simulate a threat against Mechili.

PR 5, which was leading the advance, raised a tremendous dust cloud by dragging old tank tracks and other pieces of equipment behind its vehicles.

Rommel, the master of stratagem and deception, had achieved his objective. Benghazi fell and MG 8 was able to take a rest.

Rommel's View of the Advance

General Cavallero arrived at the headquarters of *Panzerarmee Afrika* on the afternoon of January 23, 1942 to denounce Rommel's unauthorized advance and halt attack operations by the *Panzerarmee*. Rommel disagreed with the Italian General. He described the conversation in his diary:

"Cavallero brought the Duce's guidelines for the subsequent prosecution of the war. It appeared that those in Rome did not at all agree with the *Panzerarmee* launching a counterattack and wanted to end the attack as quickly as possible. Among other things Cavallero said:

'Just pull out of the position and come back!'

I resisted these demands and informed him that I had decided to settle accounts with the enemy as long as my troops and my supplies allowed, because now the *Panzerarmee* was finally on the move and the first blows had landed well. I would first strike southward and destroy the enemy south of Agedabia, then turn east and later northeast. If need be I could always fall back to the Marsa el Brega position, but that mattered little to me as my objective lay significantly farther afield.

General Cavallero implored me not to do this. But I informed him that only the *Führer* was in a position to reverse this decision, because the battle was being fought mainly by German troops.

Cavallero finally left grumbling after Kesselring unsuccessfully tried to bring me around to

Cavallero's way of thinking. I kept *General* von Rintelen (who had come with Cavallero) so that I could show him the battlefield the next day and awaken his understanding of the concerns in Africa.

Cavallero soon got even by forbidding the Italian Corps from leaving Agedabia and the area around Marsa el Brega, and thus more or less removed them from my command. Nevertheless, the German troops won back Cyrenaica."

This account by Rommel reveals the nature of his personality, but also the prevailing conditions in that theater with which he had to contend.

Rommel decided to attack in a situation where he appeared to be finished. Following the destruction of the British First Armored Division he and *Oberstleutnant* Westphal set out in Rommel's *Storch* to survey the battlefield. They were greeted by ferocious anti-aircraft fire, and the aircraft's skin was ripped by shell splinters. Rommel, however, remained cool. He gave the pilot directions to fly to get out of the hail of fire. While they were attempting to escape, Westphal sighted a dozen Hurricane fighters high above the *Storch*. But the British fighters failed to spot the German aircraft twisting and turning just above the desert floor. The machine was again hit by bullets on the return flight.

When Rommel drove into the Cyrenaican capital of Benghazi at about 12.00 on January 30, 1942, he had just received a radio message from Mussolini, the contents of which amused him greatly. It said that he — Rommel — would be permitted to take Benghazi if a favorable opportunity presented itself, *provided* it did not endanger the Italian positions near Agedabia and Marsa el Brega.

Rommel's reply consisted of three words:

"Benghazi already taken!"

In the British headquarters that evening of January 30, 1942 Commander-in-Chief General Auchinleck sat before the headquarters map in which many new tiny flags had been stuck, and shook his head worriedly. Then he wrote in his diary:

"This then is the bitter end of the winter campaign, which according to our plans was to have taken us to Tripoli."

Cyrenaica had been recaptured. Rommel paused before the enemy's Gazala Line to catch his breath for the next blow, which was inevitably to lead to the capture of Tobruk. On February 9, 1942 the Luftwaffe reoccupied the airfields at Martuba, Derna and Tmimi.

The deliveries of fresh supplies Rommel was counting on would be completed in May. Then he would decide what to do next.

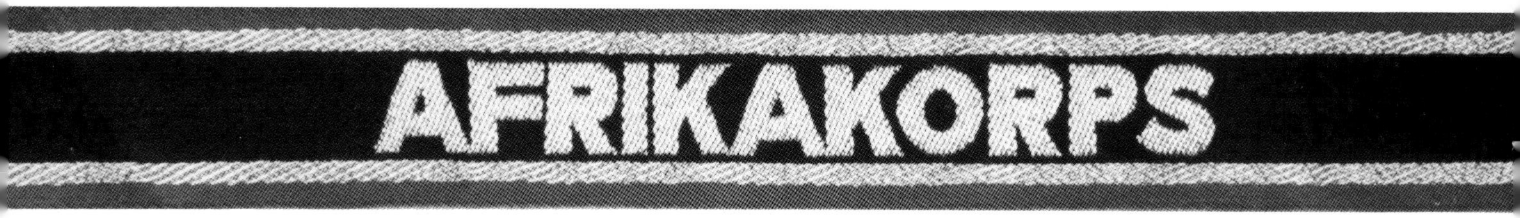
AFRIKAKORPS

The Intervening Period -
Plans of the German Command

With Cyrenaica back in Axis hands and *Panzer-armee Afrika* dug in in front of the British-held Gazala Line, early on the morning of February 15, 1942 Rommel and the Ia of the DAK, *Oberstleutnant* Westphal, flew from Misurata to Rome. It was Westphal's first meeting with the Duce, to whom he would be reporting often in the coming years. The next day the pair flew on to Wiener Neustadt so that Rommel could visit his family. A day later the He 111 landed at the *Wolfsschanze* airfield in Rastenburg. *Oberstleutnant* Westphal and his Commander-in-Chief drove into the *Wolfsschanze*. Both men were convinced that Hitler would be very interested in the North African Theater, especially after the spectacular blows handed out by the DAK and the *Panzergruppe*, therefore by the *Panzerarmee Afrika*.

Hitler was certainly pleased that Rommel had mastered the threatening situation and even begun a new offensive, but he was not very interested in the African Theater. This was as a result of the setbacks suffered by Germany on the Eastern Front and the winter retreat of 1941-42, which was still of concern. All of Hitler's attention and energy were therefore directed at regaining the initiative in Russia.

Rommel was disappointed, because he had been fighting with limited resources in Africa for over a year. He was certain that with a total of six German motorized divisions he could sweep the enemy from the African continent. But Hitler evaded all of Rommel's requests. There were not even any clear plans for the future prosecution of the war in the theater. Rommel suggested that

they must secure control of Malta. This would eliminate the flanking threat to North Africa and at the same time ensure secure supply routes across the Mediterranean. Hitler gave no clear answer.

When Westphal spoke with Jodl on the evening of February 17 the *Generaloberst* was unable to give him any information as to how the OKW planned to handle North Africa. A second discussion on 18 February also failed to result in a clear position on the problems at hand. *Oberstleutnant* Westphal made it clear that a British offensive was expected no later than early summer and that they would have to be ready to meet it.

In the Wehrmacht High Command all attention was fixed firmly on Russia, however. What was North Africa anyway? A small secondary theater which could have no decisive effect on the outcome of the war.

They had forgotten that this was the only place where Germany could strike at Britain. Not so British Prime Minister Winston Churchill. He was betting everything on the African card, which was to become his best trump. Africa, it was clear to the sly British fox, was England's decisive front. He therefore shipped everything he could lay his hands on there, strengthening not only the position of the western desert forces, but the Mediterranean Fleet and the strongpoints of Malta, Gibraltar and Alexandria as well.

A few days earlier, when *Generalleutnant* Nehring — who was on his way from Russia to become Commanding General of the DAK — had reported to Hitler, the *Führer* had been much more open-minded. On that occasion Hitler said

Top: Rommel in Umm Er Rzem, 20. 3. 1942.
Center: General Crüwell, left, celebrates his 50th birthday on 20. 3. 1942. To his right is Generalleutnant Walther K. Nehring, Commanding General of the Deutsches Afrika-Korps.
Bottom: Congratulations for General Crüwell on 20. 3. 1942 in Umm Er Rzem. From left: Oberst Menny, commander 15th Rifle Brigade; Oberst Bruer, commander 155th Motorized Artillery Regiment; DAK signals officer; Generalmajor von Bismarck, commander of the 21st Panzer Division; Hauptmann Johannes Kümmel, commander of I./PR 8; Oberst Gerhard Müller, commander of PR 5; Major Lehmann, commander III./PzAR 155; Oberst Herbert Ewert, commander 104th Rifle Regiment.

Generalmajor von Vaerst.

1. 4. 1942. K 15 is dismissed from the 15th Panzer Division by Generalleutnant von Vaerst and Oberst Menny.

that they would have to advance as far east as possible *and* tie down the maximum possible number of British forces on the African Front. Hitler enjoined Nehring:

"Tell *Generaloberst* Rommel that I admire him!"

None of this was evident during Rommel's decisive discussions in the FHQ only ten days later. *Generaloberst* Rommel and *Oberstleutnant* Westphal flew back to Rome. They met once again with Mussolini. Rommel presented his plans to the Duce and tried to win him over. In brief, Rommel's plan consisted of:

1. The capture of Malta. This would eliminate the serious threat to the supply routes to *Panzerarmee Afrika*.

2. An offensive with the initial objective of Tobruk.

"If the preparations for the conquest of Malta should demand too much time, Duce, then I would agree to change the timetable and attack Tobruk first."

Rommel's words indicated to Mussolini a good possibility of deciding the war in favor of the Axis partners, but he, too, was hesitant and gave evasive answers. Rommel felt, however, that Mussolini would keep these things in mind.

The supply situation of the DAK and *Panzergruppe Afrika* in March remained poor. In the month of March only 18,000 tons of supplies reached Africa out of a total of 60,000 tons dispatched.

Things changed in April, however. *Luftflotte* 2 succeeded in gaining air superiority over the central Mediterranean and brought the island fortress of Malta to the brink of defeat.

The air offensive against Malta began on April 2, 1942. The German-Italian air forces bombed submarine pens, harbor installations and the island's airfields.

II. *Fliegerkorps* under *General der Flieger* Loerzer attacked Malta without pause in conjunction with Italian units. These attacks, which reached their high point in mid-April, resulted in the sinking of the destroyers "Lance," "Gallant" and "Kingston," the minesweeper "Abingdon," the submarines "P 36," "Pandora" and "Glavkos," the tanker "Plumleaf" (5,916 tons) and several smaller vessels.

The cruiser "Penelope" was severely damaged and on April 10 was towed to Gibraltar. The submarine "Unbeaten" was damaged in dry dock and had to proceed to Gibraltar for repairs.

On 9 April the Polish submarine "Sokol" was assigned to the Tenth Malta Submarine Flotilla. It was severely damaged en route and arrived at Malta on April 13 with over 100 holes in its outer hull.

The Tenth Flotilla suffered an especially

BV 222 A "Viking" flying boat in repair dock.

painful loss on April 14. While attempting to attack an Italian convoy in the Tripoli area the most successful British submarine, the "Upholder," commanded by Victoria Cross winner Wanklyn, was sunk by the Italian submarine "Pegaso." The entire crew went down with the submarine.

Malta had been hard hit and discussions were already under way in the OKH and OKW on the best way of capturing the island.

Surprise Attack on Malta?

In April 1942 *General der Flieger* Kurt Student was summoned to Rome by a teletype message from *Feldmarschall* Kesselring. He found *Generalmajor* Ramcke already there. Ramcke had been in Italy since early in the year in an advisory role. He was assisting in the formation of the Italian *"Folgore"* Parachute Division, ensuring that its training and organization followed German models.

The task at hand was to work out a plan for the conquest of Malta. Together with Hermann Bernhard Ramcke, Student formulated the initial outlines of the attack. Overall command of the operation was to be in the hands of the *Comando Supremo*, and would be coordinated by Colonel General Baron Cavallero.

A considerable German-Italian force was already on hand for the operation, which had been code-named *"Herkules,"* and Mussolini had promised the support of the entire Italian Fleet. It was planned that parachute and air-landed troops under the command of *General* Student would lead the attack and gain a major foothold on the island. The main body of the attack force would follow by sea and air.

A dozen six-engined Me 323 *Gigant* transport aircraft were on hand to transport Panzer IV tanks to Malta. Also available were about 100 Go 242 transport aircraft, which could each carry a pay load of 2.5 tons, and 1,000 DFS 230 transport gliders.

Assembly and departure were to take place in Sicily. II. *Fliegerkorps* was to receive the full support of the Italian Air Force in suppressing any opposition.

While preparations were in full swing *General* Student received a telegram summoning him to *Führer* Headquarters. When he arrived there *Generaloberst* Jeschonnek, Chief of the *Luftwaffe* General Staff, said to him: "Student, you're going to have a hard time of it with the *Führer* tomorrow. *General* Crüwell of the *Afrika-Korps* was here this morning. The subject of Italian fighting morale came up. Crüwell gave a *very* negative opinion of it. As a result the entire Malta operation is in danger!"

Kurt Student had been forewarned. The next morning he explained the plans developed in Rome for the capture of Malta to a large audience. Hitler interrupted several times to ask questions which the Commanding General of XI. *Fliegerkorps* — which contained the German parachute and air-landing units — was able to answer to his satisfaction. Hitler showed himself to be well-informed and indicated that he basically considered the plan a good and feasible one. But then, as *Generaloberst* Student related to the author following the war, "Hitler broke loose!"

"The creation of the bridgehead by your air-landed troops is assured. Fine! But then I guarantee you the following: when the attack begins the British Fleet will sail from Gibraltar and Alexandria. They will see what the Italians are up to. As soon as the first radio message comes in the Italians will all return to harbor; the warships as well as the transports. Then you and your parachute troops will be sitting alone on the island."

General Student replied, "*Feldmarschall* Kesselring has prepared for this eventuality. The British will be dealt with just as they were a year ago at Crete, when Richthofen intervened and sank part of the Alexandria Squadron: but it will probably be worse for them this time because Malta is within close striking range of the Luftwaffe. The flying distance from Sicily to Malta is significantly less than from Greece to Crete. On the other side the range for the British Fleet is twice as great as it was to Crete. Malta can thus, mein *Führer*, become the grave of the British Mediterranean Fleet."

But Hitler was not convinced. Although he grasped the significance of Malta, he no longer trusted the Italians. He also recalled the catastrophic casualties suffered by the parachute troops in the invasion of Crete. Hitler therefore rejected Student's claim that, if need be, the parachute units could take Malta alone, as the island was already heavily battered. Hitler decided:

"The attack on Malta will not be carried out in 1942."

As a result of this decision an operation which could have altered the entire conduct of the war in the Mediterranean was not carried out. Following the war western historians confirmed that German parachute troops could have conquered Malta.

Final Preparations on Both Sides

Naturally the German efforts to soften up Malta and their plans for an airborne invasion of the British "aircraft carrier in the Mediterranean" did not escape the notice of the other side. Churchill, who considered the strengthening *and* defence of

the island the number one priority in the Mediterranean, assailed General Auchinleck with demands for a new offensive to take the pressure off Malta.

The result was a series of radio messages back and forth, of which Alan Brooke wrote in his diary on the evening of May 2, 1942:

"The Prime Minister sent an unfriendly radio message to Auchinleck in which he reproached him for not attacking."

In concluding the message Churchill had said:

"We believe that an attempt to drive the Germans out of Cyrenaica in the course of the following weeks is not only necessary for the security of Malta, on which so much depends, but is also the *only* hope of fighting a battle while the enemy is still comparatively weak and short of all types of equipment."

On May 8 Churchill again telegraphed Auchinleck and replied to the main points of his response:

"Prime Minister to General Auchinleck: May 8, 1942: The Chiefs of Staff, the Defence Committee and the War Cabinet have scrutinized your telegram on the overall war situation, especially in respect to Malta, whose loss would be a catastrophe of the first order for the British Empire and probably make the defence of the Nile Valley impossible in the long run.

We share your opinion that it would be appropriate, despite the risks you mentioned, if you attack the enemy and involve him in a major battle in May if possible, and the earlier the better. We are prepared to accept full responsibility for the general directive and leave you with the necessary freedom of decision for the conduct of the operation. Undoubtedly you will have to bear in mind that the enemy himself could be planning to attack you at the beginning of June" (see Lewin Ronald: *Rommel*).

General Auchinleck now accelerated the delivery of supplies to the areas close to the front around Tobruk. The Eighth Army established huge supply dumps, and on May 16 General Ritchie, the Commander-in-Chief of the Eighth Army, explained that it was his objective "to destroy the enemy's armored forces in a battle in the Gazala-Tobruk-Bir Hacheim area and thus take the first step toward recapturing Cyrenaica."

The line of fortifications known as the Gazala Line stretched from Ain el Gazala on the coast sixty kilometers south to its end point, the fortress of Bir Hacheim. In between lay a chain of strong-points, termed boxes, which were built as all-round defensive positions consisting of infantry positions and bunkers with barbed wire entanglements.

On May 20 General Auchinleck again asked General Ritchie for an assessment of Rommel's intentions and how best to meet his attack.

Auchinleck suggested to Ritchie that he mass his tanks on both sides of the Trigh Capuzzo because "in all probability Rommel will carry out a diversionary attack on Bir Hacheim so that he can attack with his main force, especially the panzer divisions, in the center, drive through the minefields and then turn toward the sea to envelop the northern part of the line and attack Tobruk."

Ritchie, the Commander-in-Chief of the Eighth Army, and his division commanders were of a different opinion. General Norrie suggested that the main weight of the German attack would fall in the north, while the Commander-in-Chief himself was of the opinion that Rommel, the sly desert fox, would go around Bir Hacheim to the south. He therefore positioned the First Armored Division behind the center of the defensive positions west and southwest of El Adem and assigned the Seventh Armored Division an assembly area farther south.

Everything was thus ready for the defence on the British side, even though the diverging opinions would later lead to a catastrophic confusion at the highest levels of command.

Feverish preparations were also under way on the German side. It was clear to Rommel that he would have to attack *before* the enemy if he wanted to win. He now had at his disposal three German divisions and a brigade of German troops as well as seven Italian divisions, only three of which were motorized.

On May 20 Rommel issued his attack orders to *Panzerarmee Afrika*:

"The prelude to the offensive will be a frontal attack by the Italian divisions in the Gazala position. These divisions will be committed against the British Fiftieth and South African Divisions. Strong artillery units under the Arko 104 will be assigned to support the attack. Tank assembly areas will be simulated behind these positions day and night. For this purpose tanks and vehicles will drive in circles there.

This should result in the concentration of British armored units close behind these infantry sectors.

By daylight all movements of motorized units are to take place in the direction of the site of the attack by the Italian infantry. Not until darkness falls will the motorized units drive into their assembly areas. They will consist of the DAK, with the 15th and 21st Panzer Divisions, and the Italian Twentieth Motorized Corps, with *"Trieste"* and *"Ariete"*, as well as the attached 90th Light Division, to which has been added the three reconnaissance battalions of the DAK.

The advance will begin at 21.00. It will lead around Bir Hacheim. From there the DAK and the Italian Twentieth Corps will advance through Acroma to the coast in order to cut off the lines of communication of the British divisions in the Gazala position as well as the British armored units assembled there and destroy them.

The 90th Light and the three attached reconnaissance battalions will advance into the El Adem-Belhamed area and prevent the withdrawal of the garrison of Tobruk and any flow of reinforcements into the Acroma area. The British will thus be cut off from the supply dumps which they have set up in the area east of Tobruk.

It is planned that the quick destruction of the Eighth Army will be followed by the speedy capture of Tobruk."

The date of the attack was fixed as May 26, 1942.

The New Offensive Gets Under Way

Rommel's Coming!

On May 26, 1942 the frontal group of *Panzergruppe Afrika* opened the new offensive. The 15th Rifle Brigade of the 90th Light Division and the Tenth and Twenty-first Italian Corps launched a frontal attack from the west to tie down enemy forces and draw the British armored divisions away from the planned points of main effort.

The Italian *"Brescia," "Pavia"* and *"Trento"* Divisions attacked shoulder to shoulder with the German infantry under *Oberst* Menny. Overall command of the battle group was in the hands of *Generalleutnant* Crüwell. The DAK's new commanding general was Walther K. Nehring.

While the infantry attacked, in the rear all sorts of vehicles were raising dust to simulate the approach of a large armored force. The artillery of Arko 104 opened fire with all available guns. Stukas appeared in the sky above the fortress. With sirens screaming they dived on the defensive boxes and recognized positions.

Soon afterward the soldiers of PGR 361 were among the British positions, but a deeper penetration was impossible as the terrain was teeming with machine-gun positions and was barricaded with dense barbed wire entanglements.

The offensive had begun, but the British

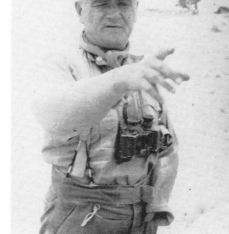

Oberst Gerhard Müller, commander of PR 5, and his adjutant in May 1942 before the offensive.

The "old man," Oberst Gerhard Müller.

Air attack alert — ready to fire!

The ninth victory ring is painted on the barrel of a successful anti-aircraft gun.

suspected that this was a diversion — which in fact it was.

When it became dark the main striking force, consisting of the DAK and the *Corpo celeri* — the Italian fast Army Corps, set off from the area around Segnali North. The night march moved southeast. Former *Oberleutnant* Josef Hišmann described that night:

"Rommel's *Panzerarmee* was on the march. Despite the star-filled night sky Egyptian blackness reigned. A misty grey, which swallowed up every feature, spread over the ground and the endlessness of the heavens absorbed all light. Someone seeing a division or the entire *Afrika-Korps* moving across open terrain in an impenetrable cloud of dust for the first time would think it a disorganized mass. But gradually he would perceive the deadly serious order and discipline which controlled this tremendous war machine. Every unit had its assigned place which guaranteed its immediate battle readiness and effective operation.

The Panzers of the DAK led the way. Their tracks tore up the desert soil and ground it to dust. Together with the tracks of the following prime movers and the many thousands of wheels of the total of 10,000 vehicles they created an impenetrable cloud which rose and shrouded everything, making the night even darker.

The otherwise quiet desert resounded with the roaring of motors, the rattling of tank tracks and the rumbling of gun tractors. The dense mass of vehicles raced forward as if on a wild, exciting chase. They were all possessed by one will, not to lose contact with the pack. The drivers drove practically blind, able to react only to the signals of the commanders standing in their turrets and the 'observers' squatting on the front mudguards. In such close quarters accidents were unavoidable. 1./Fla 617 (Hissmann's Company!) lost a tank and a self-propelled gun that night as a result of collisions. Two messengers went missing for good.

When it finally became day the DAK was attacked in series by artillery, fighter-bombers and powerful armored forces. Within the 21st PD under *Generalmajor* von Bismarck, the 617th Flak Battalion had its hands full defending against the persistent low-level strafing attacks. 2./Fla 617 under *Oberleutnant* Hilgemann opened the score, shooting down a Hurricane fighter from a small formation of three aircraft."

This ends Hissmann's report. But what was the overall picture of this flanking move through the desert, which had been initiated by Rommel at 22.00 on May 26 with the code word "*Venezia?*"

In carrying out Rommel's orders the armored and motorized divisions of the main attack force rolled through the night toward the unfamiliar objective of Bir Hacheim, which lay in the desert 65 kilometers to the south. The divisions were assembled in a bottle-shaped formation. Patrols led the way, followed by the panzer regiments driving in a wide combat formation and close behind the artillery and the division headquarters. Behind these and echeloned to the sides were the infantry battalions, combat engineers, anti-tank units, anti-aircraft units and other attached units. Driving between the two panzer divisions, roughly in line with the 15th and 21st Division Headquarters, was the DAK Corps Headquarters under *Generalleutnant* Nehring.

By the time the morning of May 27 dawned the giant column had veered around the southern wing of the Gazala Line near Bir Hacheim. Everything now turned north, while the Italian motorized Army Corps halted before Bir Hacheim to lay seige to the fortress.

Enemy resistance soon stiffened. The DAK was halted near Knightsbridge and came under attack by enemy armored forces from the north and east. The following segment describes the 8th Panzer Regiment's encounter with the British tank units.

The 15th and 21st Panzer Divisions in the Tank Battle

On the morning of May 27 both panzer divisions of the DAK were driving in the center of the spearhead with the 15th PD on the right and the 21st PD on the left. The 15th PD's PR 8 was at full strength for the first time. *Panzerarmee Afrika* had at its disposal a total of more than 560 tanks, counting those of the Italians, while the British Eighth Army had 631 tanks at the front, which were later joined by another 250.

Looking back, *Hauptmann* Hannes Kümmel could see the tremendous armada of his regiment's 180 tanks, which were led by *Oberstleutnant* Teege who was driving in the lead group.

When the specified frontal width of his battalion threatened to increase Kümmel had the companies close up, as the existing width of 3 kilometers was already difficult to oversee. The depth of the battalion wedge was 1.5 kilometers. Close behind Kümmel's I./PR 8 and to the right was Second Battalion. Kümmel called the regiment and asked about enemy reconnaissance aircraft. *Oberstleutnant* Teege replied that none had been seen so far. Somewhere in the desert was the enemy; but where?

Suddenly British tanks were sighted, emerging from a shallow depression 3 kilometers away. The crews were ordered to battle readiness. A short time later they recognized the turrets of the new American Grant tanks, camouflaged behind camel-thorn bushes in the depression.

They belonged to units of the British Fourth Armored Brigade which had apparently been waiting for the DAK. It was equipped with 65 Grant tanks and had also set up several anti-tank barricades. Kümmel gave the order to attack and drove off at the head of his battalion. His tanks followed close behind, ready to fire. Orders crackled through the commanders' headsets.

"Firing halt by platoons!"

The first shots were exchanged. Then the tanks which had fired raced on at full speed. All of a sudden from ahead came a dozen harsh flashes. Shells struck the ground to the left and right of the approaching tanks. The scene was shrouded in smoke, fire and dust. The enemy tanks discarded their camouflage. The German commanders could see that the new enemy tanks had at least 75mm guns. Their guns could not penetrate the frontal armor of the Grant.

"Get closer!" shouted Kümmel's gunner. He had already hit one of the enemy tanks without effect.

"We need artillery!" called Kümmel.

The radio message was sent. *Oberstleutnant* Teege called the artillery to support PR 8's attack. On the left flank PR 5 joined the battle under its new commander *Oberst* Gerhard Müller. During the approach the tank of II./PR 5's commander, *Oberstleutnant* Martin, took a direct hit.

"Hang on Kümmel!" Teege called to his friend, who was drawing most of the enemy fire, "I'm coming with Second Battalion!"

Oberstleutnant Teege led II./PR 8 in an arc around the center. While Kümmel constantly

Leutnante Wuth and Bönisch of 8./PR 8.

PR 8's band.

changed positions to present a moving target while trying to get close enough for a lethal shot, II./PR 8 arrived on the enemy's flank. The arrival of Teege's tanks took the British completely by surprise. The Germans poured armor-piercing rounds into the vulnerable flanks of the Grants. Soon the first was burning, then more. At that point Kümmel drove forward with the heavy company. He raced toward the enemy tanks and reached a favorable firing position. From such close range the crash of the guns and the impact of the shells were nearly simultaneous. Soon the battlefield was a scene of blazing tanks and explosions. The pall of dust became thicker and thicker.

All of a sudden the British began to pull back. The Eighth Hussars, the core formation of the Fourth Armored Brigade, pulled out, and the Third Company, Royal Tank Regiment lost 16 Grants in this phase of the German attack alone.

Just then the division commander's command panzer appeared on the scene. *Generalmajor* von Vaerst assumed the lead.

"Where to, *Herr General*?" asked *Leutnant* Max Keil, who was temporarily in command of 1./PR 8.

But before von Vaerst could answer, his adjutant shouted:

"There, men! There's Rommel!"

It was Rommel, and moments later Kümmel heard the voice of the *Generaloberst* ordering him to close up and follow.

Under the command of *General* Nehring the advance continued toward the north. The 90th Light — less the 15th Rifle Brigade which had been left behind on the western front — turned toward El Adem with the three reconnaissance battalions of the DAK and the Italian Twentieth Corps. The 21st PD drove to a point just outside Acroma. The 15th PD drove on to the north, toward the sea. At 16.00 enemy tanks were sighted. They attacked from the right flank and drove straight into the advancing columns of the 15th PD.

The panzers which tried to stop the attacking Grants had no chance. It was the German anti-aircraft guns which now came to the fore.

On February 1, 1942 *Oberst* Alwin Wolz had received orders to go to Africa and take command of the 135th Flak Regiment, which had previously been commanded by *Major* Hecht. Wolz met

Rommel soon after arriving in Africa. When asked by the author, he recalled:

"Rommel received me very cordially, but when I asked him for the assignment of an earlier transport number to get my regimental headquarters across from Naples, I received a characteristic Rommel reply:

'Guns, Wolz, are more important!'

I was able to accept this decision calmly, because I had already found a freighter with excess cargo space which could transport my regiment."

On May 24 the headquarters of the 135th Flak Regiment was transferred to Umm er Rzem, where the headquarters of *Panzerarmee Afrika* had been located since the end of March. Wolz then went to the DAK's tactical section in Bir es Sferi where he assembled his commanders to discuss the operational principles for the upcoming German offensive. The tactical disposition of the regiment on May 24, 1942 was as follows:

Regimental Headquarters and 1./Flak 43 to the Corps combat echelon.

3./Flak 43 to the Rommel combat echelon.

I./Flak 43 (less First and Third Companies) to the 15th PD.

I./Flak 18 (less Second Company) to the 21st PD.

2./Flak 18 to the 90th Light.

II./Flak 25 with Seventh and Ninth Companies to Arko 104. When, on the afternoon of May 27, the 15th PD once again encountered enemy tanks,

Oberst Wolz committed the Corps combat echelon, which he himself was leading. Widely-spaced, the "eighty-eights" drove forward over the coverless terrain. In order to get into action as quickly as possible the guns opened fire without first being emplaced. They were unlimbered from their tractors, but were not moved from the trailers onto their outrigger-type gun mounts.

The first Grants were soon ablaze on the battlefield. Then the British artillery replied. *Oberst* Wolz was forced to break off the engagement, however, as he had to follow after the DAK, which had become involved in heavy fighting.

General Nehring, the new commander of the DAK, drove over to Wolz. Together they drove ahead to ascertain the situation at the front of the column. Heavy artillery fire caused their vehicle to take evasive action and by chance they came upon the hastily retiring vehicles of the corps operations section, which were themselves being overtaken by the combat train.

Oberst Wolz saw several "eighty-eights" among the mass of vehicles. Nehring and Wolz drove into the mass to stop the guns. Then, suddenly, they saw Rommel, who was wedged amongst the heavy flow of vehicles.

"The Flak is responsible for this whole mess!" shouted Rommel angrily. "Because they didn't fire!"

Before Wolz could answer the Commander-in-

Oberleutnant Theodor Schwabach.   *Oberst Alwin Wolz.*

Chief had driven off. Wolz brought the three 88mm Flak to a halt. They were joined by the guns of I./Flak 43 which was driving close behind Wolz. When the last of the transport vehicles had roared past Wolz and Nehring saw the cause of the hasty retreat by the corps headquarters.

About 1,500 meters away a group of 35 enemy tanks was approaching. The guns, which had gone into position at 150-meter intervals, opened fire on Wolz' order. The first tank began to burn and the enemy pulled back.

A little later *Major* Gürke, the commander of I./Flak 43, appeared and moved the six guns of 2./Flak 43 into position on the left flank of the small anti-tank front. Half an hour later the *Armee* adjutant arrived with 3./Flak 43, which had been sent by Rommel.

The anti-aircraft guns now occupied a three-kilometer front. Here in the desert, for the first time in the history of warfare, anti-aircraft guns were to decide the outcome of a land battle. *Oberst* Wolz relinquished overall command to *Major* Gürke. Gürke was thus given the opportunity of commanding all three of his heavy batteries in action. Wolz drove back to *General* Nehring, who had set up his headquarters 1,000 meters behind the barrier of anti-aircraft guns, underlining its importance.

In the meantime enemy artillery had gone into position behind the tanks. During the last daylight hours of May 27 they fired without pause on the German gun positions, some of which had to be evacuated in order to save the crews. *Oberst* Wolz and *Major* Gürke went from gun to gun encouraging the men.

"We simply had to hold!" said *General* Wolz after the war. "It was the only way to repel the attack by the enemy armored group into the rear of the DAK."

A total of 24 enemy tanks were destroyed in the battle between the British armor and the German anti-aircraft guns. The Flak had saved the DAK.

The British Fourth Armored Brigade, which was the blocking force in front of the Eighth Army, had been cracked. Parallel to the Gazala Line, but in its rear, the DAK rolled onward. The 21st PD reached Acroma. Then the spearheads were on the *Via Balbia* and the men could hear the sea. Had they really done it? Had the enemy been beaten already?

The next day brought one crisis-filled situation report after another, and when darkness fell it was clear to the men of the command section that the DAK was practically surrounded in the east, north and west, while supply from the south was uncertain, because the southernmost cornerstone of the Gazala Line, the fortress of Bir Hacheim, defended by 4,400 Free French under General Pierre König, had not yet fallen. New British armored forces had been sighted driving west from El Adem.

May 29 brought no change in the situation, other than that the ring around the DAK had grown tighter and the supply situation had become more critical.

When Rommel was at the situation briefing that evening neither *Generalleutnant* Nehring nor *Generalmajor* Gause, Chief of the *Panzerarmee* General Staff, or staff officers Bayerlein and Westphal tried to minimize the fact that the situation was very serious.

Fritz Bayerlein requested a breakout from the encirclement to the west. Following initial success the frontal attack on the Gazala Line by the German and Italian units had ground to a halt. There were special reasons for this. On the evening of May 28 Rommel radioed *General* Crüwell:

"Immediate attack by the Navarrini Corps from the west through the mine field to free the rear of the DAK!"

General Crüwell sent the Arko 104, *Oberst* Krause, ahead to the Italian corps headquarters and impressed upon him:

"See to it that from 08.30 tomorrow morning a sentry is standing ready to indicate to my Storch the position of the Italian front with a signal flare!" Krause arranged this and then drove off as ordered.

Next morning the *Storch* took off punctually at 08.30. The pilot of the small machine had no proper maps. *General* Crüwell described what happened:

"Soon after we took off I noticed that we were flying directly into the sun. The pilot reassured me. 'We can't miss the signal flare!' he said. But that is exactly what happened: we found ourselves over the British lines. We were flying at a height of about 140 meters and came under machine-gun fire. The first burst struck the tail, the second holed the engine and the third hit the pilot. He fell dead to one side.

Miraculously the machine did not crash, but

flattened out and made a belly landing on its own, completely tearing off the undercarriage in the process. There was splintering and cracking all around me, but luckily the door had not jammed. I was in the British front lines, the box defended by the 150th Brigade. A lot of Tommies came running over and took me prisoner.

More than a year later *General* Krause, who had gone into captivity in Tunisia, informed me that the arranged signal flare had not been fired. The officer assigned to do the job had been called into his quarters to answer the telephone in the moment I flew past."

As a result of this incident the attack which was to have freed the DAK from encirclement did not take place.

Feldmarschall Albert Kesselring, who was in Africa, stepped into the breach and carried on on the Gazala Front. He asked to be placed under Rommel's command, even though he outranked him.

Bir Hacheim was holding out against the attack by the Italians, and the insertion of the First Battalion of the 155th motorized Infantry Regiment did not help. The attackers were met by heavy fire from Bir Hacheim's 1,200 strongpoints, forcing them to take cover. Two forward bunkers were taken but had to be given up again. Bir Hacheim held.

Attack to the West - The Hell of Got el Ualeb

In agreement with the commanding general of the DAK, Nehring, Rommel decided late on the evening of May 29 to break through the British minefield to the west. Fortunately for the DAK the Italians on the western front had managed to capture a narrow lane through the minefield, although it lay under enemy fire. For the Germans the push toward the west had become necessary in order to reestablish contact with their supply bases.

The DAK set off toward the west during the night. At first light on May 30 the Corps Headquarters, followed by the 15th PD, came upon a powerful enemy field fortification near Sidi Muftah which had not been spotted before. It was the British strongpoint of Got el Ualeb. An

attempt to overrun the strongpoint failed. Manning the position was the British 150th Brigade with 2,000 men and 80 Mark II tanks. The lane through the minefield which had been cleared by the *"Trieste"* Division was under constant artillery bombardment. At the same time near Knightsbridge the British Guards were fighting against the onrushing German units with the courage of desperation. The 90th Light as well as AA 3 and AA 33, together with the newly-formed AA 580 under *Rittmeister* von Homeyer, stormed the British positions at Knightsbridge.

General Ritchie, the Commander-in-Chief of the Eighth Army, radioed Cairo: "Rommel is retreating!"

The reply from General Auchinleck in Cairo read: "Bravo, Eighth Army! Finish him off!"

Got el Ualeb held against the storm. *Generaloberst* Rommel committed PR 5. Twelve of the attacking panzers were knocked out by British anti-tank guns and the heavy Mark II tanks. The rest were turned back.

Then it was the turn of the Kiehl combat echelon. It, too, failed to get through. It was June 1, 1942 and it looked as though General Ritchie might be proven right. But the British had lost fifty percent of their tanks and both strongpoints were weakening.

Generalleutnant Nehring and Fritz Bayerlein drove forward to scout the nests of resistance and enter them on their maps. Bayerlein suggested they commit the former 15th Motorcycle Battalion, which had been incorporated into SR 104 as the unit's Third Battalion, against the british strongpoints.

Generalmajor von Bismarck, the commander of the 21st PD, personally issued the instructions to the battalion's commander. He showed him the burned-out tanks which lay in front of the strongpoint of Got el Ualeb. Then he said:

"It's going to be difficult, Ehle! All the earlier attacks were beaten off. Have a look at the situation and let me know what you intend to do. *Major* Beil's battalion will provide you with artillery support."

Major Ehle, of medium height, wiry and the symbol of his battalion, drove forward to scout the area accompanied by *Oberleutnant* Kordel, the battalion adjutant. Along the way they ran into *Major* Beil, who was standing by an "eighty-eight" with *General* Nehring and *Oberst* Bayerlein.

As *Oberst* Bayerlein was describing the situation to the adjutant using a map, a member of the gun crew shouted: "strafing attack!"

A half-second later they heard the roar of aircraft engines and hacking bursts of machine-gun fire. Curt Ehle was wounded and out of action. *Hauptmann* Werner Reissmann took command of the battalion for the attack on Got el Ualeb. He later said:

"Everything depended on good preparation, a rapid advance and the fastest driving." Let us turn at this point to the original combat report submitted on June 2 by Third Battalion, 104th Motorized Rifle Regiment, which provides a detailed, but factual description of the battle at Got el Ualeb.

"Battle Order:
15th PD, *Kampfgruppe Major* Block, Ia Pi., DAK
Assignment of Units to the Battle Group:
III./SR 104 with Battalion Headquarters, Ninth and Eleventh Companies and attached 4./SR 104 z.b.V.
Commander: *Hauptmann* Reissmann
II./AR 155 with two light batteries and attached heavy field howitzer battery of III./PzAR 155
Commander: *Major* Beil
Elements of *Panzer-Pionier-Bataillon* 200 as mine clearing party. 12./PzJägAbt. 39
Commander: *Oberleutnant* Fahrenkamp
one platoon 20mm Flak and two 88mm guns of the DAK combat echelon
Combat Strength:
9./SR 104: 3 officers, 16 NCOs, 86 men
11./SR 104: 3 officers, 19 NCOs, 103 men."

On May 31 the battalion received orders to take the fortified position of Got el Ualeb, about 2 km south of the Trigh Capuzzo, as part of a battle group formed from elements of the division and the combat echelon of the DAK.

Previous attempts to take the position had failed. Its capture resulted from the necessity of a secure supply route to the west for the DAK. The battle plan had the battalion attacking in a north-south direction in conjunction with an armored battle group of the 15th PD from the east, which would be outflanking the position to the south.

As a result of the wounding of the commander, *Major* Ehle, during an information gathering mission at the front during the evening of May 31,

Hauptmann Reissmann, chief of Thirteenth (Infantry Gun) Company, SR 104, took command of the battalion.

Approaching nightfall made impossible a new briefing on the spot. The time of the operation had been fixed as the early morning hours of June 1; however, the precise time of the attack was not known. At about 20.30 orders arrived that the battalion was to be in position and ready in the valley of the Trigh Capuzzo at 05.00, facing west with its leading elements in line with the shot-down aircraft behind the armored combat engineer battalion. Briefing and issuing of orders at 05.00. Beginning of attack: 07.00. A telephone call came at 23.30 advising that the time of the attack had been moved to 05.15.

The battalion moved out of the regimental strongpoint into the assembly area at 03.15 after its sector had been taken over by elements of I./SR 104. 4./SR 104 was placed under the command of the Battalion CO in reserve, but on instructions from division it was held ready in the area of the division command post and was only to be committed in case of extreme urgency.

At 04.30 the battalion was in its assigned position. The men were issued rations, the supply train withdrew and the battalion made ready for the attack. The orders issued by the officer commanding the 15th PD, *Oberst* Eduard Crasemann, who had assumed command of the division on May 26 in place of its wounded commanding officer, specified an immediate attack following the completion of preparations. This was delayed as the supporting weapons of the DAK first had to be moved from their positions. At 06.10 the battalion was ready to attack in the following formation:
Right: Eleventh Company, *Hauptmann* Kraus.
Left: Ninth Company, *Hauptmann* Krüger.
Center: Battalion Headquarters.
With each company a 20mm Flak platoon, a mine-clearing party of combat engineers and a forward observer from the light battery of the Beil Battalion, with the battalion headquarters the forward observer of the heavy field howitzer battery.

The attack had to take place without reconnaissance or special preparations. The officers and men saw the enemy defensive works for the first time only a few minutes before the attack began. Attack targets could not be made out, and the exact position and frontage of the fortifications could not be seen. The enemy was quiet and — other than five tanks which were spotted — remained out of sight. The range from the forward edge of the assembly area to the works was about 1,500 meters. The assembly area in the valley of the Trigh Capuzzo was out of sight of enemy observers.

After the batteries had ranged in one after another along the whole width of the front to deceive the enemy, at 07.15 the battalion went to the attack riding in its vehicles, while at the same time the artillery began firing for effect. Fire from anti-aircraft guns and the developing dust clouds limited the effectiveness of the enemy tanks on the edge of the hill. When the firing began they pulled back behind the edge of the hill. The battalion drove half the distance to the objective and then, as planned, dismounted and continued on foot in the face of enemy machine-gun fire.

Recognizing the enemy positions was still almost impossible. The companies worked their way forward in stages with the combat engineers in the leading platoon. The forward observer with 11./SR 104 spotted flanking movement from the right section of the position and halted it with well-directed fire. At about 300 meters the ground-level frontal positions were spotted behind light barbwire entanglements. Running and firing, the company worked its way up to the minefield, suffering considerable casualties as a result of small arms and machine-gun fire. The engineers cleared lanes through the minefield under covering fire from our infantry and the following 20mm Flak.

At about 08.00 *Oberleutnant* Köppe's platoon of 11./SR 104 broke into the enemy position. *Leutnant* Miessgang's platoon was pinned down by flanking fire. Storming ahead, Eleventh Company reached the crest of the hill and barricaded the break-in point to the south and west against the position's deep flank. Shortly afterward the anti-tank guns of Eleventh Company followed into the area of penetration. On this position was now directed a half-hour of fire from machine-guns, mortars and a battery of cannon from the deep flank of the enemy position. Movement was scarcely possible. Nevertheless, the anti-tank guns were able to provide some temporary relief by firing on recognized targets with high-explosive shells.

About 15 minutes after the penetration by Eleventh Company, Ninth Company also managed to break into the position, despite the loss of an entire platoon, and linked up with Eleventh Company on the crest of the hill. On the right flank Eleventh Company knocked out two heavy British Mark II tanks, preventing the counterattack the tanks were to have accompanied.

The Ninth Company's losses were a result of the difficult to detect enemy positions in the level ground just behind the minefield. Snipers hampered both companies' advance. Seventy prisoners were brought in from the forward enemy positions.

The engineers of Ninth Company were unable to clear a path through the mines, and *Leutnant* Schröder was wounded while trying to cut a path through the barbwire. His platoon suffered heavy casualties. The company stormed forward through the minefield with *Leutnant* Thomas' still-intact platoon and the rest of the Schröder Platoon. While the breaching of the enemy position was still under way the *Panzerjäger* Company followed on orders from battalion. They set about engaging enemy machine-gun nests and 40mm self-propelled guns. Later the adjutant fetched the 20mm Flak, which was still firing from positions in the rear, into the area of penetration. It, too, effectively engaged the enemy's heavy weapons. Five officers were wounded during the attack. *Leutnant* Daute seriously, and *Leutnants* Wolf, Kielmann, Miessgang and Schröder lightly.

As a result of the fire being directed at the battalion, especially against its center, it ordered the right of the line held and the systematic elimination of recognized enemy weapons. Only then *and* after reorganizing our own artillery fire was the battle to be resumed through the deep zone.

At that moment the commander of II./AR 155, *Major* Beil, went to the front lines to see the situation there for himself. Exposed to heavy machine-gun and mortar fire, he recognized the focal point of the enemy defence on the right flank and afterward organized a change of position and opened fire with his artillery.

Soon afterward, at 08.30, a Stuka attack on the depths of the position brought the first relief from the pounding being administered by the enemy's artillery. The bombing attack was followed by extremely accurate artillery fire on the right flanking strongpoint. *Leutnant* Czymoch, who with his radio team was acting as Eleventh Company's forward observer, distinguished himself while directing the artillery fire.

At that time the Commander-in-Chief, *Generaloberst* Rommel, was with the right platoon and remained in the front lines for the duration of the battalion's attack. The Kraus Company now set out to roll up the right side of the enemy position. The British gave up following an attack with hand grenades. A heavy machine-gun and a mortar were still firing on Ninth Company.

The companies now advanced southward. More and more British surrendered to them. The pursuit of the enemy was continued in the combat vehicles which had followed the advance as well as in captured vehicles and the entire position was captured. Soon afterward the spearhead of the 15th PD approached from the east. After establishing contact the two forces — the reinforced battalion on the right beside the Kümmel Panzer Battalion —broke through to the south until they reached the Italian strongpoint.

Acting quickly, Eleventh Company was able to capture four Mark II tanks. At 15.00 all units assembled in the assembly area at the Trigh Capuzzo. The battalion was ordered back to the division by radio.''

This ends the report by former *Hauptmann* Reissmann. On August 1, 1942 Werner Reissmann received the Knight's Cross for his actions.

The breakthrough had been achieved, but the DAK had only 130 tanks. It had started with 320. Nevertheless, repaired vehicles were returning from the repair shops daily.

Bir Hacheim was still holding out, and this southern strongpoint of the Gazala Line would have to fall before the attack could continue toward the northeast to the coast — and Tobruk.

During the night of June 1-2 Rommel committed the 90th Light and the *"Trieste"* Division against Bir Hacheim. In his inimitable fashion Rommel had greeted his new chief of staff, *Oberst* Bayerlein, who on June 1 had stepped into the place of the wounded former "chief," *Generalmajor* Gause, with the words:

"Into the car, Bayerlein! I'm going to lead the attack on Bir Hacheim myself!"

Having just escaped the threat of destruction, Rommel was already thinking of a way to strike at the enemy. And striking the enemy meant taking Bir Hacheim, because only then could he begin a further advance.

The Battle of Bir Hacheim

Bir Hacheim was defended by 4,400 soldiers of the Free French Brigade, which included a Jewish battalion. Commanding the brigade was Colonel Pierre König. General Ritchie had placed one of his strongest units in this southern bulwark of the Gazala Line. The 4,400 soldiers manned about 1,200 defensive positions and artillery nests within the strongpoint.

The motorized First Battalion of the 90th Light Division had been assigned to help the *"Trieste"* Division in the storming of Bir Hacheim.

"Boys," said *Generalmajor* Ulrich Kleemann, the division commander, "this will be a glorified stroll."

This "glorified stroll" was to demand a high cost in the first week. Bir Hacheim did not fall and for a day it looked as if Rommel, the desert fox, had fallen into his own trap. The breakthrough to the west had succeeded and now Bir Hacheim had to fall. Rommel formed a battle group around the 90th Light and several tanks sent by the DAK. Also sent to help out were AA 33 and the *"Trieste"* Division.

When Rommel arrived before Bir Hacheim and had worked his way to within sight of the fort, he turned around.

"We'll soon have it," he observed. "Parlementaire! — Bring me a parlementaire!"

Oberleutnant Gellert waved a white flag several times, but the often used handkerchief tactic of Rommel's did not work on the French.

"We attack then!" was Rommel's next order.

The men stormed forward once again. However, they were met by heavy machine-gun fire from the 1,200 defensive positions and were forced to take cover.

"Radio message to *Feldmarschall* Kesselring. He is to send Stukas. Send the message under 'KR'."

Feldmarschall Kesselring sent the Stukas. A total of 22 machines flew through the curtain of Flak, peeled off and dove on Bir Hacheim, Jericho sirens howling. One machine which pulled out too late was caught in the explosion of its own bomb. The bombs tore up great craters, and while the Stukas were still attacking British fighters were taking off from Gambut and El Adem. Before Rommel's eyes Hurricanes and Spitfires flew around the Stukas and, together with the anti-aircraft guns of the fortress, shot down nine Ju 87s.

A few hours later *Feldmarschall* Kesselring flew to Africa in his He 111.

"Rommel," he said angrily, "this isn't working! This damned nest must be attacked with all available ground forces. Take the flak too, it can crack the fortress' concrete cupolas! The battle group tactic won't work here. We're squandering too much valuable time."

Kampfgruppe Wolz under *Oberst* Alwin Wolz, with its assembled flak batteries and the regimental headquarters of the 135th Flak Regiment, now attacked Bir Hacheim from the west together with AA 3 and PzJägAbt. 33. It drove through the blowing sand of a *ghibli* into the din of the enemy defence. Bursts of machine-gun fire hissed into the sand. The attackers were halted and they dug in on the western side of the attacking front. On June 5 *Generaloberst* Rommel appeared once again in the western sector. *Oberst* Wolz made his report under the burning sun. The desert fox had new orders for him:

"Wolz, you are to immediately pull AA 3, *Panzerjäger-Abteilung* 33 and II./Flak 25 out of the Bir Hacheim operation and assemble them into the fast Battle Group Wolz. With this battle group you will go to Bir Scerrara, northeast of Bir Hacheim."

When *Oberst* Wolz arrived with the new battle group at about 17.00, Rommel was already there.

"A strong enemy force today attacked *"Ariete"* east of Got el Ualeb, Wolz," declared Rommel to the *Oberst*. "The enemy was repulsed. The DAK has launched a counterattack. You will set out from here, advance on the right wing of the 15th PD, take possession of the Trigh Capuzzo east of Bellefaa and cut off the enemy's retreat."

Rommel drove forward with *Kampfgruppe* Wolz. At about 18.30 they came upon the enemy east of Bir Harmat. Acting immediately, Wolz attacked. Four Flak batteries and the tanks of the 15th PD engaged the surprised enemy in the failing light. The battle continued into June 6, and by the evening of that day the four Flak batteries had a total of nine rounds of ammunition left between them. Once again Rommel had

succeeded in isolating and destroying an enemy force in this giant witch's cauldron where no one knew where the enemy was, and where the enemy could appear anywhere. In his book the *Feldmarschall* wrote:

"Under my command *Kampfgruppe* Wolz drove into the rear of the British near Knightsbridge. The 15th PD drove into battle on our left. It was to encircle the British from the south. The guns hit the British from three sides. By evening there were over fifty knocked-out tanks on the battlefield."

Now it was back to Bir Hacheim. Rommel gave the Wolz group its orders and then said:

"We will now drive the enemy out of there and then the way will be free!"

On June 6 Flak Battalion 606 under *Hauptmann* Briel with several attached units was moved forward to a blocking position south of Bir Hacheim. Joining Briel were the "Kayser" *Panzergrenadier* Battalion and elements of the 605th Anti-tank Battalion.

With these forces Briel attempted to take the fortress in a frontal attack on June 7. The attack failed. The minefields and the heavy artillery fire were too much for Briel's men. The battle group was then assigned to prevent breakout and relief attempts to and from the south.

On the morning of June 8 Bir Hacheim was covered by dense fog. When the fog had lifted somewhat *Oberst* Alwin Wolz, who was at his battle group's new firing positions outside Bir Hacheim, saw that the terrain which lay before him was as flat as a table. He immediately moved the two batteries which had gone into position back behind a rise in the terrain.

Ten minutes later *Kampfgruppe* Kiehl launched an attack on Bir Hacheim. Despite rapid fire from the two "eighty-eight" batteries the attack was halted. When the 20mm Flak moved forward through the gap cleared in the minefield by the engineers, they were pinned down by fire from the fort. The two promised infantry companies did not show up. Rommel, who had installed himself in a large hole fifty meters from *Oberst* Wolz' command post, called off the attack. He drove to the combat engineers, who were under the command of *Oberst* Hecker.

"Hecker, pull your units out and form a battle group with the two Italian battalions which have been sent with which we can take Bir Hacheim!"

"I don't have sufficient forces for that, *Herr*

General!" replied Hecker.

"Very well, Hecker! Then I'll send you *Sonderverband* 288. Menton will support you in this attack!"

Oberst Menton led this elite unit, which had been selected for use in Iraq. It had been transferred to Africa in March 1942 after the Iraq operation was cancelled.

"In addition you will receive my Kiehl combat echelon and an eighty-eight battery."

With this force *Oberst* Hecker was to hazard a move against the fortress. He formed two battle groups. Hecker led the left group himself, while the right was commanded by *Hauptmann* Hundt.

The combat engineers set out early on the afternoon of June 8. Their job was to clear a path through the minefield. Several mines exploded, showing the French defenders the locations of the attacking units. Colonel König radioed for help. The Commander-in-Chief of the Eighth Army sent fighter-bombers, which attacked from altitudes of barely more than 50 feet, rocketing and strafing anything that moved.

The attack nevertheless rapidly gained ground. *Oberst* Hecker led the way for his battle groups, which consisted of two Italian battalions, in an armored car.

"*Avanti! - avanti!*" he called to the Italians.

The attack gained momentum until the first exploding mines tore the battle group apart and concentrated fire began to pour in. Enemy anti-tank guns opened fire from ambush positions and knocked out six of *Kampfgruppe* Kiehl's eleven supporting tanks.

Meanwhile the German 20mm anti-aircraft guns had opened fire, and when the enemy launched a counterattack with tanks the eighty-eights joined the battle and turned them back.

When evening fell Hecker's two battle groups had advanced to within 500 meters of Bir Hacheim's main defensive works. The *Gebirgsjäger* Company of the Menton unit reached a wide trench occupied by soldiers of the Jewish battalion and jumped in. The enemy gave up. Would they be given quarter by the Germans? Rommel's soldiers treated these men like any other soldiers. None of the Jewish soldiers was harmed.

Night passed. The Stukas were scheduled to attack again early on the morning of June 9. *Oberst* Hecker had driven into the minefield to assess the effectiveness of the Stuka attack.

However, the Stukas did not show up. As it was later discovered, they had not received the order to attack. Instead the French spotted Hecker's vehicle and opened fire on it. As it withdrew the armored car drove over a mine. *Oberst* Hecker was wounded. He reached a burned-out tank and took up position there.

A little later he reported to *Generaloberst* Rommel, who had appeared on the scene:

"Give me a battalion of German Panzer Grenadiers, *Herr Generaloberst*, and I'll be able do it."

Oberst Bayerlein subsequently convinced Rommel, who appeared to Bayerlein to have already decided to spare Bir Hacheim, to go along with the suggestion. *Oberstleutnant* Ernst-Günther Baade, commander of SR 115, set out with his two battalions. Before the battalions began their attack the Stukas arrived. Once again they poured a hail of bombs down on Bir Hacheim. On the morning of that day, June 10, Colonel König issued an order of the day, which said:

"In this corner of the desert we have to prove that Frenchmen know how to fight and die!"
And through the positions of the Jewish battalion went the watchword:

"Fight men! The Jews of the world are watching!"

June 10, 1942 was the day of decision. Baade's infantry worked its way forward step by step, bunker by bunker, position by position. By evening the men of SR 115 were deep inside Bir Hacheim's system of positions. The final act must take place soon and there was no longer any doubt that the fate of Bir Hacheim was sealed.

During the night of June 10 *Kampfgruppe* Briel captured a prisoner who was part of a group engaged in clearing mines. The man revealed to *Hauptmann* Briel that the surrounded troops in the fortress were to break out that night through lanes cleared in the minefield.

Hauptmann Briel and *Hauptmann* Kayser hurried from gun to gun and from machine-gun position to machine-gun position. Every weapon was trained on the location of the expected breakout. Retired *Oberst* Georg Briel described what took place:

"All available tracing ammunition was loaded into the magazines and belts. I gave strict orders to open fire only on my light signal. I had a special surprise at my disposal in the shape of six MG 42s.

One of my men had obtained these wonder-MGs from the OKH and brought them back with him to Africa when his leave was over.

At midnight we began to hear ever louder engine noises from Bir Hacheim. Tracks rattled. Wires were cut in the minefield. When the enemy fired smoke shells to conceal his movements, I nudged the combat messenger, *Gefreiter* Batz:

'Go! — Fire the signal flare!'

The green star-shell and its red advance signal illuminated the surrounding terrain. At that moment all hell broke loose — a hell of fire, explosions and death. The artificial smoke was of no avail to Colonel König's Legionaires. Bursts of tracer hissed into the enemy vehicles. The bark of the new MG 42 was heard for the first time. With a rate of fire of 25 rounds per second, it was unbelievably effective.

At other places around the encircling ring the breakout attempt by the Legionnaires came down to bitter close-quarters fighting. It was man against man with spades, pistols, knives and hand grenades. Only half of the effectives within the fortress managed to break through the encircling ring with their colonel and reach the lines of the British Seventh Armored Brigade.''

When morning dawned and *Oberstleutnant* Baade and his infantry moved into the main area of the fort they were met by waving white flags. They found only about a dozen soldiers and medics and about 500 wounded in the hospital areas. The medical teams and their nursing sisters were left undisturbed in the hospital to care for their wounded. The Battle of Bir Hacheim was over.

Generaloberst Erwin Rommel acted immediately and in typical fashion. Everything that was drivable was sent north. The desert fox was launching a blow against the main British force. Rommel — almost finished ten days earlier — had turned things around. With Bir Hacheim the key to the fortress of Tobruk had fallen. The desert fox did not hesitate to issue new orders:

"Tobruk! — Everything toward Tobruk! Our objective is the coast and the ultimate destruction of the enemy!"

Advance toward the North - Tobruk Is the Objective

During the night of June 4/5, while fighting was

still going on at Bir Hacheim, near Bir Harmat the British were making preparations for a new attack. Early on the morning of June 6 the Second and Twenty-second Armored Brigades set off following an hour-long artillery barrage. The Tenth Indian and the 201st Guards Brigade joined the attack, which was aimed at the "*Ariete*" Division.

In order to conceal the real objective of the attack, the sector to the north manned by the 21st PD was also covered with smoke shells. The sector was also showered with artillery shells, and finally an attack was launched by the British Fourth Armored Brigade and the Second Armored Battalion to split the German forces.

The "*Ariete*" Division fell back under the weight of the attack as far as the positions of the army's artillery. Here the British advance was halted. PR 8 carried out an advance on Bir el Tamar to take the pressure off "*Ariete*." Rommel then struck at this force with *Kampfgruppe* Wolz as previously described.

At 06.00 on June 6, after it had repulsed the British attack, the 21th PD set out to attack to the east. The enemy withdrew.

Ritchie's recipe, to wear down *Panzerarmee Afrika* by forcing it to fight for fortified positions, had failed, and Rommel now committed all of his forces to the northeast. On the evening of June 11, under Rommel's command, the 15th PD, the 90th Light and AA 3 and AA 33 reached the area 10 kilometers south of El Adem. The next day they were able to capture the area around El Adem and

General-leutnant Ernst-Günther Baade. Baade also served as an Oberst-leutnant and Oberst in Africa.

131

Left: The grave of Oberleutnant Werner Tomczack.

Below left: Italian artillery position.

Below: The face of a battle group commander (Hauptmann Georg Briel).

132

the Trigh Capuzzo in spite of the armoured units which general Ritchie had concentrated there. El Adem was taken by the 90th Light Division. The defending Twenty-ninth Indian Brigade suffered heavy casualties.

Also setting out toward the east on the morning of June 12 was a battle group from the 21st PD. The British tank forces would be squeezed together between the two panzer divisions and the *"Ariete"* and *"Trieste"* Divisions.

Rommel and his Kiehl combat echelon drove to the line of hills in the area southeast of El Adem and from there observed the course of the attack. The men of the 90th Light were facing the Indian troops. Heavy fighting broke out. Burning tanks littered the desert and by the afternoon of that June 12 the enemy was beaten. General Ritchie radioed Cairo:

"We have no effective armored force to set against Rommel's drive to the coast; if the Germans reach the sea both of our effective divisions in the Gazala position, the First South African and the British Fiftieth, will be cut off and lost."

A short time later the British Commander-in-Chief reported his arrival at Eighth Army headquarters in Gambut. An hour later Claude Auchinleck was on the scene. He order a continuation of the battle in the Gazala — El Adem area until Rommel ran out of steam. Before returning to Cairo he radioed London:

"Atmosphere here good! The situation has been assessed calmly and resolutely. Morale of the troops good. Enemy intentions apparently not going according to plan. — Auchinleck."

Winston Churchill telegraphed back:

"I welcome your decision to fight. Your success depends not on arms, but on strength of will. God bless you all. Winston Churchill."

The battle raged on. However, on the afternoon of June 14 General Ritchie was forced to transmit the code word "Freeborn." This was the signal for the First South African and British Fiftieth Divisions to evacuate their positions and fall back to Tobruk.

On the night of June 13/14 Rommel sent the 15th and 21st Panzer Divisions to attack in a northerly direction west of the Capuzzo — Bir Hacheim road. That morning the 90th Light set out toward the east to capture the approaches to Tobruk and set the stage for an attack on the

fortress, while *"Trieste"* and *"Ariete"* screened the eastern flank.

Rommel accompanied the attack in his command vehicle, and while the British and South Africans were blowing up their depots in the Gazala Line, the DAK rolled on through the midst of a sand storm.

The First South African Division managed to reach Tobruk. The British Fiftieth Division was able to break through the Italian Tenth Army Corps toward the south. Early on the morning of June 15, 1942 the spearheads of the 15th PD reached the sea.

On June 15 the 21th PD was withdrawn from the Acroma area and sent toward the east via El Adem. Advancing with it were the motorized elements of the 90th Light Division. The strongpoints of El Adem, Batruna and El Hatian were attacked. The tanks of PR 5 shot up nests of resistance. Batruna was stormed. 800 prisoners were taken and Sidi Rezegh was reached that evening. The 90th Light, however, was halted in front of El Hatian. The Grenadiers of the 361st Regiment under *Oberstleutnant* Panzenhagen, who had defeated the Indians near El Adem, could not get through. Rommel decided to bypass this strongpoint. He realized that it served no other purpose but to tie down his forces for as long as possible.

Nevertheless, on the morning of June 16 he ordered a resumption of the attack. The 90th Light Division failed to take the position. It did manage to penetrate the defences but was unable to expand its foothold. The defending Indian troops held on until the morning of June 17.

On June 16 the 21st PD captured the forts of El Duda and Belhamed, and the next morning, following the fall of El Hatian, Rommel committed the 90th Light Division against the remaining enemy strongpoints in the area. The DAK and *"Ariete"* received orders to attack toward Gambut. The 21st PD reached the area south of Gambut on the evening of June 17, when it was ordered by Rommel to veer toward the north. Rommel placed himself at the head with his combat echelon and at about 22.00, following a skirmish with French Foreign Legionnaires, reached Gambut. Gambut fell the next day, and during June 18 the entire area between Tobruk in the west and Gambut 450 kilometers farther east was cleared. Fifteen serviceable British aircraft

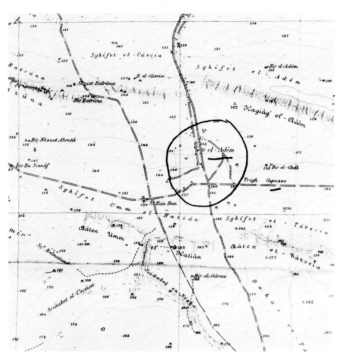

THE EL ADEM BATTLE ZONE

Drawing by G. Briel

were captured at Gambut airfield.

Once again Tobruk was encircled.

Tobruk Falls

On the afternoon of June 19 Rommel again turned both of the DAK's Panzer Divisions toward the west, while the 90th Light was instructed to set out toward the east to capture a British supply base located between Bardia and Tobruk and conceal his real intention of capturing Tobruk.

The 90th Light reached Bardia that same day. As part of the effort to mislead the British, communications were transmitted in the clear. That afternoon a British operator sent the following message:

"Attention, Rommel is driving toward the Egyptian frontier!"

The feint attack had succeeded.

The attack on Tobruk began early on the morning of June 20, 1942. The Twenty-first Italian Corps launched a diversionary attack against the fortress' southwestern front. Several tanks were placed under its command to provide support. The DAK and the motorized Italian Twentieth Corps were to carry out the main attack from the southeast.

Air attacks on the fortress and the planned point of penetration in the southeast began at 05.30.

Rommel, who had moved into a forward command post with his operations staff early that morning, watched the air attack. Eighty Stukas and 100 bombers dropped their loads. Gaps were ripped in the wire entanglements and the attack began.

The 21st Panzer Division under *Generalmajor* von Bismarck and the 15th PD commanded by *Oberst* Crasemann rolled toward the break-in point. The 15th Rifle Brigade under Oberst Menny, which had been committed independently, supported the attack and many other units and sections advanced with it: combat engineers and anti-aircraft guns, as well as the Grenadiers of GR 361 under *Oberstleutnant* Panzenhagen.

PR 5, led by *Oberst* Müller, stormed forward, as did PR 8. The crossroads near Sidi Mahmud was reached. By then the two panzer regiments had destroyed fifty enemy tanks.

The panzers approached the fort of Gabr Gasem. By evening the 15th PD had driven the enemy forces from the fort. A half hour later Fort Pilastrino surrendered. The incline to the city had been reached.

We will now follow one of the assault groups into Tobruk.

On the afternoon of June 20 GR 361 had advanced to within range of Tobruk's airfield. *Oberstleutnant* Panzenhagen gave *Hauptmann* Klärmann, the commander of II./GR 361, the order to take the field. Klärmann reached his objective and decided to push on to the harbor. By the evening of June 20 the Grenadiers had captured the harbor and taken several thousand prisoners.

Panzenhagen recommended Hans Klärmann for the Knight's Cross. On September 18, 1942 he became the first "legionnaire" to receive the decoration.

1./Flak 617 under *Hauptmann* Hissmann, which was standing by with *Generalmajor* von Bismarck as division reserve for the 21st PD, intervened in the battle when the advancing infantry began to take flanking machine-gun fire. The company eliminated the enemy's flanking weapons with its 20mm anti-aircraft guns, and in the afternoon attacked the British artillery batteries which were firing from the hills east of the harbor. During the advance *Hauptmann* Hissmann captured a British Colonel and his staff. The batteries were silenced.

Afterward the company rolled into the city. On the way it encountered Rommel. The following is a brief description by Hissmann of what happened:

"I made my report and handed the British Colonel over to Rommel. Just as I was about to climb into my vehicle, Rommel called after me:

'You're due for a rest!'

'I know, *herr Generaloberst!* But Tobruk comes first!'

'Drive!' shouted Rommel, and I drove off. All hell had broken loose in the harbor. Tanks of the DAK were firing on the British ships. My 1./Flak 617 joined in enthusiastically. Then began the battle for the city."

As Hissmann drove round a corner he found himself heading straight toward a British tank repair shop. A tank appeared and opened fire from 300 meters. Hissmann felt the shell strike home. A spurt of flame shot up close beside his feet. An enemy machine-gun joined in. Following an exchange of fire, in which 1./Flak 617 destroyed the tank and the machine-gun, the company captured the repair shop and a number of serviceable tanks. The British pulled back into a *wadi*. *Generalmajor* von Bismarck appeared early the next morning and ordered Hissmann to demand that the enemy forces holding out there surrender. He drove off with the Battalion Medical Officer, Dr. Sydow. They presented the German demands to the British General. He agreed with an "all right!" The battle there was over.

The tanks of the 15th and 21st Panzer Divisions finished the job. Early on the morning of June 21, 1942, at about 05.00, Rommel drove into Tobruk at the head of his combat echelon. He saw the sunken ships in the harbor which had been destroyed by *Oberstleutnant* Mildebrath's I./PR 5. At 09.40 he accepted the surrender of the fortress commander, General Klopper.

33,000 prisoners were taken. In his book *African Trilogy*, Alan Moorehead wrote of the fall of Tobruk:

"It was a serious, total defeat. The road to Egypt was open, and Rommel, who had conquered Tobruk in exactly one day, was determined to take that road to Egypt."

Rommel's order of the day to *Panzerarmee Afrika* on June 21 read:

Soldiers!
The great battle in the Marmarica has been crowned with the storming of Tobruk. Altogether, more than 45,000 prisoners were taken, more than 1,000 tanks, almost 400 guns destroyed or captured. Through your incomparable bravery and tenacity you have traded the enemy blow for blow in the long hard battles of the last four weeks. Through your attacking spirit the enemy has lost the core of his field army, especially his powerful armored forces, which was poised for an attack against us. My special recognition goes out to the commanders and troops for this outstanding accomplishment.

Soldiers of *Panzerarmee Afrika*!
It is now vital to completely destroy the enemy. We will not rest until we have smashed the last part of the Eighth Army. In the coming days I will once again make great demands of you so that we may our objective.

Rommel.

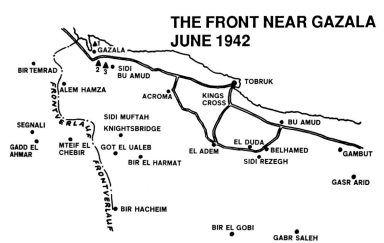

THE FRONT NEAR GAZALA JUNE 1942

Drawing by G. Briel

135

Top left: General der Panzertruppe Walther K. Nehring, Commanding General of the DAK from 8. 3. to 31. 8. 1942 (wounded). From 15.11. to 9.12.1942 Nehring was in charge of the creation of a new front in Tunisia.
Below left: Rommel and Bayerlein at the fall of Tobruk, 21. 6. 1942.

Tobruk on 21. 6. 1942.

Captured British Mark IV tanks near Tobruk.

"To Victory - to the Nile"

The Battle of Marsa Matruk

The Battle of Tobruk had been decided. After previously withstanding every effort by the DAK for 28 weeks, this time it had fallen in 30 hours. The Commander-in-Chief of *Panzerarmee Afrika*, Rommel, was promoted to *Generalfeldmarschall*. Walther K. Nehring, the Commanding General of the DAK, received a promotion to the rank of *General der Panzertruppe*. Siegfried Westphal,

who had been wounded near Got el Ualeb on June 1, 1942, became an *Oberst*. The battle had nevertheless been difficult. The fighting for the Gazala Line and its boxes had demanded sacrifices. *Feldmarschall* Rommel wrote in his diary:

"We achieved victory at Tobruk by calling on the last of our strength, because the weeks of major battles against an enemy superior in personnel

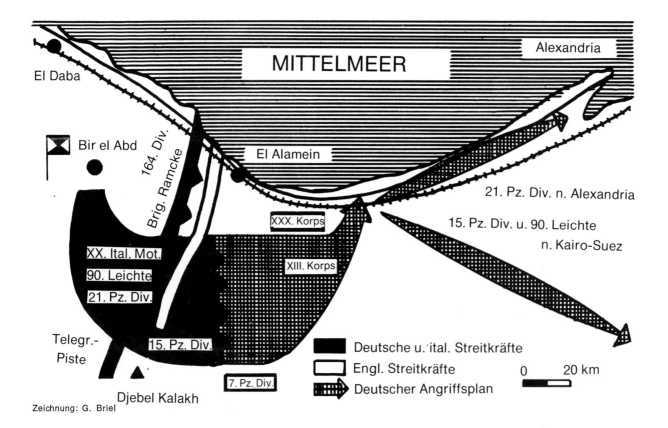

Zeichnung: G. Briel

and materiel had not been without cost to my units. But now, as a result of our giant booty in munitions, gasoline, rations and materiel of all kinds, it had become possible to stockpile for a further offensive."

This strengthened my resolve to exploit the British weakness after the Battle of Tobruk and advance as far as possible into Egypt."

Rommel's main reason, however, was that he wished "at all costs" to prevent the British from establishing a new front somewhere else and then sending fresh troops to this new front from the Near East. He said:

"The divisions of the Eighth Army should be overtaken in a rapid advance and brought to battle *before* they have linked up with other units from the Near East."

On June 20 *Feldmarschall* Rommel stood before his troops in Bardia and gave the new order for the attack to the east. The 90th Light Division took over the lead, followed by *Oberstleutnant* Panzenhagen with GR 361. Behind them came the 15th and 21st Panzer Divisions and the Twentieth Italian Army Corps. Rommel was everywhere. Wherever he appeared his watchword was, "Forward! — Exploit!"

Rommel had learned from captured British documents that the enemy intended to make a stand near Marsa Matruk. More than once the advancing German soldiers overtook fleeing British columns. But the fuel shortage began to make itself felt as early as June 24. German supply lines were now over 1,500 kilometers long. On reaching the British supply station at Habata, the advancing troops were able to rescue part of the giant supply dump there; a smaller part went up in flames. However, the vehicles were able to refuel in Habata, and the advance continued. On June 25 the advancing units reached the area 50 kilometers west of Marsa Matruk. During this phase of the pursuit the German columns were bombed relentlessly by the Royal Air Force.

The advance went on with three spearheads leading the way: in the north the 90th Light, in the center the 21st PD and on the southern flank the 15th PD. The Italian Twentieth Corps with the "Ariete," "Trieste" and "Littorio" Divisions was stalled for lack of fuel and was delayed.

The expected and intended encounter with the enemy occurred on the morning of June 26. Rommel's move, to bring the enemy's armored forces to battle and surround his infantry, was once again successful. The 15th and 21st Panzer Divisions met the enemy's armored forces about 40 kilometers south of Marsa Matruk. The British unit farthest to the west was the motorized Seventh Brigade. Behind it were the Twenty-second and Fourth Armored Brigades, and farther to the southwest was the Second New Zealand Division with the Fourth and Fifth Brigades and the First Armored Brigade.

While the 90th Light veered north and *Kampfgruppe* Marcks barricaded the coast road east of Marsa Matruk assisted by I./Flak 6, the tank battle began in the south.

General Ritchie wanted to stop the German advance here between Marsa Matruk and Bir Khalda. During its march to the north the 90th Light succeeded in barricading the fortress to the east and west. In Marsa Matruk was the Tenth Indian Division and elements of the Fiftieth British and Fifth Indian Divisions.

While the objective of the day there was being reached, the two panzer divisions, together with divisions of the Italian Twentieth Corps, especially "Ariete," were locked in battle with the British armored units which had been brought back up to strength with new medium and heavy tanks.

Once again it was PR 5 and PR 8 which engaged the enemy tanks, destroying 18. However, the attempt to prevent a breakthrough to the north and Marsa Matruk by the Second New Zealand Division failed. The New Zealanders fought their way through, suffering heavy losses.

The next day the forces of the British Tenth Corps surrounded in Marsa Matruk attempted to break through the encircling ring. The New Zealanders, too, tried to break out to the south.

Feldmarschall Rommel committed the Kiehl combat echelon and elements of the "Littorio" Division. Nevertheless, some of the New Zealanders managed to break out.

By early morning on June 28 *Feldmarschall* Rommel was already at the breakout position. Reports indicated that the main British force was withdrawing in the direction of Fuka, while elements of the Tenth Indian and Second New Zealand Divisions, as well as the British Fiftieth, together with the recently-deployed Fourth Armored Brigade, defended Marsa Matruk.

That afternoon at about 17.00 the attacking

Oberst Wolz (left), commander of the 135th Flak Regiment, with Major Briel.

Rommel with Oberstleutnant Panzenhagen at the III./IR 347 command post in Acroma on 6. 12. 1941.

units set out against Marsa Matruk. The attack force consisted of the 90th Light Division, AA 580 and a series of battle groups, Flak-Battalion 606 under *Hauptmann* Briel, Special Unit 288 under *Oberst* Menton and elements of the Italian Tenth and Twenty-first Italian Army Corps.

Stukas approached from the west and dropped their loads on the fortress. The soldiers under Albert Panzenhagen stormed into Marsa Matruk. By the time darkness fell they had reached the inner belt of fortifications. The attackers were met by fire from the two main works. An *Oberfeldwebel* took out one of the bunkers with a demolition charge. The attackers immediately pushed on and were met by fire from the left from machine-guns and rapid-firing cannon. They went around an anti-tank front and soon afterwards found themselves facing a heavily-manned trench. *Oberstleutnant* Panzenhagen jumped in; his men followed. They rolled up the trench with hand grenades and bursts of fire from their submachine-guns. Another bunker was taken out and then they were in the center of the fortress.

When enemy tanks rolled past the Panzenhagen Regiment to the left they were intercepted and fired on by *Kampfgruppe* Briel. The first enemy tank began to burn; the counterattack failed.

A little later *Oberstleutnant* Panzenhagen's men saw that the advancing Kiehl combat echelon was taking fire from machine-guns and artillery situated in a somewhat higher strongpoint.

"We must eliminate that enemy position," said Panzenhagen to his aide.

"But it's not in our lane of attack," replied the latter.

"If it isn't attacked and destroyed the whole division will be stopped! We're going to attack! — All company commanders to me!"

Oberstleutnant Panzenhagen quickly briefed his men. He led the way at the head of 2./GR 361. Quite by surprise they took the enemy in his flank. Panzenhagen led his men forward with great élan, personally taking out the first bunker accompanied by several combat messengers. The attack made rapid progress and ten minutes later the main strongpoint of the fortress of Marsa Matruk had fallen.

Generalmajor Kleemann recommended Panzenhagen for the Knight's Cross. For the first time in its brief history the 90th Light Division was mentioned in the Wehrmacht communiqué. On October 2, 1942 Albert Panzenhagen was presented the Knight's Cross.

Marsa Matruk had fallen. 6,000 British soldiers were taken prisoner.

Advance on Alexandria

Immediately after the fall of the fortress *Feldmarschall* Rommel sent all his motorized units on a further advance to the east. The next objective was Fuka.

On June 29 *Kampfgruppe* Briel was given a special assignment. Between June 11 and June 28 the battle group had driven and fought its way from Bir Hacheim to Marsa Matruk, over 250 kilometers. Several men were suffering from desert sickness. Symptoms of exhaustion spread and many suffered fainting spells. Then the battle group found a supply dump which had been buried deep underground, which even included a freezing plant. *Major* Briel ordered:

"Refuel! - Load up! - Gather what you can!"

The men did exactly that and it looked as if they were about to have a good rest — until *Feldmarschall* Rommel suddenly appeared. It was 11.00 on June 29, 1942 when he gave the battle group's commander the following order:

"Advance on Alexandria, Briel! Afterward we'll have coffee together at the Hotel Sheppard in Cairo."

Briel knew what Rommel meant. He had received similar orders in the past. His battle group had been designated as the advance detachment of the 90th Light Division.

Five minutes after receiving the order the battle group set off. Briel had divided his advance detachment into three groups. Each of the groups was of similar strength, composition and was strictly organized. In this way Briel was ready to handle any opposition "Rommel style."

"Rommel style" meant that the leading detachment opened fire and attacked frontally. The second group then attacked from the right or left flank, depending on terrain and the disposition of

Rommel orders Kampfgruppe Briel to patrol toward Alexandria.

Top left: A supply canister (a so-called "rations bomb") dropped to surrounded soldiers.
Center left: Mail call.
Bottom: Anti-aircraft position.
Above: Rest break.

Facing page above: Cigarette break.
Above right: 3,553 kilometers to Berlin.
Bottom right: Division headquarters of the 5th Light Division (later 21st Panzer Division).

the enemy, while the third group was held in reserve to be committed if it became necessary.

The lead group was commanded by *Hauptmann* Kayser, battalion commander of II./GR 155. *Hauptmann* Briel himself led the second group, while *Hauptmann* Franz was in charge of the third. The battle group had been given three objectives. They were:

Objective 1: Point 216 - Alam Hiwig
Objective 2: Point 128 - 5 km west of Fuka
Objective 3: Area south of Ras Abu Girab - 25 km east of Fuka.

The advance detachment drove forward along the road. New Zealand rearguards were overtaken and overpowered. Objective 1 was reached at 14.30. Objective 2 fell twenty minutes later. At 15.35 the enemy appeared with armored cars.

"Attack!" ordered Briel. The 40mm guns and the 20mm cannon opened fire on the armored cars, knocking out three. The battle group lost three guns.

The advance went on and at 18.02 the battle group reached its final objective, 25 kilometers before El Daba. Briel called for a rest stop, then received a radio message from the *Panzerarmee:*

"Continue the advance as far as El Daba!"

At 22.10 Briel radioed back: "El Daba taken -advancing farther; eventually as far as Sidi Abd el Rahman."

And that is what happened. In a ghostly night drive the battle group rolled through the British rearguard camp, past airfields and defensive positions.

It was midnight when the spearhead reached Sidi Abd el Rahman. On the hill stood a mosque. South of it was a train station on the Sollum-Alexandria line which had been built by the British. Here the battle group halted. Sentries were placed on the road, and several 20mm Flak were moved into position. A machine-gun was stationed on the hill near the mosque.

Studying his map by flashlight, *Major* Briel determined that in twelve hours his force had penetrated 120 kilometers into enemy territory. But the battle group was now exhausted. It had finally reached the limits of its endurance.

Early on the morning of June 30 Georg Briel received a radio message from the *Feldmarschall*:

"Halt advance! Pull back and join the 90th Light. Await further orders."

The following day, July 1, 1942, the advance detachment was relieved and, as *Kampfgruppe Briel*, made Rommel's mobile reserve. The battle group was beefed up with the addition of anti-tank gun units, artillery, combat engineers and Grenadiers. The force moved into an assembly area opposite Deir el Shein.

On the afternoon of June 30 all commanders were assembled at *Panzerarmee* headquarters between El Daba and Sidi Abd el Rahman. *Feld-marschall* Rommel gave the order everyone had been expecting:

"Advance at maximum speed through El Fajade toward Cairo!"

That same day the DAK, which was in the center of *Panzerarmee Afrika*, was to attack south along the Quattara depression and feign a southern enveloping attack against the 60-kilometer-deep defensive positions near El Alamein. When darkness fell, however, the DAK was to turn, drive toward the northeast and capture jumping-off positions for the decisive thrust between the strongpoints of El Alamein and Deir el Abyad.

The Battle of El Alamein could begin. The question was, would it lead to a breakthrough and a final decisive advance on Alexandria?

The Battle of El Alamein

Deir el Shein

The march by the DAK during the night of July 1, 1942 led over difficult terrain. What was more the turn to the north was hindered by a sand storm. At 02.30 *Feldmarschall* Rommel drove from his headquarters south of El Daba to the front. He spoke with *General* Nehring at the DAK's headquarters and then drove on to Hill 31, where the new headquarters of the *Panzerarmee* was set up next to the road.

When the 21st PD arrived near Deir el Abyad it found that there was no British strongpoint there. It in fact was situated several kilometers away near Deir el Shein.

Reconnaissance results received by *General* Nehring showed that there was an additional fortification north of the Ruweisat Ridge held by the First South African Brigade. This forced him to attack Deir el Shein *and* attempt a strategic breakthrough.

The first attack by the 21st Panzer Division against Deir el Shein began at 09.00. In position there was the Eighth Indian Division fresh from Iraq. The attack was halted by heavy artillery fire and deep minefields.

The 90th Light Division had also gone to the attack that morning, but after a few hours it became bogged down in front of the El Alamein fortifications. *General* Nehring had the division swing out to south and advance into the area southeast of El Alamein at about noon. The division made slow progress and after establishing defensive fronts to the north and south it began an attempt to break through to the sea and encircle the fortress. However the enemy recognized this threat in time and blanketed the advancing division with extremely heavy artillery fire. The assault groups were pinned down by the hail of fire.

The *Feldmarschall* sent his combat echelon south of the 90th Light. As he drove forward to see the situation for himself he came under such heavy artillery fire that he was forced to turn back. But what had transpired at Deir el Shein?

THe 21st Panzer Division launched another attack at midday. The tanks accompanied the attack against the heavily-fortified strongpoint. They lost 18 of their number in duels with anti-tank guns and several British tanks, but managed to break through into the center of the defences. By evening Deir el Shein had fallen. 2,000 Indian troops went into captivity.

The 90th Light, however, made no progress. By late evening that day it had only 1,300 effectives left. In the north it had run up against an extremely well-constructed system of concrete emplacements, and to the east was a powerful system of British field positions.

When *Feldmarschall* Rommel learned from the *Fliegerführer Afrika* that the British Fleet had sailed from Alexandria, he became determined to force a decision in the next few days.

"I was convinced," he wrote later, "that a major breakthrough by my troops would lead to panic on the British side."

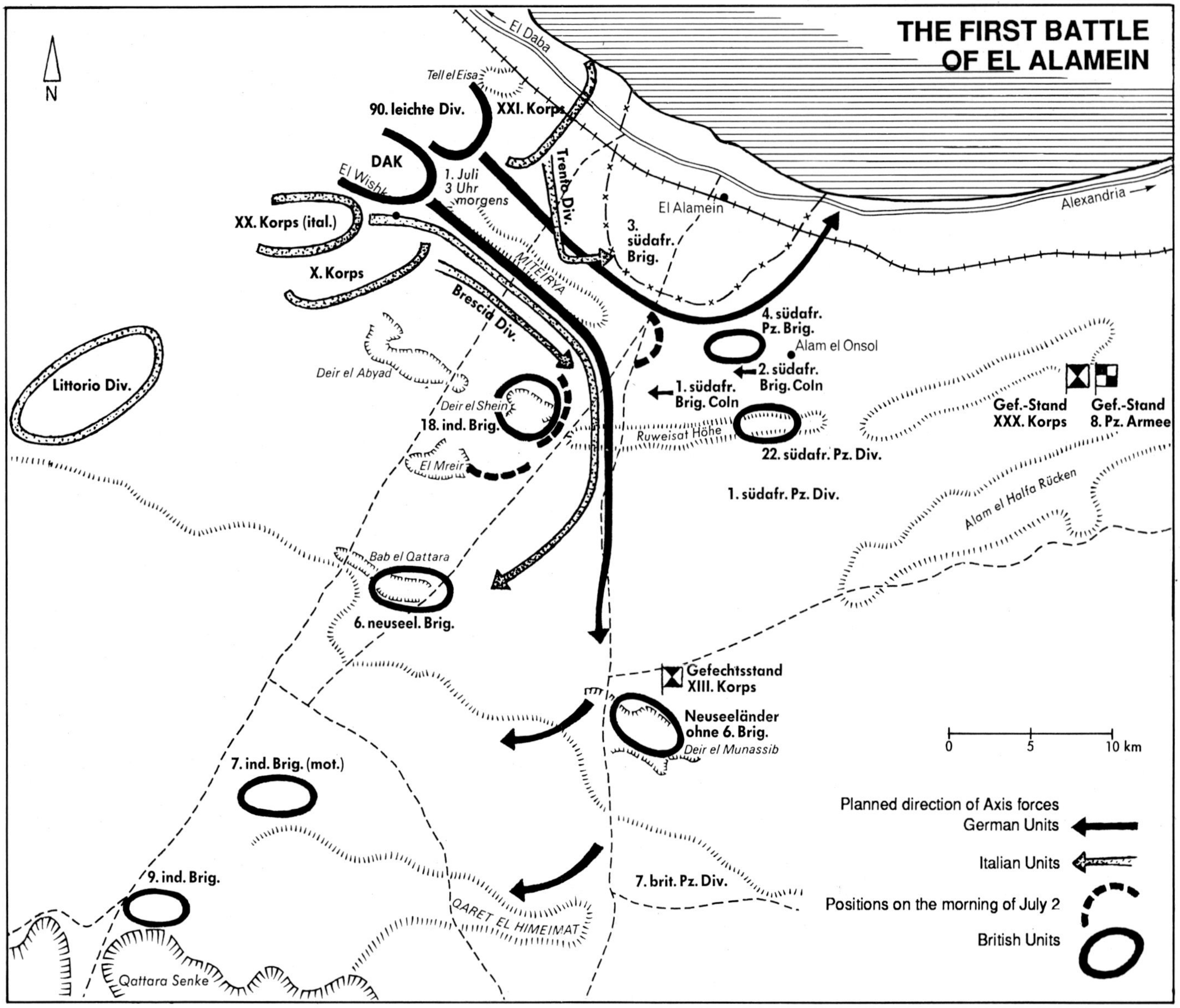
THE FIRST BATTLE OF EL ALAMEIN
N
El Daba
Tell el Eisa
90. leichte Div.
XXI. Korps
DAK
El Wishka
1. Juli
3 Uhr
morgens
Trento Div.
XX. Korps (ital.)
X. Korps
MITEIRYA
El Alamein
3. südafr. Brig.
Alexandria
Brescia Div.
4. südafr. Pz. Brig.
Alam el Onsol
2. südafr. Brig. Coln
1. südafr. Brig. Coln
Littorio Div.
Deir el Abyad
Deir el Shein
18. ind. Brig.
Ruweisat Höhe
22. südafr. Pz. Div.
Gef.-Stand XXX. Korps
Gef.-Stand 8. Pz. Armee
El Mreir
1. südafr. Pz. Div.
Alam el Halfa Rücken
Bab el Qattara
6. neuseel. Brig.
Gefechtsstand XIII. Korps
Neuseeländer ohne 6. Brig.
Deir el Munassib
0
5
10 km
7. ind. Brig. (mot.)
Planned direction of Axis forces
German Units
Italian Units
Positions on the morning of July 2
British Units
9. ind. Brig.
7. brit. Pz. Div.
QARET EL HIMEIMAT
Qattara Senke

From *Rommel*, by Ron Lewin

On July 2 the DAK set off again to achieve a breakthrough to the coast 12 kilometers east of El Alamein. Both panzer divisions were soon embroiled in an engagement with about 100 enemy tanks and 10 batteries of artillery.

General Claude Auchinleck, who had come from Cairo and was commanding in place of General Ritchie, knew only too well what was at stake. The battle for Deir el Shein had given him a chance to regroup the British First Armored Division, and when the DAK attacked again on July 3, it was halted by heavy British artillery fire after initial success. By that evening Rommel was convinced that continuing the attack would have meant "only a useless exhausting of our strength." He must give the troops a day of rest *and* bring forward supplies of all kinds. Then he would try again.

In the days that followed the motorized units and panzer divisions were pulled out of the line one after another. The first to pull back into positions in the rear was the 21st PD. When sufficient supplies of mines arrived Rommel had dense minefields placed around El Alamein. Antiaircraft guns were emplaced at the most threatened sectors of the front. Captured British guns were also used to beef up the firepower of the defensive front. New tanks reached the front in the following days and General Auchinleck had thus lost his chance to finish off Rommel.

The state of *Panzerarmee Afrika* facing the Commander-in-Chief on July 8 was as follows:

Within the 15th and 21st Panzer Divisions the *Deutsche Afrika-Korps* had at its disposal a total of 50 tanks; each division had an infantry regiment with 300 men, ten anti-tank guns and an artillery regiment with seven batteries.

With its four infantry regiments the 90th Light Division had available 1,500 men, as well as 30 anti-tank guns and two batteries of artillery.

The three reconnaissance battalions possessed 15 armored cars, 20 armored personnel carriers and 3 batteries of captured enemy artillery. The *Armee* artillery under *Generalmajor* Weber consisted of 11 heavy and 4 light batteries. The *Armee* flak had twenty-six 88mm and twenty-five 20mm guns.

The situation of the Italian units was no better. The Twentieth Motorized Army Corps, with two armored divisions and one motorized division, had a total of 54 tanks and 8 motorized battalions with a total strength of 1,600 men. There were also 40 anti-tank guns and 6 light batteries.

The elements of the Tenth and Twenty-first Army Corps totalled 11 infantry battalions with 200 men each as well as 30 light and 11 heavy batteries. The Italian Army artillery had four additional batteries.

Rommel's comment was, "One can see from this report that my units do not deserve the title of divisions."

Nevertheless, the *Feldmarschall* was confident and on July 8 decided to carry out an attack against the New Zealand positions the following morning in an attempt to break through.

During the night of July 8/9 a strong patrol from the 21st PD fought its way into the Quaret el Abd position, and a little later *Panzerarmee Afrika* launched an attack against the British southern front with the 21st Panzer Division, the Italian *"Littorio"* Armored Division and the 90th Light Division. The important position of Quaret el Abd was stormed and taken.

Early in the afternoon *Feldmarschall* Rommel arrived there with *Generalmajor* von Bismarck. Both became convinced that it must be possible to advance east from there and so bring about the fall of the enemy positions near El Alamein.

Things turned out quite differently, however. In the early morning hours of July 10 the British launched an attack in the northern sector, over-running the Italian *"Sabrata"* Division. The British counterattack spoiled the planned attack

to the east from Quaret el Abd.

Rommel rolled northward with his combat echelon and a hastily-assembled battle group. However, it was due to the efforts of the Ic of *Panzerarmee Afrika, Oberstleutnant* von Mellenthin, that the British attack was stopped. With a scratch force of troops from headquarters and anti-aircraft units and the leading elements of IR 382 of the 164th Light Division, which was approaching along the coast road, he was able to stop the British and hold on until the arrival of the battle groups from the south.

The battle group under the command of *Oberst* Hecker played a major role, along with GR 382, in ensuring that the enemy got no farther.

A counterattack from the southern flank was halted by heavy British artillery fire. The enemy resumed his attack on July 11. Once again an Italian unit, this time the *"Trieste"* Division, was overrun and its soldiers taken prisoner. By the time the British attack there subsided, there was no longer any question of an Axis attack in the south.

On July 15 New Zealand and Indian troops broke into the German front at Ruweisat Ridge. The 15th PD, AA 3 and AA 33 launched a counterattack and recovered the lost territory.

Two days later a more powerful British attack struck the *"Trento"* and *"Trieste"* Divisions which had been deployed to the southwest. The resulting penetration was sealed off and a counterattack recovered the lost territory.

Feldmarschall Albert Kesselring arrived at *Armee* headquarters on the evening of July 17. Rommel informed him that if there was not a decisive improvement in the area of supply, *Panzerarmee Afrika* would soon be facing collapse. Field Marshall Count Cavallero, who had accompanied Kesselring, attempted to play down the Army's predicament, but Kesselring, as well as Rommel, demanded a definite promise from the Italian Chief-of-Staff.

During the following days of quiet the units were brought back to a semblance of order. However, on July 20 British assembly areas were detected opposite the central sector of the El Alamein front which was held by the 15th Panzer Division.

The first penetration was sealed off. Nevertheless the units were forced to pull back to a shortened line in line with the captured defensive works of Deir el Shein and Quaret el Abd.

The main assault against the central sector followed at about 08.00. The British attack force consisted of the First Armored Division and the Second New Zealand and Fifth Indian Divisions. These units were later joined by the reformed and reequipped Twenty-third Armored Brigade with over one hundred tanks.

South of Deir el Shein the German lines were overrun. An hour after the attack began the attacking units, especially the Twenty-third Armored Brigade, were far behind the German front. Only a few kilometers from the headquarters of the 21st PD the British armored spearhead came upon an anti-tank gun platoon of the headquarters company of PGR 104 (formerly the 104th Rifle Regiment). Platoon leader *Leutnant* Skubowius had observed the approach of the enemy tanks from the position of the number one gun commanded by *Unteroffizier* Jabeck. They counted no fewer than thirty enemy tanks. Gunner Halm targeted the first British tank and destroyed it with his first shot. Within two minutes the lone anti-tank gun had destroyed four tanks. By this time the enemy tanks had opened fire on the anti-tank gun, which soon destroyed its fifth, sixth, seventh, eighth and then ninth tanks. The number two gun had meanwhile joined the battle and knocked out several of the approaching tanks.

By now the number of enemy tanks sighted had climbed to eighty, and then to ninety. If they all sped up and rolled through, then . . .

But they halted. They were engaged and knocked out, and then — then the rest turned away.

The commander of GR 104, *Oberst* Ewert, who had witnessed the duel, came roaring forward in his *Kübelwagen*. He had immediately alerted the Stukas and requested help from the 21st PD.

By the time the Stukas arrived and plunged down on the tanks *Unteroffizier* Jabeck's gun had been destroyed and Halm, like all the others, had been wounded.

Afterward the tanks of PR 5 appeared, led by *Oberst* Gerhard Müller. The panzers fired in salvoes. They rolled forward by companies, attacked the enemy on both flanks, and put him to flight.

Halm had destroyed nine enemy tanks. The platoon's number two gun accounted for another six. The rest were taken care of by the Stukas and PR 5. When the battle was over 96 of the fresh armored brigade's tanks lay on the battlefield —

knocked out, burning or with their tracks smashed. The British Twenty-third Armored Brigade had been wiped out.

On August 7, 1942 *Gefreiter* Günther Halm received the Knight's Cross for breaking the back of the British attack.

On the German side the same units were sent into battle again and again. The same panzer units had to go out and face fresh enemy formations. Rommel had failed to realize his plans.

In the period May 25 to July 30 *Panzerarmee Afrika* had taken more than 60,000 prisoners. Over 2,000 enemy tanks had been destroyed or captured. However, German losses in the same period had also been high. Casualties were:

2,300 officers and men killed.

7,500 officers and men wounded.

2,700 officers and men taken prisoner.

Italian losses were:

1,000 officers and men killed.

10,000 officers and men wounded.

5,000 officers and men taken prisoner.

Losses of materiel were high. The attack had come to an end before El Alamein. Finally, the tide of war was to turn there. Before this, however, both sides were forced to pause and catch their breath.

Attack and counterattack had ebbed away. In the front lines near El Alamein both sides were at readiness. In the meantime all of the units of the 164th Light Division had been brought across from Crete to Africa, and *Fallschirmbrigade* (Parachute Brigade) Ramcke had moved into position near the Quattara depression.

The German headquarters signals intelligence section was providing a continuous flow of information on the mighty supply convoys en route to the Eighth Army. Soon it was able to forecast when the enemy would be ready for his next offensive: mid-September 1942.

The new British Commander-in-Chief in the desert was to have been General Gott. However on August 7, 1942 the aircraft carrying Gott was shot down over the front. His successor was General Bernard Montgomery. With the new Commander-in-Chief came the new commander of Thirteenth Corps, Lieutenant General Brian Horrocks.

The threatened offensive forced the German Commander-in-Chief in the desert to consider two options: either he could withdraw to more favorable positions from which to meet the enemy, or he could launch his own attack before the enemy. The commands in Rome and Berlin ordered Rommel not to withdraw under any circumstances. As a result Rommel was forced to go to the attack again.

On August 20 Rommel still needed 16,000 replacement personnel, 210 tanks, 175 armored personnel carriers and armored cars and at least 1,500 vehicles to make his army fully mobile. However, since a major convoy carrying 100,000 tons of the most modern weapons and materiel for the Eighth Army was expected in Suez at the beginning of September, he was forced to act.

It became the end of August. The British forces in the northern sector consisted of the Thirtieth Corps with the Fifth Indian, the Fiftieth British and Ninth Australian Divisions. Behind at the coast in reserve was the First South African Infantry Division.

The southern sector had been assigned to the Thirteenth Corps, with the Seventh Armored Division and the reconnaissance units at the front. The northern part of the southern sector was held by the Second New Zealand Division, and behind the central and southern parts were the British First and Tenth Armored Divisions.

Rommel formulated the intentions of *Panzerarmee Afrika* as follows:

"The offensive group of the *Panzerarmee* is to move into assembly areas in the southern sector observing all security measures. (The offensive group included: the DAK, the Twentieth Italian Corps and the 90th Light Division.)

As part of this action the armored units are to be transferred into the new attack positions over the course of several days and assembled there under cover. The wheeled elements are subsequently to be moved into the assembly area in one go, and their places taken in the rear by assembling the supply columns. Our intentions must be concealed under all circumstances."

German patrols had revealed only weak minefields in the southern part of the El Alamein front. The positions behind them were to be taken at night by Italian and German infantry and then the enemy thrown back by the armored units which would move out at once. Together with elements of the Italian Motorized Corps, the DAK was to "advancing rapidly eastward, reach the area southwest of El Hamman — 50 km from the point of departure — during the night."

"In planning this operation," wrote Rommel, "we reckoned on the customary long reaction time of the British command and troops. We therefore hoped to engage the British before they were fully aware that the operation was under way."

The "Six Day Race"

On August 30 the soldiers of *Panzerarmee Afrika* were surprised by a new Army order of the day:

Panzerarmee Afrika
The Commander-in-Chief
Armee Headquarters, 30. 8. 1942

Army order of the day
Soldiers!
Today the Armee goes to the attack, reinforced with new divisions, to achieve the final destruction of the enemy. I expect that in these decisive days every soldier in my army will do his utmost.

The Commander-in-Chief
signed Rommel
Generalfeldmarschall

At 20.00, after darkness had fallen, the divisions of the DAK rolled off. The 15th Panzer Division arrived in the new sector with 70 tanks, and the 21st PD's strength had risen again to over 120 Panzers.

At first all went well. The leading vehicles of I./PGR 115 under *Major* Busch first came upon the British mine barrier just before midnight. This barrier, which was backed up by artillery, tanks and infantry, proved a serious obstacle. II./PGR 115, which was following close behind First Battalion, attacked across the minefield under the command of *Hauptmann* Weichsel. It captured a bridgehead, enabling the combat engineers to begin clearing a lane through the mines.

The vehicles of the 21st PD reached the mine barrier at nearly the same time. There, too, the British defences opened fire on the Germans, who were plainly visible in the moonlit night.

Accompanying the 21st PD was the commanding general of the DAK, *General der Panzertruppe* Nehring, and his staff. He, too, drove into the minefield. Trucks were blown up and the RAF appeared on the scene. They dropped parachute flares and "Christmas trees," illuminating the battlefield. *Generalmajor* von Bismarck was killed at the head of the 21st PD. *Generalmajor* von Kleemann, commander of the 90th Light Division, was wounded.

When daylight arrived on August 31, 1942 British close-support aircraft dived down on the German attacking forces crawling around the minefields. One of the aircraft spotted the commanding general's armored personnel carrier and bombed it. A bomb exploded close to the front axle. Fragments pierced the armor plate and *General* Nehring collapsed bleeding inside the vehicle. *Oberst* Bayerlein was saved, because the radio equipment took the full force of the shrapnel. *Oberstleutnant* Walter Schmitt, the DAK's supply officer, and *Hauptmann* von Burgsdorff, who had just left the command vehicle, were killed.

Oberst Bayerlein assumed command of the DAK until *Generalmajor* von Vaerst, who was hurrying to the scene on Rommel's orders, could take over. *Oberst* Crasemann once again took command of the 15th PD.

Throughout August 31 the divisions fought on in the midst of the British minefields. Then enemy resistance began to collapse. Rommel's wish, to advance fifty kilometers east that day, had come to nothing. *Oberst* Bayerlein was asked by Rommel if it was advisable to continue the attack. The reached the conclusion that it *must* be, even if the "great solution" planned by Rommel was now out of the question. The *Panzerarmee* would therefore have to turn north sooner than planned.

However, as a result of this early change of direction the divisions of the DAK ran into the strongly fortified ridge at Alam Halfa with the vitally important Hill 132. Unnoticed by German reconnaissance the British Forty-fourth Infantry Division, just arrived from England, had gone into position on this hill. It was backed up by powerful armored forces, the majority of which were dug in.

The attack on the ridge by the 15th and 21st Panzer Divisions began in the midst of a *ghibli* at about 13.00. Initial progress was good; however, the attack by the Italian Twentieth Corps did not begin until 15.00. Rommel drove there from DAK headquarters and urged the Italians to hurry. But at 16.00 the attack had to be called off due to the very low fuel state.

The 15th PD resumed the attack on September 1. British heavy tanks which came out to meet the division's Panzers were knocked out. *Major* Hannes Kümmel and his I./PR 8 managed to push back the enemy and reach an area just south of Hill 132. *Oberstleutnant* Teege, the regimental commander, swore when Kümmel reported that he had been forced to halt for lack of fuel.

Everything now depended on the 21st Panzer Division's 5th Panzer Regiment, which was advancing to the left of PR 8; however, the regiment was halted in front of the strong British defensive positions.

That evening Rommel was forced to call off the attack. Alam Halfa had become the "Stalingrad in the desert." The divisions pulled back to their departure positions.

One of the main factors which led to the suspension of the attack was the loss of 6,000 tons of fuel through the sinking of the majority of the Axis tankers in the Mediterranean.

Meanwhile, Montgomery's plans were bearing fruit. Between Alam Halfa and Bab el Quattara were powerful armored forces of the Eighth Army. General Montgomery had directed them there — and from now on he also directed events near El Alamein, because he was stronger in materiel and possessed greater air forces than *Panzerarmee Afrika*. Also, Montgomery did not risk lightly what he had achieved. The advocate of the risk-free battle of materiel, he did not pursue Rommel; that would have been too uncertain for him. He waited for his chance, which must come soon.

Major Briel as commander of the 200th Panzer Grenadier Regiment (90th Light) near Deir Alinda (Alamein Front) in September 1942.

Recon patrol.

The Great Retreat

The Prelude to El Alamein

In the Alamein position the days passed with the same routine of fortification building, nightly patrols, watch duty and free time. Along the German front near El Alamein the commander of the *Armee* combat engineers, *Oberst* Hecker, had laid a devil's garden of mines between Tel el Eissa in the north and the Quattara Depression in the south. In the sixty kilometers between the two cornerstones of the Axis line stood five Italian infantry divisions and one German, as well as the German 90th Light Division and the 15th and 21st Panzer Divisions. The six infantry divisions were dug in in their field positions, the three fast divisions behind them in reserve. The 21st PD was on the southern wing, while the 15th PD was in position behind the center of the front. *Feldmarschall* Rommel had the 90th Light on the coast road as his mobile reserve.

Each day that passed saw the Eighth Army grow stronger. As hard as *Feldmarschall* Rommel and *Oberst* Bayerlein tried to obtain supplies, they simply were not getting through. The OKW promised speedy help, as did the Duce, but good words were no substitute for tanks.

Feldmarschall Rommel, who had been serving in North Africa for 18 months and was suffering constantly from a throat inflammation and liver disease, now got the opportunity to take a long-overdue rest cure. It was estimated that the enemy would be ready for action again in November. By then he would have completed his cure and returned to Africa.

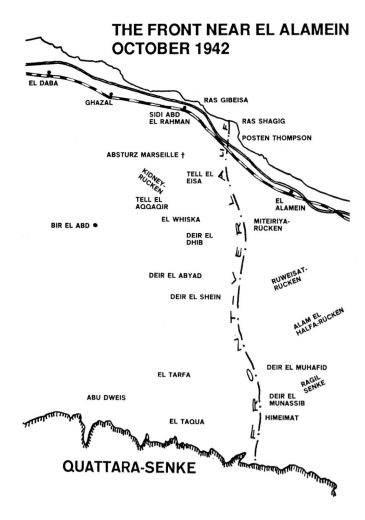

THE FRONT NEAR EL ALAMEIN OCTOBER 1942

EL DABA

GHAZAL

RAS GIBEISA

SIDI ABD EL RAHMAN

RAS SHAGIG

POSTEN THOMPSON

ABSTURZ MARSEILLE †

KIDNEY-RÜCKEN

TELL EL EISA

TELL EL AQQAQIR

EL ALAMEIN

BIR EL ABD

EL WHISKA

MITEIRIYA-RÜCKEN

DEIR EL DHIB

DEIR EL ABYAD

RUWEISAT-RÜCKEN

DEIR EL SHEIN

ALAM EL HALFA-RÜCKEN

DEIR EL MUHAFID

EL TARFA

RAGIL SENKE

DEIR EL MUNASSIB

ABU DWEIS

HIMEIMAT

EL TAQUA

QUATTARA-SENKE

THE SECOND BATTLE OF EL ALAMEIN

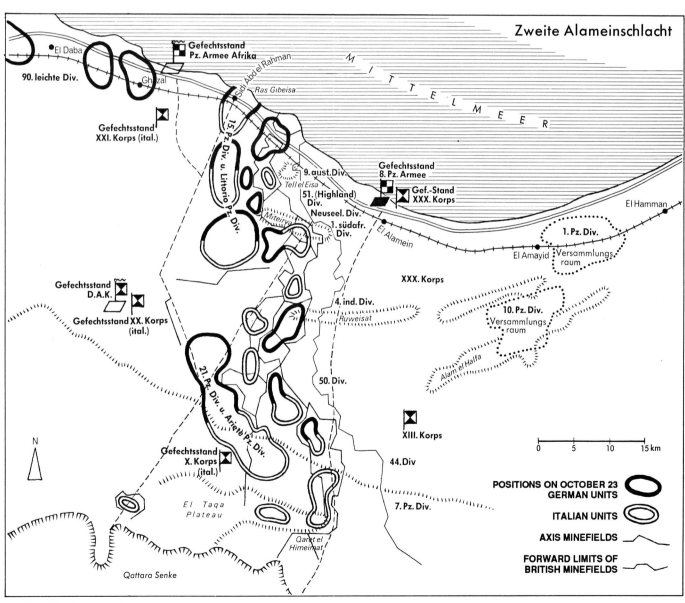

Zweite Alameinschlacht

MITTELMEER

El Daba
90. leichte Div.
Ghazal
Gefechtsstand
Pz. Armee Afrika
Sidi Abd el Rahman
Ras Gibeisa

Gefechtsstand
XXI. Korps (ital.)

15. Pz. Div. u. Litorio Pz. Div.

Tell el Eisa
9. aust. Div.
Gefechtsstand
8. Pz. Armee
Gef.-Stand
XXX. Korps
El Hamman

51. (Highland) Div.
Neuseel. Div.
Miteirya
1. südafr. Div.
El Alamein

1. Pz. Div.
Versammlungsraum
El Amayid

Gefechtsstand
D.A.K.
Gefechtsstand XX. Korps (ital.)

XXX. Korps

4. ind. Div.
Ruweisat

10. Pz. Div.
Versammlungsraum

50. Div.

21. Pz. Div. u. Ariete Pz. Div.

Alam el Halfa

N

Gefechtsstand
X. Korps (ital.)

XIII. Korps

44. Div

El Taqa Plateau

0   5   10   15 km

7. Pz. Div.

Qaret el Himeimat

POSITIONS ON OCTOBER 23 GERMAN UNITS

ITALIAN UNITS

AXIS MINEFIELDS

FORWARD LIMITS OF BRITISH MINEFIELDS

Qattara Senke

aus Ronald Lewin: »Rommel«

On September 19, 1942 Rommel began the flight to Germany. His stand-in, *General* Stumme, had arrived in Africa from Russia. But first Rommel flew to Derna on September 22 and the next day went on to Rome, where he visited the Duce in Forli, on the Adriatic coast.

On September 25 he met with Hitler in the FHQ, where the *Führer* personally presented him with his Field Marshall's baton. He then flew on to Summering, near Vienna, to begin his cure. He was not to complete the cure, however, because on October 23 the storm broke near El Alamein. The British offensive had begun.

The Storm Breaks

The Eighth Army opened its offensive at 20.40 on the evening of October 23, 1942 with a barrage from 1,000 guns. The barrage lasted five hours, then the Ninth Australian and Fifty-first Highlands Divisions stormed forward toward the El Alamein positions, beginning a ten-day battle the like of which the North African campaign had not seen before.

The Eighth Army attacked *Panzerarmee Afrika* with more than 1,000 tanks. At that time the *Armee* had available over 200 German and 300 Italian tanks.

The barrage fire disrupted all communications and at about 01.00 on October 24 British units broke through the front in the sector held by the Italian Sixty-second Infantry Regiment. Two battalions of the 164th Light Division, which had been brought over from Crete in late summer, were also destroyed in the first charge which resulted in a ten-kilometer breach in the Axis main line of resistance.

When morning came and still no reports had reached the headquarters of the *Panzerarmee*, *General* Stumme decided to drive to the front and check the situation.

"*Herr General*," said the acting Chief of Staff of *Panzerarmee Afrika*, *Oberst* Westphal (*Oberst* Bayerlein was on leave), "take your escort car and radio station with you so we can remain in constant touch."

"That will not be necessary, Westphal. I will drive with *Oberst* Büchting to the headquarters of the 90th Light, and under these circumstances I

can dispense with the escort vehicle."

A little later the General drove off. When the two officers reached Hill 28 they were fired on by anti-tank guns and machine-guns. The *Armee* Signals Officer, *Oberst* Büchtig was shot in the head and killed. *General* Stumme suffered a heart attack. Overall command of the *Panzerarmee* was assumed temporarily by *General* Ritter von Thoma. He remained at DAK headquarters.

Oberst Westphal had already sent the first situation report to FHQ. He received a message back from FHQ which requested that he reply within an hour. Hitler wanted to know if this was a large-scale raid or the British offensive. Westphal sent the following message:

"The long awaited British offensive has begun. Return of *Feldmarschall* Rommel necessary!"

At noon on October 24 Rommel received a call in Semmering. On the other end of the line was *Feldmarschall* Keitel. He said:

"The British began offensive operations on the Alamein front last night with strong artillery and bomber support. General Stumme is missing. Are you well enough to return to Africa and assume command?"

"I can and I will!" replied Rommel, and Keitel promised to keep him apprised on the situation.

That evening Hitler also called the Commander-in-Chief of *Panzerarmee Afrika* and asked if he could take off for Africa at once. Rommel replied in the affirmative once again. He ordered his aircraft to be ready at 07.00 on October 25 and immediately drove to Wiener Neustadt. There he received Hitler's second call shortly after midnight. Hitler confirmed that the situation in Africa had become so threatening that he had to ask Rommel to fly to Africa and take command. Rommel noted in his diary:

"I knew that I would win no further laurels in Africa, because I had learned from my officers that the requested minimum level of supply had not come close to being met. But as it soon turned out, I had no idea *how* bad the supply situation was in reality."

When Rommel landed in Rome at about 11.00 *General* Rintelen was waiting there for him and informed him of the latest events in the African Theater.

That evening he arrived at DAK headquarters and *General* Ritter von Thoma and *Oberst* Westphal briefed him on the situation.

The Battle of El Alamein

The units of the Eighth Army continued to attack on the south of the front on October 24. In position there was the 15th Panzer Division under *Generalleutnant* von Vaerst, who had recovered from his wounds in mid-August. He had returned to the division and assumed command with his faithful Ia, General Staff *Oberstleutnant* Heinrich Müller. Battle Group South was led by *Oberst* Teege, the commander of PR 8.

When the Italians there fell back under the overpowering pressure of the British units and the first Grant tanks appeared, 1./PzArtRgt. 33, which had gone into position there, opened fire. The company was directed personally by *Oberleutnant* Orth. The first enemy tank was hit and when the enemy tank spearhead had been brought to a halt *Oberst* Teege committed his I./PR 8 under *Hauptmann* Stiefelmayer. The violent attack by the Panzer battalion drove the enemy into a broad minefield, and within a short time 35 tanks were left shattered and burning there. The rest pulled back. This breakthrough attempt had been foiled.

Montgomery now shifted the focus of his attack to the north. On October 25 the 15th PD repulsed another attack and was left with only 31 tanks; it had destroyed 88 of the enemy's.

Rommel, who had just arrived, concentrated all his mobile forces — with the exception of the 21st PD — in the northern sector for a counterattack. When reconnaissance revealed that Montgomery was moving all of his armored forces in the south to the north, Rommel also moved the 21st PD north. He also pulled half of the artillery units from the south of the front. As a result of this move Rommel succeeded in closing the gaping hole in the northern front at least temporarily.

Early on the morning of October 28 the 21st PD reached the threatened northern sector and immediately attacked past the elements of the 15th PD still holding out there.

Generalmajor von Randow drove at the head of the division with his Ia, General Staff *Major* von Heuduck. Close behind followed the Panzers of PR 5, led by *Oberstleutnant* Mildebrath (*Oberst* gerhard Müller was on leave.)

Oberst Teege joined the attack with his remaining tanks. Heavy artillery fire met the attackers. Nevertheless, they forced their way through and came within firing range of the enemy armor. The Panzers engaged the enemy tanks and forced them back.

In the following days every unit was drawn into the whirlwind of the Battle of El Alamein. The Royal Air Force carried out massed air attacks all day. The new "General Sherman" tank proved superior to the German Panzers.

On the afternoon of October 27 the 90th Light Division undertook a counterattack on the enemy-occupied Hill 28, while the 15th and 21st Panzer Divisions and a battle group from the Italian "*Ariete*" Division set out against the british positions between minefields L and I. The 90th Light failed to take the hill. That evening the DAK was inserted where the infantry divisions had suffered heavy losses and could no longer hold on alone.

During the night of October 28/29 and the next morning the 125th Grenadier Regiment of the 164th Light Division was smashed. The remnants were able to withdraw under cover of a relief attack by the 90th Light Division or fight their way through to neighboring units.

At 07.00 that day *Oberst* Bayerlein returned from leave. Following a short briefing and discussion with *Feldmarschall* Rommel he immediately made his way to the DAK where he was urgently needed.

The British regrouped on October 29. It looked as if the expected offensive was not going to take place that day. However, just as *Feldmarschall* Rommel was discussing the Fuka Plan — the defence of the Fuka position — with *Oberst* Westphal, a report arrived that the enemy had broken through the Quattara Depression with two divisions. However, this report turned out to be a hoax. The Fuka position was reconnoitered that same day.

October 30 passed with lasting skirmishes and small battles all along the front. The 21st PD was pulled out of the front during the night of October 30/31 to act as a mobile fire-brigade to clear up any penetrations. The "*Trieste*" Division was to take its place in the line.

During this reorganization the British opened up on GR 125 in the northern sector with heavy artillery. Soon afterward the Australian Ninth Division launched an attack into GR 125's flank from the southeast. At the same time powerful British armored forces drove northward from the area north of Hill 28 and soon had more than 30 tanks on the coast road. There they encountered GR 361 which was manning the second line of defence. Once again the veteran Albert Panzenhagen, who had meanwhile been promoted to the rank of *Oberst*, was in the center of a defensive battle. He stopped the breakthrough and put out of action the tanks which had broken through. His action gave Rommel time to organize a counterattack, initially with AA 33, later joined by the 21. PD which was engaged in withdrawing from the front line.

Feldmarschall Rommel drove to Sidi Abd el Rahman and set up his headquarters east of the mosque there. At about 10.00 *General* von Thoma and *Oberst* Bayerlein arrived and Rommel assigned von Thoma to lead the counterattack, which was to be carried out by the relieved units of the 21st PD and elements of the 90th Light. The attack was to be preceded by a Stuka attack and a massed artillery barrage.

The attack began at 12.00. It was stopped by the concentrated fire of the enemy, by bombing attacks as well as infantry and armored forces. Nevertheless, following heavy fighting the counterattack did succeed in establishing contact with GR 125. The two surrounded battalions were relieved the next day when a fresh attack led by *General* von Thoma threw the enemy back to the south across the railway line.

Early on the morning of November 1, 1942 *Feldmarschall* Rommel stood on Hill 16 with *General* Ritter von Thoma, *Generalmajor* Graf Sponeck, who had commanded the 90th Light Division since September 2, and *Oberst* Bayerlein. From there they could survey the scene of the past two days' fighting with the train station buildings and could see seven knocked-out enemy tanks at the station and an estimated 40 more in the vicinity.

A red and white flag fluttered over the station and the German artillery had ceased firing while the British recovered their wounded.

By now the enemy had committed several divisions and still had more than 800 tanks. These were now assembled opposite the *Panzerarmee*'s northern sector for the decisive attack.

Facing this armored phalanx were 90 German and 140 Italian tanks. Rome was still optimistic, however, as a radio message which reached *Armee* headquarters on the evening of November 1 showed:

"For *Feldmarschall* Rommel.
The Duce has asked me to express to you his deep appreciation for the successful counterattacks personally led by you. What is more the Duce has expressed that he is fully confident that under your command the battle which is under way will be brought to a victorious conclusion.

Ugo Cavallero."

This was a total misjudgment of the facts. The British attack began during the night of November 1-2. Every available division went to the attack after a three-hour artillery barrage, supported by bombing attacks. GR 200, which was in position on both sides of Hill 28, was overwhelmed and destroyed. Tanks and armored cars broke through to the west. This attack was finally halted when the reserves of the 90th Light were committed.

A short time later massed British units breached the front of the 15th PD southwest of Hill 28. 400 enemy tanks plunged through the gap smashed in the front. Driving west, by dawn on November 2 they had reached the telegraph road. Reports by forward artillery observers indicated that a further 400 tanks were still waiting east of the minefields.

The DAK launched a counterattack early on the morning of November 2. The 15th and 21st Panzer Divisions achieved initial success, at the cost of many tanks, however. Nevertheless, the German divisions did manage to seal off the 4-kilometer-wide penetration into which the enemy had sent 15 artillery regiments on the heels of his tanks. This was achieved by the German artillery and Flak opening up with a desperate rapid fire in spite of their low ammunition states.

The 21st PD was committed from the north and the 15th PD from the south against the British spearhead, resulting in a tank-versus-tank engagement. The Panzer crews fought with the courage of desperation.

When evening fell on this costly day, reconnaissance reported that the second wave of enemy tanks had moved forward in to ready positions. The DAK now had a total of 35 tanks. The moment to withdraw to the Fuka position had come. The strength of *Panzerarmee Afrika* had been exhausted by the ten-day battle. November 3 dawned. It was to be the decisive day.

That morning *Feldmarschall* Rommel ordered the withdrawal. As *Oberst* Westphal was eating lunch a *Führerbefehl* (order direct from Hitler) came in. The order arrived just as Rommel drove up in his command vehicle. Westphal handed Rommel the brief message which read:

"Win or die!"

The order arrived at the moment when Rommel was awaiting a reply to the sending of an executive officer — *Hauptmann* Berndt — to FHQ. Berndt, whom Hitler knew well, was to try and obtain full freedom of action for *Panzerarmee Afrika*.

Was this Hitler's reply?

"This message could not have been written with a knowledge of our situation report, *Herr Feldmarschall*," said Westphal suspiciously. He sensed what Hitler had in mind, and expressed this clearly to Rommel when he continued, "it's nothing more than a shot in the arm, *Herr Feldmarschall*. Who knows how many days ago this decree was written."

Rommel hesitated. On the evening of November 3, 1942 he issued the order Hitler expected:

"Fight to the last round!"

The next morning *Feldmarschall* Albert Kesselring, the Commander-in-Chief South, arrived at the headquarters of the *Panzerarmee*. Following a discussion with Rommel and Westphal he agreed that Hitler's order was impracticable.

Rommel and Kesselring reported this to the OKW and asked for a withdrawal of the *Führerbefehl*. Rommel then drove to DAK headquarters and on his own ordered a withdrawal to the Fuka line. The remaining corps and divisions of the DAK received orders to withdraw by radio.

Early on the morning of November 4, while Rommel was still having discussions with Kesselring, the DAK's 90th Light Division was holding a weak front line on both sides of the low, but nevertheless commanding sand dunes of Tel el Mampsra. *Generalleutnant* Ritter von Thoma, the DAK's commanding general, took his leave of *Oberst* Bayerlein, who was to drive to El Daba and set up a new corps headquarters there. As he left he said to the staff officer:

"Bayerlein, this *Führerbefehl* is madness. It's a death sentence for the army. How am I to advocate *that* to my soldiers?"

The high-ranking officer, who had been wounded twenty times in the First World War,

turned to Bayerlein once again and said, "go to El Daba, I'm going to stay here and personally take over the defence of Tel el Mampsra."

Oberst Fritz Bayerlein drove to El Daba. He had just finished setting up a provisional headquarters when, at about 11.00, *Oberleutnant* Hartdegen, *Generalleutnant* von Thoma's executive officer, arrived and reported to the chief of staff:

"Our tanks, flak and anti-aircraft guns of the combat echelon on the Tel el Mampsra have been destroyed, *Herr Oberst!*"

Oberst Bayerlein jumped into his scout car and drove off toward the east. When he was fired on by enemy tanks he got out and continued on foot. He reached the edge of the dunes and climbed up. Before him was scene of devastation. Burning and shot-up tanks, wrecked anti-tank and anti-aircraft guns and dead —many, many dead.

Then he found *Generalleutnant* von Thoma. He was standing in the open about 2000 meters ahead, as if he were waiting for a bullet to end it all. But the enemy abruptly ceased fire and Thoma was taken prisoner. Bayerlein drove back to El Daba. Rommel arrived soon afterward. The Chief of Staff reported and finally Rommel said:

"Our front is broken, Bayerlein. We'll pull back to the Fuka position to save what we can." After a brief pause Rommel added:

"Bayerlein, I'm handing command of the DAK over to you. You know what that means. If we're brought before a court martial for insubordination we'll have to answer for our decision. Do everything correctly. All orders you give the DAK are given in my name. Tell this to the senior commanders in case you should have difficulties."

"I will do my best, *Herr Feldmarschall*," replied Bayerlein following a few seconds of silence.

The withdrawal began. The *"Ariete"* Division's final radio message arrived during the initial stages of the withdrawal:

"Enemy tanks have penetrated south of 'Ariete,' and 'Ariete' is now surrounded. Situated about 5 km northwest of Bir el Abd. Tanks of 'Ariete' are fighting."

By the evening of that day the tanks of the Italian Twentieth Motorized Corps had been destroyed and the enemy had smashed a breach in the defensive front twenty kilometers wide.

During the battle at El Alamein the Luftwaffe flew as many as 180 missions per day. This was not enough, however, because the Royal Air Force was able to fly about 800 bomber and 2,500 fighter sorties daily at the high point of the battle. The few remaining Stukas supported the ground troops, but it was not enough to prevail in a battle of materiel such as the one General Montgomery was directing.

The withdrawal into the Fuka position took place during the night of November 4/5 on a wide front. The retreat was a race with the British tanks and night bombers, which illuminated the roads with flares and bombed everything they could see.

The road to Fuka was 100 kilometers long. The *Panzerarmee* staff, which had set off just before darkness, strayed from the road several times and became stuck. When this happened everyone had to get out and push the vehicle free. Nevertheless, by early morning on November 5 they had reached the barbwire barricades at the Fuka airfield. On November 5 the main body of the DAK, the 90th Light Division and elements of the Italian Twentieth Corps reached Fuka. The DAK rearguards fought desperately against the pursuing British, who were following close behind the retreating Axis forces with 200 tanks and 200 armored personnel carriers.

When midday came the rest of the DAK and the soldiers of the 90th Light were battling the enemy tanks. When a British armored column drove through a sand storm and approached the open German southern flank Rommel was forced to continue the withdrawal. Soon afterward the headquarters of the *Panzerarmee* was subjected by a heavy bombing attack which was followed by a second, equally heavy attack. Rommel cowered in a foxhole with his Chief of the General Staff, *Oberst* Westphal. When Sherman tanks broke through the thin front held by the 15th and 21st Panzer Divisions, Rommel had to pull back to Marsa Matruk, even though not all of his units had yet got back.

One of these non-motorized units in the southern sector was *Fallschirmbrigade* Ramcke. Its experiences are representative of those of the other, similar units.

Battles and Retreat by Fallschirmbrigade Ramcke

On the evening of July 22, 1942 *Generalmajor* Ramcke had received orders to take his newly-formed parachute brigade to Africa.

A few days later he was standing before *Feldmarschall* Rommel, reporting his brigade present with 2,000 men and an artillery and anti-tank battalion on the way. The brigade was deployed in the area of Fort Bab el Quattara. It was there that the paratroops endured the miseries of the African summer — the burning sun, sand storms and myriads of flies. They were engaged in nightly offensive patrols against the Indian and Malayan troops in position opposite them.

On August 30 the brigade, which had been transferred to the north of the Alamein position, went to the attack. Together with Italian units it was to tie down the enemy until the DAK could complete its enveloping movement and encircle the enemy forces.

In the following days the paratroops fought shoulder to shoulder with the 164th Light Division and reached the objective of Deir el Munassib. The enemy struck back on the evening of September 3. The One-hundred-and-Thirty-second Armoured Brigade attempted to break through the paratroops' front. Sixteen tanks and 80 personnel carriers were destroyed by the paratroops. Among the prisoners taken was Major General Clifton, the British brigade's commander.

When the enemy began his offensive on the evening of October 23, 250 bombs hammered the Quattara defensive works alone. The parachute brigade, reinforced by the Italian *"Folgore"* Parachute Division, lay ready in its defensive positions. However, the attack came in the north and not against them.

The probing enemy forces were turned back. On November 2 a radio message arrived from the *Panzerarmee* instructing the brigade to disengage and occupy new positions between Duweir el Tarfa and the Deir el Quatani mine belt. This meant a foot march of 30 kilometers, as the brigade was not motorized. The journey was completed on foot and the new position was reached on the morning of November 3. That evening new orders arrived instructing the brigade to regroup to the north. A battalion under *Hauptmann* Straehler-Pohl set off in the 40 available trucks. They had just disappeared when yet another order arrived. The brigade was to pull back and occupy new positions west of Fuka.

The new positions were 100 kilometers as the

crow flies and would mean a full four day's march through the desert under constant air attack for the paratroops. The brigade would be wiped out. However, Ramcke did not give up.

The enemy attacked as the brigade moved out. The anti-tank battalion, which had been left behind as a rearguard, knocked out the pursuing enemy tanks. Then it, too, rolled westward.

A rest was called at an hour past midnight. *Generalmajor* Ramcke drove ahead to reconnoiter with *Major* Kroh, *Major* Fenski and *Oberleutnant* Wetter. On a plateau they ran into a British armored regiment. Fleeing at high speed, they managed to escape. Ramcke directed his brigade south, into the desert.

The next morning the brigade was discovered by patrolling British aircraft. Within an hour tanks were on the way. Once again the anti-tank guns stayed behind and destroyed all of the British tanks save one. Nevertheless, the enemy continued to attack. The brigade's route was marked by a trail of knocked-out British tanks. By evening the anti-tank guns were out of ammunition and the crews were forced to spike their guns. Then they made their way back to the brigade.

During the night of November 4/5 brigade units came upon a long British vehicle column which included tanks. Bernhard Hermann Ramcke saw his chance.

The paratroops snuck toward the column in small groups. All at once they made their move. The British were taken completely by surprise. The trucks were found to contain food, weapons and ammunition. Its former owners were put out and the column continued on its way.

The brigade met up with a German reconnaissance battalion on the morning of November 7. *Generalmajor* Ramcke arrived in time to attend a *Panzerarmee* briefing in which the parachute brigade had just been written off.

"We're not finished yet!" declared the small, iron-hard man. On November 16, 1942 Ramcke was awarded the Oak Leaves to the Knight's Cross.

The Retreat Continues - The Allied Invasion

On the morning of November 6, 1942 the staff of the *Panzerarmee* added up the cost of the El Alamein battle. The Italian Twentieth Army Corps had largely been destroyed, while the Italian Tenth Corps was retreating southeast of Fuka with only limited supplies of water and ammunition. The Twenty-first Corps had likewise been destroyed or was in retreat.

The 90th Light Division had been decimated. Its fighting strength was limited, as was that of the divisions of the DAK which had been reduced to battle groups. *Panzergrenadier-Regiment Afrika*, several hastily-assembled battle groups and elements of the 164th Light Division were still intact.

After the vehicles had been assembled the tactical operations staff and the remaining staffs of the *Panzerarmee* drove through the mined southern zone into the area east of Marsa Matruk. There they set up *Armee* headquarters.

The 15th Panzer Division and the 90th Light Division reached the area southwest of Marsa Matruk which they had been ordered to defend. As a result of a fuel shortage the 21st PD was forced to assume an all-round defensive position southwest of Quasaba. There it was attacked by a British armored brigade with 60 tanks. The division was just able to hold off the attacking British. Suddenly *Kampfgruppe* Voss, which had been left behind in Fuka as a rearguard unit and had been bypassed by the British tank force, approached from the east. *Hauptmann* Voss, Rommel's former executive officer and now commander of AA 580, attacked the British armored brigade from the rear and inflicted heavy losses on it.

In the battle with the British Twenty-second Armoured brigade the 21st PD had lost 16 tanks. At noon a further ten had to be blown up for lack of fuel and the crews made their way west in the division's wheeled vehicles. By the evening of November 6 the 21st PD had four tanks left.

The new army headquarters was to be located in Sidi Barani. When enemy tanks bypassed Marsa Matruk to the south, the *Panzerarmee* was forced to withdraw to Sidi Barani. The 90th Light formed the rearguard. Once again the Panzer Grenadiers of PGR 361 under *Oberst* Panzenhagen were involved in bitter fighting. By the time the enemy turned north to trap the *Panzerarmee* on the night of November 1 Rommel had already withdrawn his units.

In the morning *Feldmarschall* Rommel heard the first reports of the Anglo-American landings in West Africa. In the headquarters of the DAK he met *Oberst* Bayerlein and informed him of the events. Then he said what Bayerlein was already thinking:

"The campaign is lost, Bayerlein. Africa is lost. If they don't recognize this in time in Rome and Rastenburg and take measures to save my soldiers, then one of the bravest German armies will be captured. Then who will defend Italy against invasion?"

During those hours the fleeing units of *Panzer-armee Afrika* were moving through the passes near Halfaya and Sollum. The *Panzerarmee* was to halt in the Sollum position and hold off the approach of several hundred enemy tanks.

In the meantime the full extent of the landings in West Africa, near Casablanca, Oran and Algiers, had become known, and Rommel asked *Feldmarschall* Kesselring and Marshall Cavallero to come to Africa. He noted in his diary:

"I wanted to ask them for a precise report as to whether it was possible to hold Tunisia and nevertheless supply and refit my army in the Marsa el Brega position. However, neither Marshall Cavallero nor *Feldmarschall* Kesselring felt it was necessary to come to Africa. I therefore decided to send *Hauptmann* Berndt to FHQ the next day and have him present our situation there.

When Berndt returned a few days later, he told me that he had met with little sympathy. The *Führer* had him tell me not to be concerned with Tunisia and simply accept that the bridgehead would be held."

While the largest invasion to that time was taking place in West Africa, the Eighth Army had already begun its pursuit south of Sidi Omar, assigning an armored division the task. Rommel withdrew the *Panzerarmee* toward Tobruk. Tobruk was to be held until the 10,000 tons of materiel stored there could be removed.

But what was going on in Tunisia in the rapidly forming German bridgehead?

Oberst Ewert, left.

The Invasion in West Africa

The Prehistory of "Torch" - Planning in London - German Speculations

On June 23, 1942 Lieutenant General Dwight D. Eisenhower and Major General Mark Clark took off from Washington. Their destination was London.

Immediately after landing General Eisenhower assumed command of all American troops in Europe. A few days later the press in England and the USA publicized the Soviet wish for a second front. It was still too early, however. The only American forces in Great Britain at that time were the 34th US Infantry Division and the 1st US Armored Division in England and several units of the USAAF in Northern Ireland.

In joint discussions the Allies came to the conclusion that the Soviets would not be able to hold out without the second front they were so urgently demanding.

President Roosevelt gave the American Chiefs of Staff the assignment of undertaking a landing operation somewhere in the European Theater in 1942.

By July 24 they were in agreement. The objective of the first attack would be the occupation of Northwest Africa by a force combining all elements of the Allied armed forces. For tactical reasons the force was to be led by an American. The operation was code-named "Torch."

The occupation of Tunisia would relieve the pressure on Malta once and for all. What was more, from there the Allies would be able to interdict the supply lines to *Panzerarmee Afrika* by land, sea and air.

Casablanca was chosen as the target for one landing group because a railway line led from there through Oran and Algiers to Tunisia. The railway line was important as a supply route. Oran and Algiers were to be the two other objectives. Both were major seaports. Allied bomber and fighter units would be able to use the airfields around Oran. It was hoped that the landings could be carried out unopposed.

The troops for Casablanca were to come direct from the United States. Major General Patton was given command of this group of forces. The central group of forces — the US II Corps — was under the command of Major General Fredenhall.

The Algiers battle group was to be led by Major General Ryder. Immediately following the capture of Algiers, however, General Anderson, the Commander-in-Chief of the British First Army, was to assume command of this most important group of forces. Its task was to advance to Tunis with its motorized units as quickly as possible and occupy the city.

Advance convoys sailed from England for Gibraltar in early October. Four major convoys carrying attack forces followed in the period October 22 — November 1, 1942. The warships, on the other hand, a total of 160 ships, did not leave Scapa Flow until the end of October.

On November 4 those in Rome decided that the operation in progress might involve a landing in North Africa. On November 6 Mussolini was convinced that the Allied forces could *only* be heading for North Africa.

The American convoys, consisting of a total of 102 warships, transports and freighters, were designated Task Force 34, which was under the command of Rear Admiral H.K. Hewitt. The first ships began weighing anchor from Casco Bay, Maine, on the morning of 23 October. They carried the troops for the landings at Safi and Mehdia. The second convoy sailed the next morning. It was bound for Fedala. The warship group left Casco Bay the same day to rendezvous with the first convoy on October 26. The air escort group sailed on October 28. Leading the way was the aircraft carrier "Ranger," followed by the escort carriers "Suwannee," "Sangamon," "Santee" and "Chenango."

The American force detailed to land at Casablanca was divided into four landing groups, and it was escorted by a naval group comprising the battleships "Massachusetts," "New York" and "Texas," the five aircraft carriers, seven cruisers and a number of destroyers and minesweepers.

On November 5 General Eisenhower and his entire staff flew to Gibraltar aboard five Flying Fortresses. On arrival he was welcomed by Governor General Sir F.N. Mason-MacFarlane.

The first reports of the approach of a large-scale enemy operation reached FdU-Italy on the morning of November 6. Two hours later, at about midday, *Konteradmiral* Kreisch received a radio message from *Führer* Headquarters:

"The fate of the Africa army depends on the smashing of Gibraltar convoys. Expect bold and victorious action. — Adolf Hitler."

On the evening of November 6 these convoys reached the coastal waters of West Africa. *Konteradmiral* Kreisch immediately dispatched all available U-boats, which was only a few, in the direction of the convoys.

The Landings

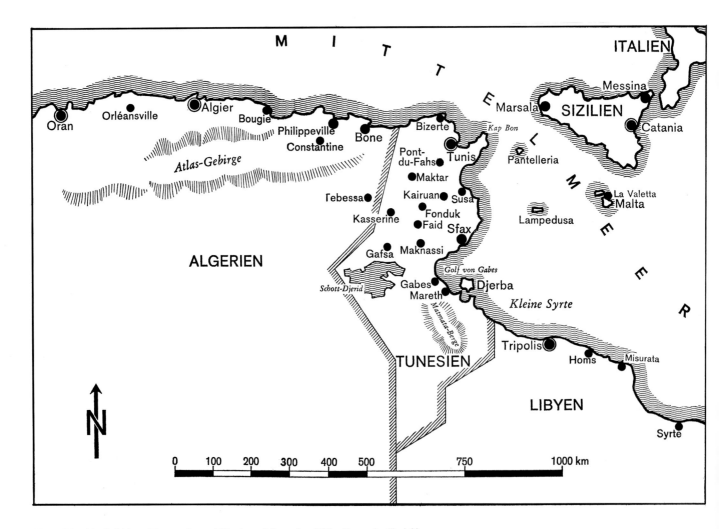

Map of the North African Theater from, *Ritterkreuzträger des Afrika-Korps*, by Karl Alman.

Oran, Casablanca, Algiers - Hitler's Reaction

At 04.00 on November 8, 1942 the signal "play ball" was given to the southern attack group of Western Task Force 43. The attack on the northwest African coast near Safi had begun. There, as at all the other landing sites, the French forces offered resistance, which was not broken until November 9. All of the landing contingents made it ashore.

The first optimistic reports reached Allied headquarters during the night of November 8/9 and the following morning. The landings near Algiers had gone without a hitch. Only token resistance was offered, because General Mast, who was commanding the French Army units there, had already been influenced by Ambassador Murphy. Moreover General Alphonse Pierre Juin, the French commander in Algiers, sympathized with the Allies.

The landings near Oran were more difficult. The assault troops got ashore but French Marines continued to resist after the landings. It was here that the 1st US Infantry Division received its baptism of fire. The infantry was supported by elements of the 1st Armored Division — Battle Group B under Colonel, later Brigadier General Robinett — which had landed in two groups east and west of Oran. The fighting was not over until November 10.

News of the imminent Allied landings reached Hitler during the night of November 7/8, 1942 at a train station in Thuringia. He and his inner circle were on their way from the *"Wolfsschanze"* to Munich where he was to make his traditional speech in the Bürgerbräukeller on the evening of November 8.

In a brief discussion with his advisors Hitler brushed off suggestions of evacuating Africa. One thing was certain: giving up Africa meant giving up the Mediterranean. This would leave the entire Mediterranean Theater in the hands of the Allies by the end of 1942. The loss of prestige was unthinkable. Such a setback would strike Italian resistance to the core. What was more, such a move would give the Allies the freedom to assume the strategic initiative.

The wire to Rom, to the *Oberbefehlshaber Süd*, *Generalfeldmarschall* Kesselring, began to glow. It was Hitler who put the decisive question to the Field Marshall:

"Kesselring, what troops can you throw into Africa?"

"Two battalions of *Fallschirmjäger-Regiment* 5 and my headquarters company, *mein Führer!*"

"Good! Send across what you have on hand," was Hitler's order to the Field Marshal. It was now up to him to prevent the enemy from breaking through from Algiers to Tunis.

At 06.30 on November 8, 1942 Admiral Dönitz, the commander of the German U-boat arm, received the following information by telephone from Navy headquarters:

"The Americans have landed on the Moroccan coast!"

Without waiting for further orders the BdU sent every available U-boat in position between the Bay of Biscay and the Cape Verde Islands toward the Moroccan coast. Following a discussion with the Skl all submarines operating in the North Atlantic were redirected to the Gibraltar area.

In the following days the U-boats U 515 (Henke), U 130 (Kals), U 155 (Pienig), U 173 (Schweichel), U 92 (Oelrich) and U 263 (Nölke) scored successes against the Allied invasion fleet. This series of sinkings west of Gibraltar ended on November 20.

The few boats which had left Mediterranean bases and joined the battle also scored some successes, but were unable to interfere with the landings.

U 605, which was patrolling off Algiers, was sunk on November 7 by the British corvettes "Lotus" and "Poppy." A few days later U 660 suffered the same fate when it was sunk off Oran by "Lotus" and the corvette "Starwort." On November 14 U 595 was sent to the bottom by an air attack northeast of Oran. With the loss of U 331 (on 17. 11.) and U 411 (on 28. 11.) a large part of the operational Mediterranean U-boat fleet had been sunk off the Northwest African coast.

Deliberations by OB-Süd - General Nehring Goes to Tunis

Before the Allied landings an avalanche of contradictory rumors had been flowing into the headquarters of the *Oberbefehlshaber Süd*, *Feldmarschall* Kesselring, in Frascati, near Rome. *Feldmarschall* Kesselring strove to keep informed of the enemy's latest movements.

He devised his countermeasures. One of these was a strengthening of *Luftflotte* 2. Reconnaissance activity was doubled. In addition the *Feldmarschall* asked the OKW to move at least one division to Sicily. Wherever the Allies landed this division would be in a position to intervene quickly. It could be sent across to Tunis or counter an Allied landing on Sicily. The request was approved by the OKW.

All that was left the *Feldmarschall* was his Guard Battalion and, from the beginning of November, the first elements of the 5th Parachute Regiment. The regiment had originally been intended for Rommel's *Panzerarmee*, but was sent to Italy instead.

On November 9 — 24 hours after the initial landings — Hitler personally called Kesselring and gave him a free hand in Tunisia. He forbid him, however, to go to Tunisia himself. The Wehrmacht command staff received approval from Marshal Pétain for the landing of German troops.

The first German troops — the paratroops and elements of the Guard Battalion — landed in Tunis on November 11. A few fighters and Stukas were sent over at the same time.

It was clear to the OB-Süd that strong German forces would have to be committed against the enemy in Tunisia as quickly as possible. If this was not done they faced the total loss of the German-Italian *Panzerarmee Afrika*. In the face of unhindered cooperation between the landing forces and the British Eighth Army in the east, as well as the unchallenged Allied command of the sea, there would be little chance of extracting the members of *Panzerarmee Afrika* from the trap. The only way would be by air and that would mean the loss of all the army's equipment.

The German tactical demands were drawn up in the face of these alternatives. They were as follows:

Delay the Allied landing operations. Secure Tunis and deploy German troops as far to the south and west as possible for the creation of a Tunisian bridgehead.

On November 9, 1942 *General der Panzertruppe* Walther K. Nehring received a call from Berlin. The General, who was in hospital in Wunsdorf recovering from the wounds he had received on August 31 at the beginning of Rommel's advance on the Nile Delta, picked up the receiver. On the other end of the line was *Generalmajor* Gause,

Chief of Staff of *Panzerarmee Afrika*.

Gause requested that Nehring come to Berlin for an urgent discussion in his apartment. Gause was home in Germany on sick leave. Taking part in the discussion besides the two generals was Rommel's executive officer, Reserve *Hauptmann* Ingemar Berndt.

Generalmajor Gause asked Nehring whether he was able and willing to take over the expansion of the positions near Marsa el Brega, where the retreating *Panzerarmee Afrika* was going to halt. *Hauptmann* Berndt was to take Nehring's answer to Africa while he, Gause, would notify the OKW.

Under the pressure of the situation the General immediately decided to reply in the affirmative at once. Despite his only partially healed arm wound the General flew to Rome on November 11. In Rome an order reached Nehring instructing him to divert to Tunis at once and take over command there. The General was taken completely by surprise. Before flying to Tunis he was to report to the *Oberfehlshaber Süd* in Frascati.

Feldmarschall Kesselring himself informed Nehring of his assignment and stressed the difficulty and urgency of the situation. *General* Nehring took the following order with him from Frascati:

"It is vital to advance far to the west in order to have freedom of movement. A line approximately along the Tunisian-Algerian border is desirable. The OKW and I hope that you will succeed in mastering Assignment 'Tunis.'

It is true that there are few German troops there. The XC. *Armeekorps* staff will be assembled for you. Until this is done you will have to manage as best you can. A chief of staff is not yet available, however we have found a Ia, General Staff *Major* Moll."

This conversation took place in Frascati on November 13.

German and Italian Troops for Tunisia - Landings and Surprise Moves - Dealings with the French - Unopposed Advance to Medjez el Bab

On November 8, the day of the Allied landings in

North Africa, the Sauer Parachute Company was formed in Athens from the remnants of the 27 companies and batteries of the Ramcke Parachute Brigade. Commanded by *Hauptmann* Paul Sauer, the company was flown via Brindisi and Catania to Tunis. It arrived on November 10, the first German unit in Tunisia. The company, which was brought up to strength and eventually became a battle group, was under the direct command of the *Fliegerführer Tunesien, Oberst* Harlinghausen. The latter gave Sauer the task of securing the airfields at La Marsa and El Aouina for the landings of the following paratroops.

Hauptmann Sauer and his battle group took over the Tunisia-South security sector during the night of November 13/14 and occupied the entire city of Tunis on the morning of the 14th. In the days that followed the battle group received a steady flow of reinforcements from the Italian division "*Superga.*"

The first company of the Tunisian Field Battalion, which was in Athens waiting to be sent to *Feldmarschall* Rommel, landed at Bizerta airfield on November 11. The company, which was led by *Oberleutnant* Wolff, was reinforced by the Arent Pionier Platoon from FJR 5.

The 5th Parachute Regiment, which had been formed in May 1942 under *Oberstleutnant* Koch, was stationed in France. With news of the invasion the unit was placed on alert and sent by rail to Caserta, where the unit's Third Battalion arrived on the evening of November 10.

An advance party was formed while the unit was still being unloaded and was flown to El Aouina on November 11 under the command of *Leutnant* Baltinger. German fighter aircraft and anti-aircraft guns were already there.

Baltinger received orders to push through to Tunis with the men of 10./FJR 5 and secure the arterial road to the west. The order was carried out.

The next elements of the regiment flown to Tunisia as part of the advance detachment were 3./FJR 5 under *Hauptmann* Langbein and 9./FJR 5 under *Hauptmann* Becker. They landed at El Aouina early on the morning of November 12. *Oberst* Harlinghausen deployed the units to secure La Marsa airfield.

Thus the German troops for Tunisia arrived in North Africa piecemeal, in company strength, while the highly mobile and heavily-armed mass of 100,000 Anglo-American troops drove cross-country toward Tunis.

The next German units, which arrived on November 13, were 10./FJR 5 under *Oberleutnant* Jahn and part of 12./FJR 5 under the battalion commander, *Hauptmann* Knoche. That day *Oberst* Harlinghausen held discussions with *Hauptleuten* Knoche, Sauer and Becker. Security sectors were assigned. These were allocated as follows:

> *Gruppe* Schirmer: Tunis-West sector
> *Gruppe* Sauer: Tunis-South sector

When the remaining elements of *Hauptmann* Knoche's III./FJR 5 were flown over on November 14 and 15 they were sent to Security Sector West.

Beginning November 15 the soldiers of I./FJR 5 under the command of *Hauptmann* Jungwirt began arriving at La Marsa airfield. The regimental headquarters arrived on November 16 with *Oberstleutnant* Walter Koch, Regimental Medical Officer Dr. Weizel and Signals Officer *Hauptmann* Graubartz in the lead aircraft.

On November 16 the Becker Company marched to Djedeida to secure the Medjerda Bridge there.

On November 14 *General* Nehring had landed at La Marsa for his initial inspection accompanied by his Ia, *Major* Moll, *major* Hinkelbein and his aide *Leutnant* Sell. Nehring subsequently flew on to Bizerta and instructed the *Oberst* in command there to send his troops west and reconnoiter in the direction of Bône.

He then flew back to the mainland and reported to the OB-Süd in Frascati. He described the situation in Tunisia and stated the following demands:

"(a) Formation of Corps Headquarters XC. Army Corps.

(b) Delivery of signals equipment.

(c) Soonest possible arrival of self-contained, battle-ready units with commanders and staffs."

The Tunisian bridgehead demanded by *General* Nehring was vitally important for several reasons:

1. It was a moral support for the withdrawing *Panzerarmee Afrika*, which would know that its rear was secure.

2. The bridgehead provided a vital supply base for Rommel's withdrawal.

3. The sudden occupation of Tunis eliminated significant elements of the French occupation force and denied the enemy the two major air and seaports of Bizerta and Tunis and held the latter

open for *Panzerarmee Afrika*.

4. The Tunisian bridgehead was a standing threat to the Allied landing forces which must influence their actions. If they attacked the Bizerta-Tunis Line to eliminate the threat, then nothing would happen to *Panzerarmee Afrika*. If they took the shortest route to Rommel's army, the forces in the bridgehead would pose a threat to their flank.

If the Allies attempted to carry out both moves simultaneously, which would be the most dangerous for the German command, and the most correct for the enemy, they would have to divide their strength and send considerable forces in each direction.

The result of these considerations for both parties was the "race to Tunis."

November 16, the day that saw the arrival of the last of the 5th Parachute Regiment's units, saw *General* Nehring land in Tunis as the Commanding General of XC. *Armeekorps*. The same day the Wehrmacht communiqué reported:

"German and Italian troops have landed in Tunis with the complete approval of the French President and the military authorities."

On November 16 the Corps Headquarters of the XC. AK had at its disposal the following units:
1. 5th Parachute Regiment, *Oberstleutnant* Koch
2. Corps Parachute Engineer Battalion, *Major* Witzig
3. a German replacement training battalion
4. a battery of 88mm Flak with four guns
5. an armored car company, *Oberleutnant* Kahle
6. an Italian Admiral with 2 battalions of Marine Infantry in the Bizerta area
7. two battalions of the Italian "Superga" Division in the Pont du Fahs area. At that time the entire command staff of the XC. AK consisted of the Commanding General, Nehring, *Major* Moll as Ia, Luftwaffe General Staff *Major* Hinkelbein and *Oberleutnant* Sell as aide.

Major von Seubert arrived a few days later as adjutant and *Oberleutnant* Theil as O1. The man named as Chief of the Corps Staff, *Oberst* Pomtow, was still acting as Ia of a Panzer Division in the Caucasus. He did not arrive in Tunisia until the end of November.

Oberstleutnant Broccoli served as liaison officer between the Italian forces and XC. AK.

General Nehring faced a difficult task. He had received the following instructions from the OB-Süd:

"Immediate advance to the Algerian-Tunisian border. Reach the country's western slope in order to create better defensive possibilities and a deep bridgehead."

The Initial Battles

The units spearheading the advance by the Seventy-eighth Infantry Division, which had been ordered by General Anderson, Commander-in-Chief of the British First Army, to advance on Bizerta, ran into the *Fallschirmpioniere* under *Major* Witzig at the Djebel Abiod, east of Abiod.

The paratroops were dug in on the hills alongside and east of the road and held off the British, who gradually threw the entire division into the battle, for 48 hours. Contributing to this defensive success were the heavy weapons of the Italian "Superga" Division, which had sent a battalion to help out.

The Luftwaffe also intervened in the battle, relieving the pressure on *Major* Witzig and allowing him to establish a favorable defensive position near the Djebel Abiod.

At the same time British paratroops, who had jumped near Souk el Arba on November 15 and captured Béja without a shot being fired (with support from Blade Force), attacked Oued Zarga and took the town, which lay halfway between Béja and Medjez el Bab. The British unit was the First Battalion of the First Airborne Brigade under Colonel Hill. The Blade Force was an improvised unit formed after the landings under Colonel Dick Hull which was equipped with 25 tanks.

On the second day of the attack by the Seventy-eighth Infantry Division General Anderson committed tanks against the Djebel Abiod. Witzig's force had to make a fighting withdrawal. It found a favorable defensive position in the Jefna Tunnel. The British Seventy-eighth Infantry Division was diverted southward toward Medjez el Bab.

Early on the morning of November 18 the paratroops of FJR 5 which had been despatched to Medjez el Bab reached the town. There they were fired on by French troops. *Oberleutnant* Hoge, commander of 10./FJR 5, determined that the French had established a bridgehead on the east bank of the Medjerda. At noon the decision was made in the headquarters of the XC. AK to send Stukas to attack the French near Medjez el Bab and support FJR 5's attack.

Hauptmann Knoche, commander of III./FJR 5, received orders to "attack Medjez el Bab taking advantage of the Stuka attack" on November 19. Knoche and part of his signals platoon reached the Hoge group near Medjez el Bab shortly after midnight.

Since the cities of southern Tunisia were not occupied by German troops, but could become of decisive importance to *Panzerarmee Afrika*, measures were taken by XC. AK for their speedy occupation.

The first action began on the morning of November 17. *Leutnant* Kempa took off from La Marsa airfield. Accompanying him were his wheeled vehicle platoon and the Third Guard Company of the OB-Süd under *Oberleutnant* Salg. The small force's objective was Gabes.

When the first aircraft approached to land it was met by heavy flak and machine-gun fire. The machines turned away. The majority flew back toward the north, but the six Ju 52s with the paratroops on board reassembled. Following a brief discussion between *Leutnant* Kempa and *Hauptmann* Grund, who was to become commandant of Gabes airfield, the six Ju 52s flew on about 40 km from Gabes and landed in an open field.

Leutnant Kempa sent the first patrol toward Gabes. Just outside the town it was discovered by a French armored car patrol and fired upon. The six men were able to hide in a small valley.

The second patrol sent out by Kempa was captured by French defenders. Just as the seven German paratroops were being brought in for questioning on the morning of November 18, columns of Ju 52s suddenly droned overhead escorted by a pair of Bf 109 fighters. The transports were carrying the air landing troops.

The French took to their heels and when the aircraft landed they were greeted by the seven paratroopers. When the first American tanks appeared before Gabes two days later they would be given a hot reception by the German paratroops.

Two battalions of "Brigade L" under General Imperiali, which had been sent to reinforce the small group, reached Gabes following a forced march and relieved the small force of paratroops.

In the Medjez el Bab area the paratroops under *Hauptmann* Knoche readied themselves late on the evening of November 18. Patrols reported the enemy's strength as a motorized infantry regiment with light tanks and armored cars as well as a battery of anti-aircraft guns. Observers reported to *Hauptmann* Knoche that four American tanks and the spearhead of an Allied motorized unit had arrived in the French assembly area.

His own battle group consisted of the following:
Staff and 1/3 of signals platoon FJR 5
Tenth Company less First Rifle Squad
1/2 of Twelfth Company with heavy machine-guns and 80mm mortars and light infantry guns
1/2 of Fourteenth Company, IR 104 with five 50mm anti-tank guns
2 Flak combat groups

Still in Tunis were two Italian companies, including an anti-tank company.

The 19th of November dawned brightly and the battle group waited for the promised Stuka attack. The Stukas were to be supported by strong units from Sicily. By 09.00 two Bf 109s flew over the battle zone and two hours later — hours after the time promised — 12 Stukas approached, escorted by four Bf 109s. Enemy anti-aircraft guns opened fire. Infantry and artillery joined in. With sirens screaming the Stukas dived toward their targets and bombed the French troops assembly areas.

The air attack and the opening of fire by the French was the signal for the waiting paratroops and the German anti-tank guns to open fire. The two eighty-eights and the two-centimeter guns, the mortars and machine-guns all fired shells and bursts of fire into the enemy positions.

The paratroops attacked and took almost all of the city east of the Medjerda in the first rush. Only the train station was still held by French troops. The German paratroops advanced as far as the bridge over the Medjerda. They could get no farther, however, as the ceaseless artillery fire pinned them down and they were raked by heavy machine-gun fire.

Oberleutnant Bundt lead an assault team across the river!" ordered *Hauptmann* Knoche.

The assault team got some distance into Medjez el Bab but then it was fired upon from several sides and lost most of its men killed or wounded. *Oberleutnant* Bundt was among the fallen. Four survivors dodged their way back to the Medjerda River. They swam across below the city and reported to *Hauptmann* Knoche.

The Italian reinforcements finally arrived late in the afternoon. Shortly afterward *Hauptmann* Koch arrived among his paratroops. He had brought demolition materials from Tunis by truck. Koch formed ten assault teams armed with submachine-guns, satchel charges and hollow charges. Each team was given a target.

The assault teams began to move out at designated intervals at midnight. They forded the Medjerda at previously chosen locations. One of the most daring paratroops operations had begun.

The first hollow charge went off in the city a good hour later. Satchel charges blasted machine-gun positions from the roofs of houses where most had been set up by the French. Groups of paratroops attacked in ten different places, and the numerous explosions and tremendous columns of smoke and flame from the blasted depots sent the French into a state of panic.

At dawn the enemy climbed aboard his vehicles and set off to the west as fast as he could go. Medjez el Bab had been cleared of the enemy.

The paratroops secured the city. *Hauptmann* Knoche, who had gone four days and nights without sleep, was relieved by *Hauptmann* Gerhard Schirmer. Schirmer led the paratroops to Oued Zarga and attacked the town that night from the left flank. While the attack was under way an order arrived from regiment to break off the attack and pull back to the starting positions. The paratroops took up position near Medjez el Bab.

The 10th Panzer Division Arrives

The first elements of the 10th Panzer Division, which had been sent to Africa from southern France, arrived in the area of Teboura-Djedeida on the night of November 20/21 and relieved the paratroops of *Kampfgruppe* Knoche. They were then sent into the area of Medjez el Bab-El Aroussa and established contact with *Kampfgruppe* Schirmer to the north.

When the first American tanks reached El Aroussa on the afternoon of November 21 and tried to take the town, they were turned back by the fully-motorized 14./IR 104 and the Flak combat group.

That same day *Hauptmann* Schirmer was forced to evacuate the section of Medjez el Bab west of the Medjerda because of the threat of being outflanked to the north and south by fast enemy armored units. *General* Nehring ordered the whole front pulled back to an area 30 km west of Tunis. Some elements remained behind near Medjez el Bab as rearguards.

An Interim Balance

Just as the Germans had quickly taken Gabes, they also occupied Sousse and Sfax. The cities had to be held in order to secure the road to Tripoli for *Panzerarmee Afrika*.

The occupation force for Gafsa arrived by air. There, too, the enemy was halted a few days later. Demolition teams were sent far ahead to the west to blow up bridges, roads and other important targets.

General Nehring's only local reserve was the patrols of the 190th Armored reconnaissance Company, which he employed where they were most urgently needed.

Another pillar during the initial days of the race to Tunis was the Barenthin Parachute Regiment. Its commander, *Oberst* Walther Barenthin, was the combat engineer commander of XI. Parachute Corps. His most powerful weapon was the Witzig Corps Pionier Battalion. *Oberst* Barenthin took over as corps commander in the Mateur area.

Motorized paratroop patrols ranged as far as 250 kilometers into the countryside and reached Pont du Fahs and Enfidaville.

"Nevertheless," wrote *General* Nehring, "the south remained my greatest worry, because developments were possible at any time from the unwatched hinterland which at one blow could sever communications with Tripoli. This would negate the main purpose of the Tunisian bridgehead."

Enemy air attacks grew in strength. Allied fighters were already operating in the air over Bizerta and Tunis. A battery of 88mm Flak with four guns was on hand to defend Tunis. However, these had to be used as anti-tank weapons to prevent a breakthrough to Tunis by enemy armored forces.

On November 19 *Feldmarschall* Kesselring arrived in Tunis. *General* Nehring briefed him on the situation. He referred in particular to the existing difficulties and requested the earliest possible provision of German staff personnel *and* signals equipment for the now 500-kilometer-long front. In addition, he asked for self-contained combat units with heavy weapons.

The following German units had meanwhile arrived:
1 artillery battalion with two batteries
1 additional infantry personnel replacement battalion
1 Panzer battalion with 35 tanks
elements of a signals battalion
advance elements of the 10th Panzer Division

Surprising was the quick crossing by the Italian "*Superga*" Division. Elements of the division were already in position near Mateur. They were supported by a battalion of Italian self-propelled artillery, which was located southwest of Mateur. The situation was as follows:
(a) Offensive defensive in the Medjez el Bab area by FJR 5.
(b) Offensive defence on the roads leading to Bizerta and Mateur by *Fallschirm-Pionier-Battalion* Witzig.
(c) Defence of the city of Tunis to the south by the Italian "*Superga*" Division in a line southern edge of Sebkret es Sedjoumi-Hammabach to the sea.
(d) Direct defence of the city of Tunis to guard against surprises.

On November 19 the steamers "Viminale" and "Puccini" reached the harbor of Bizerta and landed the rest of the "*Superga*" Division. Division commander General Lorenzelli arrived at the same time at La Marsa airfield. Lorenzelli divided his battle groups among the German units and began an advance from Mateur in the direction of Sidi bou Acid and Sidi Belkai. The attack was a success and the three tactical groups of the "*Superga*" Division occupied several important crossroads.

General Eisenhower in Algiers

On November 23, 1942 General Eisenhower arrived in Algeria from Gibraltar. In the headquarters of the Allied forces he found General Clark and General Oliver in deliberating over the continuation of the advance by Brigadier General Robinett's Battle Group B. Eisenhower approved the further advance and in the following two days elements of the 1st Armored Division under Colonel Waters and the Blade Force under Colonel R.C. Hull drove toward Teboura. Following a brief engagement with the paratroops of the *Barenthin* Regiment the American force turned east in the direction of Djedeida. A patrol under Lieutenant Hoker reported:

"The way to Djedeida is open. The airfield is packed with German aircraft. Only weak opposition expected."

The German 20mm Flak positioned near Djedeida opened fire but were unable to knock out the heavy tanks, which subsequently shot up the anti-aircraft guns.

Several Ju 52s and Bf 109s tried to take off. They became bogged down in the rain-softened earth, however, and were destroyed by the tanks. When the tanks had completed their work of destruction and rolled on toward Tunis they left behind on the Djedeida airfield 14 destroyed Bf 109s and 24 Ju 52s.

About 15 kilometers from the city the tanks came upon two of the eighty-eights of the 20th Flak-Division which *General* Nehring had placed there personally. The two guns opened up with a rapid fire. Within two minutes they destroyed six of the American tanks. The rest turned and pulled back to Djedeida. Tunis had been saved at the last second.

Early on the morning of November 26 followed the German counterattack from Mateur. The first German Panzer IV tanks in the theater joined the attack. The American armored advance was stopped.

The British Seventy-eighth Infantry Division had launched an attack from Oued Zarga toward Medjez el Bab on the morning of November 25 under the command of Major General Evelegh. The British division was later joined by elements of the US 1st Armored Division and Battle Group B under Brigadier General Robinett.

Oberstleutnant Koch, who had engaged the Americans near Medjez el Bab, withdrew FJR 5 from there and halted near Massicault, occupying new positions on both sides of the road. The next few days were quiet.

As a result of this move the enemy thrust met no opposition. The tanks of Battle Group B now rolled south of Medjez el Bab toward Goubellat.

Since a latent danger remained in the Djedeida-Teboura area, *General* Nehring ordered the just-arrived Panzer battalion of the 10th Panzer Division inserted into the area north of Teboura. The battalion was to bar the enemy's way from the highlands to the coastal plain.

In the battles near Teboura on November 27 and 28 the Allies lost a series of tanks. Two events now took place which resulted in a new crisis. Arabs reported the landing of Allied troops near Cap Serrat, north of the positions held by the Witzig Battalion. The Allied landing force was roughly 2,000 men. Since these troops were in a position to bring about the fall of Bizerta, *General* Nehring immediately sent the forces which had just landed at the airfield against them. The German troops overpowered the landing force in the mountains north of the Sedjenane River. The bulk of the Allied landing force returned to their boats.

The second Arab report was more discouraging. It read:

"Approximately 1,000 enemy paratroops have jumped into the area north of Zaghouan."

If the report was true then there was danger ahead. The report was true. The Allied force was the Second Parachute Battalion of the Sixth Airborne under Major Frost. It had taken off at 12.30 on November 29 for Depienne. The battalion jumped unhindered, as there were no Germans in the area. From Depienne the paratroops marched toward Oudna. On the way they learned that there were no German aircraft left there. They found the airfield — their objective — abandoned. Over the next two days the battalion was attacked several times by German paratroops and decimated. The battle lasted until December 2 and by the time the battalion fought its way to Allied positions it had lost 16 officers and 250 men killed. Captain Richard Spencer, one of the participants in the futile raid, said:

"Silence fell over the Medjerda Valley, where so many of my comrades had died senselessly."

The Race to Tunis

Overall Situation

The situation in the Tunisian bridgehead at the end of November was marked by worry over the supply situation and the transport in of further combat units to defend the bridgehead.

As a result of increased enemy activity the transport tonnage had shrunk in a threatening fashion. On the other hand requirements had climbed significantly, as *Panzerarmee Afrika* also had to be supplied through Bizerta and Tunis.

With the uncertain situation in the area around Tunis *Panzerarmee Afrika* was pulled back farther during November. Tobruk had been reoccupied by the British on November 13 after the city was abandoned by the 90th Light Division. That same day the first elements of the *Panzerarmee* reached the Marsa el Brega position. The next day brought a general fuel crisis. Only 60 of the promised 250 tons had been flown over.

The rearguards withdrew in stages. It was the 90. *Leichte* which had the job of slowing the pursuing enemy forces. The rearguard reached Zuentia, then Agedabia, while in the Marsa el Brega position all efforts were being made to extend the defensive position. Marshal Bastico intercepted the retreating Italian units there, assembled and reorganized them and placed them in the line with other units arriving from Italy. These included the *"Pistoia"* and *"Spezia"* Divisions and the *"Centauro"* Armored Division.

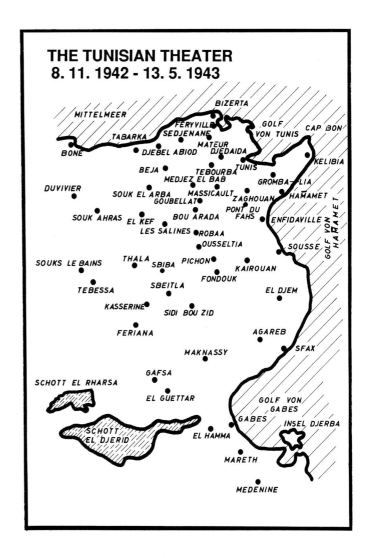

THE TUNISIAN THEATER
8. 11. 1942 - 13. 5. 1943

On November 24 *Feldmarschall* Kesselring and Marshal Cavallero went to the *Arco dei Fileni* where they met with Rommel and Marshal Bastico. Rommel decided to fly to *Führer* Headquarters to personally request a strategic decision and ask Hitler for the evacuation of Africa in the long run.

Rommel took off on the morning of November 28 and arrived in Rastenburg that afternoon. The first discussion between himself and Keitel, Jodl and Schmundt took place at about 16.00. An hour later he was summoned to see Hitler.

The Commander-in-Chief of *Panzerarmee Afrika* did not mince words. When he demanded that they must pan an evacuation of North Africa in the long run in order to save the soldiers Hitler flew into a rage. The result was a bitter argument, and Rommel defended his soldiers when Hitler said that they had thrown away their weapons during the retreat. In closing Hitler said:

"There will be no withdrawal from the Marsa el Brega position. We will do all that we can to get the necessary supplies to you. *Reichsmarschall* Göring will accompany you to Italy with full authority and will negotiate with the Italian authorities."

Together with Göring *Feldmarschall* Rommel travelled to Rome. However, Göring was of no help. He had to be corrected by Mussolini when he asserted during one discussion that he — Rommel — had left the Italians in the lurch before El Alamein.

"I know nothing of that," replied Mussolini. "Your retreat, Marshal Rommel, was a masterly accomplishment."

When Rommel flew back to Africa he knew that he was on his own and that it "would require the greatest good fortune to prevent the army's destruction as a result of an insane order."

The fact that Sicily and Tunisia were linked by German-Italian air transport, it appeared that a rapid consolidation of all Axis forces in Africa was possible. Such a consolidation under a unified command would give the Axis a chance of holding off the enemy.

In the meantime nearly all the elements of the 10th PD had arrived in the Tunis area. The commanding general now had a fully-trained division on hand in addition to FJR 5. Further anti-aircraft units of the 20th Flak Division under *Generalleutnant* Neuffer had also arrived, significantly strengthening the defences.

THE BATTLE OF TEBOURA - 1. - 3. 12. 1942

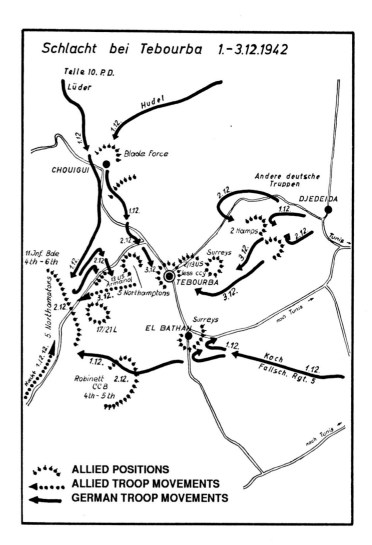

Schlacht bei Tebourba 1.-3.12.1942

▸▸▸▸ ALLIED POSITIONS
◀▪▪▪▪ ALLIED TROOP MOVEMENTS
◀━━ GERMAN TROOP MOVEMENTS

Top: Six-engined Gigant (Giant) transport aircraft bring the wheeled elements of sPzAbt. 501 to Africa.

Disembarking in Tripoli Harbor.

175

Left: An Allied tank knocked out near Tebourba.
Top right: Major Lueder with sPzAbt. 501's signals officer.
Bottom right: Tebourba assembly area. The German panzers tipped the scales of battle at Tebourba in favor of the Axis forces.

176

The situation on November 29 prompted *General* Nehring to act. He decided to take the battle to the enemy.

The Battle of Tebourba

Elements of the 10th PD had assembled between Bizerta and Tunis so that they could be deployed in any direction. Disembarkation of the Panzer battalion had been completed that day in Bizerta and the unit rested southeast of the city so as to be ready for action. On November 30 it was to move to Sidi Athman. The new command structure was as follows:

Northern Sector:*Oberst* Frhr. von Broich
Western Sector:*Generalmajor* Fischer, commander 10th PD
Southern Sector:General Lorenzelli, commander *"Superga"* Division
North of Tunis:*Generalmajor* Neuffer, commander 20th Flak-Division
Fortress Bizerta:*Generalmajor* Neuffer

The enemy's intentions were directed toward attacking from the Tebourba area toward Tunis and moving out of the Mateur area to capture Bizerta. The attack was to come soon.

On November 30 *General* Nehring gave the order for an attack in the Tebourba area. His major decision was to commit FJR 5 from the Medjez el Bab area through El Bathan against the Allied rear to complete an encirclement of the enemy. *Generalmajor* Fischer was given the task of carrying out the job, because he had the necessary signals and command assets. According to the corps order the 10th PD was to attack from the north and northeast, while the Tiger company under *Hauptmann* Baron Nolde and two replacement battalions advanced from the Djedeida area.

The Tiger unit was First Company of *schwere Panzer-Abteilung* 501 (501st Heavy Tank Battalion), which was the first of the battalion's companies to be sent to Africa. Transfer of the company to Tunisia had begun on November 10 and the first of the heavy tanks arrived on the 23rd.

Kampfgruppe Lueder was formed on November 24. The battle group was led by the commander of sPzAbt.501, *Major* Lueder, and included two

Tiger 131 near Tebourba; all still quiet.

The Tigers assemble in the Djedeida olive grove.

Panzer companies of PzAbt.190, whose commander, *Major* von Blomberg, had been killed just before, and a motorcycle company under *Oberleutnant* Pschorr of the 10th PD.

Kampfgruppe Lueder assembled for the attack on Tebourba on November 27. The first effort stalled in the face of fire from British anti-tank guns on both sides of the Djedeida-Tebourba road. Eight Panzer IIIs and IVs were lost in the duel between the tanks and anti-tank guns.

Then began the Battle of Tebourba. *Kampfgruppe* Lueder, reinforced by a company of *Panzergrenadiere* under *Hauptmann* Pomme (of the 10th PD), moved into position on the hills north of Chouigui.

Early on the morning of December 1 the tanks of the 10. PD's PR 7, *Kampfgruppe* Lueder and all the other combat units of the 10. PD launched their attack. Less than 30 (!) soldiers remained in Tunis itself.

Still surrounded in Tebourba were a company of the Barenthin Regiment and the regiment's Pionier Platoon. Brigadier General Robinett's Battle Group B had so far been unable to smoke out the German defenders.

The German attack quickly gained ground to the south. Chouigui and the southern hills were taken. On the morning of December 2 *Kampfgruppe* Lueder was one kilometer northwest of Teboura, preventing a breakout to the west by the enemy armor. The commander of 1./sPzAbt.501, *Hauptmann* Baron Nolde, joined the battle from Djedeida. He raced toward the enemy with his three platoon leaders, *Hauptmann* Deichmann, *Leutnant* Vermehren and *Leutnant* Joschko.

The three battalions of the US 13th Armored Regiment under the command of Colonel Waters, Colonel Bruss and Colonel Todd attempted to stop the onrushing German tanks. The Tigers blasted the American tanks with their long-barrelled 88mm guns. *Hauptmann* Nolde, wearing gym shoes as he always did in combat, led his small force forward. They reached and cleared an olive grove. Direct hits set the American tanks ablaze.

The enemy was defending tenaciously, however, and *Generalmajor* Fischer soon appeared to break the resistance with a renewed attack.

The American Battle Group B, which had received orders on the evening of December 1 to destroy the German armored force, first made

contact at 11.00. Company E under Captain Mayshark attacked. Within 15 minutes it had been destroyed. When Companies D and F — the 1st Battalion of the 1st Armored Regiment — attacked, they were beaten back by six Tigers. By evening the Americans had had enough and Major General Robinnet drove back to headquarters and informed General Oliver that he was unable to continue the attack. He advocated a withdrawal of the units in the olive grove between Hill 259 and the bank of the Medjerda. General Oliver approved the suggestion.

On the German side the fighting of December 2 had been an outstanding success, although one gained at some cost. The British Eleventh Brigade and the American Battle Group B had been scattered, but *Hauptmann* Nolde, whose Tigers had smashed the enemy at the much fought for olive grove, was killed. He had just left his tank to give an order to his platoon leader, *Hauptmann* Deichmann, when two enemy tanks opened fire. An armour-piercing shell tore off both of Nolde's legs. *Hauptmann* Teddy Deichmann assumed command. His Tigers destroyed both enemy tanks. A short time later *Hauptmann* Deichmann climbed from the turret hatch of his tank to explore the surrounding terrain. A single rifle shot rang out and Deichmann fell to the ground badly wounded.

The *Werhmacht* communiqué that day stated:

"More than 200 prisoners were taken, 34 tanks and 6 armored cars destroyed in local battles in Tunisia."

Generalmajor Fischer deployed his motorized units to outflank the enemy by moving northwest to south, link up with the paratroops of FJR 5 in the southwest and together close the ring behind the enemy.

Fallschirmjäger-Regiment 5

Oberstleutnant Koch received the commanding general's order to move into attack positions on November 30. The same day he sent elements of his forces along both sides of the road toward Medjez el Bab in order to deceive the enemy. During the night he turned toward El Bathan to cut off the enemy's retreat.

A meeting of two worlds: Bf 110 and camel.

As Third battalion turned north near a farmhouse not far from Furna, the Second Platoon of 10./FJR 5 was ordered to veer northeastward. Leaving behind its heavy equipment, it was to establish contact with the Arent Pionier Platoon, which, in true paratroop fashion, had been sent ahead on a special mission by *Oberstleutnant* Koch on November 30. Arent and his platoon were to occupy a bridge about 4 kilometers west of El Bathan and hold until the following units of the regiment arrived.

The closer the paratroops came to El Bathan on the morning of December 1, the heavier became the enemy fire, occasionally forcing them to take cover. The Jungwirt, Schirmer and Knoche Battalions slowly worked their way forward.

Driving toward El Bathan at the head of Twelfth Company was *Leutnant* Kauz. Taking side roads Kauz and his troops reached a position behind the town, which was supposed to be held by an American battle group. Cork-oaks and olive groves concealed the move at first, but then the Americans spotted movement and opened fire with artillery and mortars. Machine-guns rattled to life east of El Bathan where the spearhead group of PGR 86 (10.PD) had run into the enemy.

Suddenly there was the sound of engines overhead. Nine Stukas, escorted by two Bf 109s, raced toward the enemy positions, dove through the curtain of fire and dropped their bombs or strafed the enemy positions. Explosions rocked the center of Tebourba and El Bathan. In Tebourba the Americans' main depot went up in smoke and flame.

Kauz' platoon, which had meanwhile left its vehicles, worked its way forward step by step. The *Leutnant* and his men reached the American headquarters. Behind them an enemy tank pushed its way through a narrow alley. It was followed by a second, third and fourth. There were flashes as the tanks opened fire.

Leutnant Kauz, *Jäger* Bohley and *Gefreiter* Vogel were killed when a shell landed in their midst. The remaining troops ran forward. They stormed the house. The enemy artillery ceased firing.

An enemy battery firing from the western edge of El Bathan was silenced by four Panzers. Then six Churchill tanks appeared. Three were destroyed within two minutes and the rest turned and fled as fast as they could go.

British and American staff vehicles raced over

the road to the southwest in a wild flight. Tanks, guns and signals vehicles fled for their lives.

Leading the pursuers was 12./FJR 5 under *Oberleutnant* Wöhler. Not until they reached the hills of the Djebel Lanserine and Bou Aoukaz were they halted by massed enemy fire.

In the late afternoon of December 4 all available units were committed to storm the foremost hills. The Panzers rolled ahead of the attack force silencing nests of resistance. Koch's and Barenthin's paratroops took out the crews manning the foxholes and trenches. But what had become of the Arent Pionier Platoon?

At the head of his platoon, *Feldwebel* Arent broke through the British rear positions on the evening of November 30. He and his small group of 50 men fought their way through to Teboura with hand grenades and demolition charges. Four kilometers west of El Bathan they reached the bridge over the Medjerda. There Arent placed his two machine-guns to the left and right of the

bridge. The bridge itself was mined.

When the first British vehicle column approached from the direction of Medjez el Bab and reached the bridge, the leading truck was shattered by a mine. A second truck swerved around the burning vehicle and was likewise blown up. The bridge was blocked. *Oberfeldwebel* Peter Arent fired the agreed-upon red signal flare and both MG 42s opened fire. The attackers were driven back.

During the night of November 30/December 1 the enemy forces which had been halted in front of the bridge again tried to drive away the Pionier. They had to open the bridge and deliver vital supplies and ammunition to the Eleventh Brigade and elements of the US 1st Armored Division which were far ahead. Again they failed and on December 1 Arent's men were still in control of the bridge.

That night an enemy company crossed the Medjerda and tried to clear out the German

Bf 110 fighters over the Tunisian Scots (salt lakes).

180

combat engineers. Leading ten of his men Arent drove the enemy back across the river. When dawn came Arent and his men were still masters of the bridge.

Shortly after midday the men of Second Platoon/10./FJR 5, who had been sent ahead by *Oberstleutnant* Koch, arrived. The important bridge remained in German hands.

The Battle of Tebourba was over. On the way back to the regiment Peter Arent was killed near Hill 154 — Khoumet el Diab — by a British artillery shell. For his outstanding accomplishments at the bridge he was posthumously awarded the Knight's Cross. *Oberstleutnant* Walther Koch laid the Knight's Cross on the dead man's coffin.

The Anglo-American forces had lost 134 tanks on the Teboura battlefield. The Germans took 1,100 prisoners. Elements of the Blade Force, Battle group B and the US 1st Armored Division had been destroyed or decimated. Forty-seven Allied aircraft were shot down over the battlefield,
23 of these by German fighters.

A map found in one of the knocked-out tanks showed that the enemy, as *General* Nehring had suspected, had intended to break through between Bizerta and Tunis before veering south to take the airfield and city of Tunis from the rear. A large red arrow with the inscription "headquarters" pointed to the headquarters of the German commander-in-chief at the northern edge of Tunis.

The victory at Teboura relieved the XC. AK of one of its greatest worries. The existence of the bridgehead was assured for the time being. *Panzermee Afrika*'s withdrawal to Tunis now looked promising.

General Nehring combined cold-blooded opportunism and improvisational skills to score a success which the 1943 official American General Staff account of the war in North Africa characterized in the following manner:

"The Germans won the race for Tunis."

Formation of the Fifth Panzerarmee

The New 5. Panzerarmee Corps Headquarters - Special Operation Bizerta

Despite the limited troop strength, there the extraordinary circumstances in the Tunisia area called for the creation of an army headquarters command structure. The OB-Süd's instructions to establish such a formation resulted in the arrival of the Panzer AOK 5, *Generaloberst* von Arnim. Von Arnim and *Generalleutnant* Ziegler, as Chief of Staff, arrived at *Führer* Headquarters in Rastenburg on December 3. Hitler had had them summoned from the Eastern front to personally brief them on the situation. In a subsequent discussion with Keitel, Hitler stated that the 5. *Panzerarmee* was to be sent three Panzer divisions and three motorized infantry divisions.

At that time the corps headquarters of the XC. AK knew nothing of this development.

On December 6 *Generalmajor* Gause and *Oberst* Hasso von Manteuffel arrived in Bizerta from Rome. They had been tasked by the OKW to bring to the Commander-in-Chief of French troops in Tunisia, Admiral Dérien, Hitler's ultimatum to hand over all military installations in Tunisia. Furthermore all French troops were to be assembled, after which would be sent to Italy or France as prisoners of war. Soldiers who were native to Tunisia could be released directly. In the event Admiral Dérien should be unwilling to comply, *Generalmajor* Gause was authorized to use force to back up Hitler's demands.

Fortunately for this risky operation the second armored battalion of the 10. *Panzer-Division* had disembarked on the evening of December 5. Also available was a just-arrived infantry battalion as well as the two Italian Marine Infantry Battalions in Bizerta. *Generalmajor* Neuffer placed the trucks of the 20. Flak-Division at Gause's disposal as well as several 20mm Flak. *Oberst* Harlingshausen assured air support in the event the French offered any resistance.

Later *Generalmajor* Gause casually mentioned to the commanding general that *Generaloberst* von Arnim would shortly be taking over command in Tunisia. He was expected to arrive on December 8. For *General* Nehring this was an unpleasant surprise.

When *Generaloberst* von Arnim arrived in Tunis-North on the evening of December 8 accompanied by *Generalleutnant* Ziegler, *General* Nehring had already ordered a continuation of the attack for the following day.

After regrouping and taking on supplies the western group was to attack south of the Medjerda River in a southwesterly direction toward the line Medjez el Bab-Goubellat.

The northern Mateur group was to defend its positions and the southern group, consisting of Italian units of the *"Superga"* Division now under General Gelich, was to push its strongpoints farther west.

While the attack was beginning on December 9 *General der Panzertruppen* Nehring said farewell to his troops in an order of the day and thanked the commanders and soldiers for their efforts.

Special Operation Bizerta

Also beginning on that morning was the special operation against the French troops in Bizerta. *Generalmajor* Gause later described the decisive part of his discussion with Admiral Dérien:

"Admiral Dérien appeared with his chief of staff and accepted Hitler's ultimatum with dignity. He was, understandably, rather bitter that they no longer trusted him, even though he had provided proof of his loyalty and they had assured him of their complete confidence.

Following a brief discussion with his chief of staff Admiral Dérien decided to accept the ultimatum and hand over all military installations intact. He asked only to be allowed to keep a company under arms until 17.00 in order to take down the French flag with military honors. This was naturally approved. The entire operation was carried out in a loyal fashion."

The disarming of the French in Ferryville and aboard the French warships in Ferryville and Bizerta was carried out in a similar fashion. Other French units were disarmed all the way down the coast to Gabes.

The neutralizing of seven heavy French coastal batteries, the torpedo boats and auxiliary ships eliminated a potential threat.

On December 6 and 7 The Witzig group of forces repelled enemy armored advances in strength. A limited attack by the *Panzergrenadiere* of 10. PD against enemy forces 8 kilometers southwest of Tebourba resulted in the capture of Hill 145. The enemy withdrew to the west bank of the Medjerda.

Reconnaissance aircraft reported light enemy forces near Bir Mcherga and Ain el Asker, northwest of Depienne. German aircraft also discovered 40 enemy tanks and 100 other vehicles northeast of Souk el Khemis.

Short-range reconnaissance aircraft reported 20 enemy tanks in front of FJR 5 near Fourna. Finally, on December 8 General Imperiali, commander of "Battle Group L," reported a large enemy armored concentration in the Sidi bou Zid area. The enemy was preparing for an attack.

The attack by 10. PD struck these enemy pre-

parations on December 9 and resulted in another success, with which *General* Nehring left the African Theater. The tanks and *Panzergrenadiere* broke through the enemy positions and destroyed 37 enemy tanks.

As a result of this success, on December 13 *Generalmajor* Fischer was awarded the Oak Leaves to the Knight's Cross and was promoted to *Generalleutnant.*

The situation was not so bleak now, especially since the first elements of the 334. ID under *Oberst* Weber had arrived in Tunisia. Among these was GJR 756, which soon proved itself at the Chouigui Pass and at the notorious Djebel Lanserine — the Christmas Mountain.

By December 10 the German armored thrust southwest of Tebourba had reached the Toum area. By evening of that day the attack force had advanced to a point 3 kilometers from Medjez el Bab. III./FJR 5 moved forward on December 12. The Tenth Company took up position on a farm north of Sebkhet el Kourzia salt lake. The farm later came to be known as the Christmas Farm. A 50mm anti-tank gun and two Italian guns were set up on the road to Goubellat.

On the left wing the 10. PD and the *"Superga"* Division had been moved forward into the line Pont du Fahs — pass north of Djebel Saidar — pass southwest of Djebel Garce, 15 km west of Enfidaville — southwest edge of the lake south of Enfidaville.

Available to the 5. *Panzerarmee* on December 17 were 100 Panzer III and IV tanks and 7 Tigers. That day also saw the supreme command in Tunisia transferred to the Comando Supremo, at least on paper.

On December 23 the British and elements of Battle group B attacked the positions of III./FJR 5 with artillery support. The attackers were beaten back. A German patrol wiped out an advancing enemy cavalry troop.

On December 24 the enemy launched several attacks in battalion strength northeast of Medjez el Bab. The Allied forces charged the positions held by I./FJR 5 and the 10. PD. and were beaten off in both locations.

The same day a battle group from 10. PD under the command of the Division Ia, General Staff *Oberstleutnant* Bürker, launched an attack in the direction of the Weihnachtsberg. Defending there was the British Seventy-eighth Infantry Division.

Fighting was extremely heavy but the British were driven back, leaving behind many dead and 300 prisoners.

Next morning General Evelegh committed his Guards Brigade, which had just arrived in Medjez el Bab from the rear, against the hill. "Longstop Hill," as the Allied troops soon named the Weihnachtsberg, changed hands once again.

Advancing to the right of the British force at the same time was a unit of the Sixth Armoured Division. The British tanks reached Massicault, while their infantry strove to reach Tebourba plateau. The British appeared poised to break through to Tunis. Just then, however, it began to rain heavily. Two hours later every one of their vehicles was bogged down in the thick mud.

On December 26 *Kampfgruppe* Bürker again stormed the line of hills. They occupied three of the six hills in the first rush and in subsequent attacks overpowered the British defenders on the three remaining hills. 500 British soldiers surrendered. The hills, which screened Bridgehead Tunisia to the west, were again in German hands.

On January 26, 1943 General Staff *Oberstleutnant* Ulrich Bürker was awarded the Knight's Cross.

The Other Side

The Allies had selected December 24 as the date to begin their new offensive, but the reports arriving in Allied headquarters were bad. General Eisenhower and General Anderson therefore drove to Souk el Khemis, where the headquarters of the British Fifth Corps were located. Major General Allfrey, the commanding general, reported that small preparatory attacks had started and that a diversionary attack toward Goubellat was under way.

The two American Generals drove to the front in streaming rain. Eisenhower became convinced that an attack during the rainy period was impossible. Eisenhower returned to the headquarters. He decided to postpone the attack.

General Eisenhower had the US II Corps moved from Oran into the Tebessa area. There the 1st Armored Division was assigned to Major General Fredenhall. Three further divisions were to be sent to him; first the US 1st Infantry Division and later the US 9th and 34th Infantry Divisions, which were still guarding the Oran-Béja supply road. As soon as the US II Corps had assembled in the south, it was to advance in the direction of Sfax or Gabes to interdict the line of retreat of Rommel's *Panzerarmee Afrika* into Tunisia.

On December 28, 1942 the general battle line ran Mateur —northeast of Medjez el Bab-Pont du Fahs-Djebebina-Djebel bou Dabous — north of Pichon. At the end of December the Axis front was divided into four sectors:
Sector A: Mateur area — Gruppe von Broich
Sector B: area around Medjez el Bab — 10. PD
Sector C: Tunis-South area — "Superga" Division
Sector D: Brigade L, Brigadegeneral Imperiali

On the night of December 27/28 US paratroops under Colonel Edson D. Raff landed south of Sousse and blew up the railway line north of the bridge at El Djem.

The Luftwaffe also struck a major blow. It bombed and destroyed the bridge over the Medjerda near Medjez el Bab. Thus the situation on December 31, 1942 was a satisfactory one for the defenders of Bridgehead Tunisia. They had 103 Panzer IIIs and IVs and 11 Tigers on hand. On the way was PzAbt.190 with its 53 tanks.

The Link-Up

Operation Eilbote (Special Delivery)

Following several limited advances and some straightening of the front the 10. PD and the 334. ID, most of which had arrived in the meantime, were granted a period of rest. The January rains prevented any major troops movements. Snow even fell on some of the hill positions. The front froze. Only in the south, in the area held by the *"Superga"* Division, was there any offensive activity. Three divisions and a brigade of the French Nineteenth Corps under General Koeltz set out from the interior toward Tebessa. The units involved were:

"Oran" Division — General Boissau
"Morocco" Division — General Methenet
"Algiers" Division — General Conne
Light Brigade — General Le Couteux de Chaumont

Unhindered by any enemy countermeasures, the French reached the mouth of the valley of the

Left: Generalleutnant Friederich Weber.
Right: Generaloberst von Arnim (left) and Generalmajor Weber near Ponts du Fahs.

Top: The "Light" Platoon on a typically poor Tunisian road.
Center: Oberst Lang (center) and Oberst Barenthin (left) assess the situation before Operation Eilbote I.
Bottom:The advance is under way.

Three photographs taken during Operation Eilbote I.

eastern Dorsale. An advance was planned which, supported by several US units, aimed at driving through Sbeitla and the Faid Pass to Sfax and Gabes. This would cut off *Panzerarmee Afrika*'s line of retreat once and for all.

The German command recognized this threat and reacted immediately with an attack from the Pont du Fahs area. The attack was code-named *"Eilbote I."*

The operation began in mid-January. Under the command of *Generalmajor* Weber, elements of the 10. PD, sPzAbt. 501, GJR 756, two artillery batteries and PiBatl. 49 advanced toward the southwest. Farther south of this battle group were two battalions of IR 47 and I./IR 92 of the *"Superga"* Division. Commander of this battle group was *Oberstleutnant* Buhse, the commanding officer of IR 47.

The attack began early on the morning of January 18. The battle groups met the first resistance at Djebel Solbia. The French Foreign Legionnaires were smashed. The Weber group continued its advance in the direction of the 648-meter-high Djebel Mansour. The initial assault failed to capture the important hill.

The French Nineteenth Corps suffered heavy losses. The Germans took 4,000 prisoners. A significant portion of the commanding hill positions and passes between Pont du Fahs and Pichon were in German hands. Following the war *Generalleutnant* Friedrich Weber described the battle. The following are the most important extracts from his description:

"At about 06.30 on January 19 the battle group commander and his personal tactical staff made their way to the battalions at the front and issued the following orders:

1. *Kampfgruppe* Lueder, consisting of sPzAbt. 501 reinforced by II./GR 69 under the command of *Major* Lueder, was to veer southward southwest of the El Kabir coffer-dam and advance through the hill country along the road to Ousseltia, disrupting the enemy's rear communications.

2. Regiment 756 was to follow as the second echelon after assembling its units dispersed during the night battle.

Top: A Tiger in the Tunisian mud.
Center: A knocked-out Crusader III.
Bottom: American Sherman destroyed during Eilbote I.

3. The "*Superga*" Division was to tie down the enemy by launching a frontal attack from its present position. The advance by the Lueder group began at 07.00. By 10.00, and after heavy fighting, the battle group had reached the crossroads to Spika. Ousseltia lay ahead as a tempting target for the tanks. However it was reported to the battle group commander that new enemy forces were on the move on the eastern slope of Djebel bou Dabouss. Despite the Italian attack Djebel bou Dabouss had remained in enemy hands. The Nebana Gorge was also firmly in the hands of the enemy. *Major* Lueder therefore decided to enter the Nebana Gorge and drive through there.

Pressured from the rear, the enemy was forced out of the defile. Contact was made with the Italian troops at about 13.00. General Staff *Major* Strymieschny waved a flag from the front lines, signalling to the Italians that help was on its way."

This concludes Weber's report, which could not be presented in its entirety due to space limitations.

On January 20 Djebel bou Dabouss was occupied by the *Gebirgsjäger* of Regiment 756, which was operating in a supporting role.

During the night of January 2⎰2 the Lueder group was withdrawn and sent via Kairouan into the northern sector, while GJR 756 was sent there via Spika.

Oberleutnant Hartmann, platoon leader of 1./sPzAbt.501, who had taken command of the First Tiger Company following the wounding of *Oberleutnant* Schmidt-Bonarius, received the Iron Cross, First Class. *Leutnant* Vermehren, *Oberfeldwebel* Augustin and *Gefreiter* Vogel were also decorated with the Iron Cross, First Class.

The objective of Operation "*Eilbote II*" was the capture of Djebel Mansour and Pichon. The attack was launched on January 31 by units under *Generalmajor* Weber and Oberstleutnant Buhse. The Weber group's direction of attack was toward Djebel Mansour and Djebel Sidi Salem, while the Buhse group was directed toward Pichon.

The French, who had meanwhile been reinforced bu the US 1st Armored Division and batteries of US heavy artillery, delayed the advance.

Top: Tank crewmen are briefed on the advance toward Kairouan.
Bottom: Signpost leading the way to the front: names which were written in blood.

There was bitter fighting south of Djebel Chirich. The attacking forces stormed Djebel Mansour. The British Guards won it back. Again the *Gebirgsjäger* of the 334. ID attacked and again took the hill, which was subsequently held against several enemy attacks.

The attack now went toward Pichon. The French were there and it was not too far from Pichon to Sousse. *Panzerarmee Afrika* had arrived in Tripoli after heavy fighting, and the area between Pichon and Gafsa had to be secured to hold open its line of retreat.

More dangerous than the threat from Pichon was that from the Faid Pass, which was held by the French and Americans. Facing them was only a single battalion of the "*Superga*" Division. The Italians were clinging to the rocky slopes and defending the pass courageously. A German replacement battalion was supporting the Italians. To the west, in the Maknassy and Sened area, were the divisions *Bersaglieri* (mountain troops). Next to them were the first elements of the "*Centauro*" Armored Division from Libya, which had reached the Gafsa area.

The danger from Faid Pass had to be eliminated. Under the command of *Oberstleutnant* Buhse, IR 47 stormed out of the area west of Kairouan into Pichon and captured part of the town in house-to-house fighting. However the regiment was forced back by strength of numbers and pulled back to the hills east of Pichon.

Following a two day battle the main attack by the tanks and six infantry battalions, as well as the artillery battalion of the 334. ID, reached Ousseltia. The French units were scattered. More than 2,000 soldiers of the "Oran" and "Constantine" Divisions were captured.

The Retreat by Panzerarmee Afrika

The withdrawing *Panzerarmee Afrika* had held in the Buerat position until January 15, 1943 and repelled a major attack there by the British Eighth Army. On the southern wing of the position was the 15. PD's PR 8, which had been led by *Oberst* Joseph Franz Irkens since the end of September.

At that time *Oberst* Irkens had available only the approximately 30 tanks of *Hauptmann* Stotten's I./PR 8, because II./PR 8 under *Hauptmann* Schnelle, had been withdrawn to the Gabes area to regain its strength.

The British attacked under the full moon and their tanks were received by the 88mm Flak. Some British tanks which broke through were destroyed in a counterattack by I./PR 8. Thirty British tanks were destroyed with very low losses to the German forces.

The Buerat position was evacuated the following night. *Panzerarmee Afrika* conducted a fighting withdrawal which covered 350 kilometers by January 22, 1943. On the 23rd Tripoli was abandoned, the last Libyan port in Axis hands. With this the battle to hold the Italian African colonies was for all practical purposes over.

The Panzers in the rearguard under the command of *Oberst* Irkens were able to turn back the enemy along the way near Homs, Tarhuna, south of Tripoli and near Ben Gardane. The tanks were aided in their efforts by Panzer Grenadiers, anti-aircraft guns, combat engineers and artillery. The German tanks also struck a sharp blow at the pursuing enemy forces near Meatameur.

On January 25 Rommel formed three divisions from the remnants of seven shattered Italian divisions and sent them toward Tunisia. Even if the 15. and 21. Panzer Divisions, as well as the 90. and 164. Light Divisions, had been decimated, their arrival in southern Tunisia still resulted in a major strengthening of the 5. *Panzerarmee*.

The "*Centauro*" Division under General Calvi di Bergolo joined the southern group, adding a capable division to this group of forces. Battle Group Mannerini, which had fought in the Sahara and had withdrawn from the Fezzan to Tripoli, went into position in southern Tunisia between Schott el Djerid and the Matmata range of hills.

The Italian divisions "*Pistoia*" (General Falugi), "*Trieste*" (General La Ferla), "*Giovani Fascisti*" (General Sozzani) and "*Spezia*" (General Pizzolato) arrived in the Mareth position one after another.

The units of the DAK were also to be deployed there. The 90. *Leichte* had already been inserted between "*Trieste*," which was against the sea, and "*Spezia*," while the 164. *Leichte* was in the same front west of Medenine. AA 3 and the "*Nizza*" Reconnaissance Battalion were standing by near Rhoumrassene.

The Comando Supremo tried to bring all units withdrawing from Tripolitania into the Mareth position under Italian command. It formed the First Army, commanded by General Messe.

THE MARETH POSITION 1.2.1943

H.K.L.

Vorgesch. Stellungen

Vorposten der Sahara-Truppe

But Rommel himself had also worked out a new plan following the murderous retreat, with which he hoped to "pull another rabbit out of his hat." After allowing his *Panzerarmee Afrika* time to rest and refit he wanted to drive from the south into the rear of the Anglo-American front and roll it up. Then he would turn all his forces against Montgomery's Eighth Army pursuing from Libya and drive it back toward the east.

This plan was rejected by the Comando Supremo as well as by the OKW. It was too daring for them and the ratio of forces appeared too unfavorable. Instead the Mareth Line was to be held against the Eighth Army. By doing so *Panzerarmee Afrika* might save Tunisia, as the enemy would now be forced to intervene in the south with major forces and deal with this new player.

Since the Faid Pass and its powerful garrison represented a continuous threat to *Panzerarmee Afrika*, *Generaloberst* von Arnim had major elements of the 10. PD withdrawn from the central sector of the western front, where it was quiet, and regrouped to the south.

Up to that time the 21. PD was the only division

of the DAK to have all of its units in the Mareth position, and had come under the command of the 5. *Panzerarmee*. The division was scheduled for rest and refitting following months of fighting. However, it had arrived just at the right time to take the Faid Pass together with the 10. PD.

Both divisions set off on January 30 under the command of *Generalleutnant* Ziegler. Enveloping the pass from both sides, the two Panzer divisions carried out the first joint attack in Tunisia. Wherever the enemy offered resistance he was caught in a pincer attack and destroyed.

The battle lasted 48 hours. When it was over the Faid Pass was in German hands. The French and Americans withdrew toward Sidi bou Zid. A counterattack with tanks by the US II Corps on February 2 was rebuffed.

A second German attack force, consisting of the "Centauro" Armored Division reinforced by German armored forces, attacked through Maknassy toward Gafsa. The attack was supported by German air forces. The US 1st Armored Division pulled back, abandoning Gafsa.

In Allied Forces Headquarters in Algiers things looked black. If the Germans achieved any further successes Tebessa would be in danger of attack. Supply of the Allied forces depended on possession of that city.

The US II Corps sent several groups toward Sened. However, this failed to help the situation, especially since Sened was given up again.

On February 5 *Generalleutnant* Fischer drove over a mine in the sector held by the "Superga" Division. The General died moments later. The

Major Grün, a battalion commander in PR 5, achieved great success in Tunisia.

191

Division Ia, General Staff *Oberstleutnant* Bürker was seriously injured, while Fischer's chief aide was killed instantly.

Generalmajor von Broich assumed command of the battered division. General Staff *Oberstleutnant* Graf Stauffenberg became his new Ia.

An American attack toward Maknassy was beaten back by the Italians. Powerful Allied forces were being assembled in the Tebessa-Sbeitla-Sidi bou Zid area. Apparently General Eisenhower, like *Feldmarschall* Rommel, was planning an offensive. To counter this enemy attack the staff of the 5. *Panzerarmee* worked out a plan which would see the 10. and 21. PD launch a surprise attack on the American forces assembled west of the Faid Pass. The plan was code-named "*Frühlingswind*" (Spring Wind). *Generalleutnant* Ziegler was given overall command of the operation. Spearheading the attack would be sPzAbt. 501. *Oberst* Pomtow was named Chief of Staff of this battle group. He and *Generalleutnant* Ziegler made their way to La Fauconnerie. Just as they were making their final preparations they were contacted by *Feldmarschall* Rommel. Rommel made the suggestion that he send his fast units from the Mareth Line to support the advance. He was in a position do so, because the Eighth Army was not yet ready to resume fighting, allowing Rommel to withdraw his armored units.

Rommel wanted to realize his secret plan and drive deep into the Allied rear toward Tebessa. In a second phase Rommel wanted to turn north from Tebessa and drive to the Mediterranean coast. If this daring plan succeeded, the entire Allied front in Tunisia would be finished.

However, *Generaloberst* von Arnim rejected Rommel's suggestions and plans because "a series of conditions were missing necessary to carry out such a major attack. For one thing their own forces were too weak; for another it would be impossible to maintain the necessary supply lines."

Since the OKW could not make up its mind to hand over to Rommel supreme command of *all* troops in Africa there remained two separate commands and two different plans. This was a great mistake on the part of the German High Command. There is a number of Allied historians who believe that Rommel's plan stood a real chance of success.

Allied Preparations

The Allies were also making new plans. On the morning of February 13, 1943 General Eisenhower arrived at General Fredenhall's headquarters. He toured the front with Lieutenant Colonel "Red" Akers and visited the sectors held by the 1st Armored and 34th Infantry Divisions. The 9th Infantry Division had not yet reached the combat zone.

In a valley near Fonduk he visited Battle Group B, which was under the command of his old friend Robinett. Afterward Eisenhower drove back to corps headquarters. The Allied combat forces were reorganized. The 18th Army Group was formed under the supreme command of General Eisenhower and his Chief of Staff, Major General Bedell Smith. On February 14 General Harold Alexander assumed command of the new army group. Combined within the army group were the British First and Eighth Armies, the US II Corps, the French XIX Corps and several further units.

Several command changes also took place in the Italian headquarters with the assuming of command of the Italian First Army by General Messe. Ugo Count Cavallero, Chief of the Comando Supremo, was replaced by General Ambrosio. Following the evacuation of Tripolitania General Bastico was removed from the African Theater.

General Messe decided to bolster his depleted front-line units with personnel from the rear echelon. The latter was significantly larger than the fighting forces. As opposed to 30,000 fighting men at the front, the rear echelon units possessed a strength of 55,000 men.

On February 1 General Messe reported the state of the First Army to his new high commander, General Ambrosio. According to the report Battle Group "*Centauro*" was almost without heavy weapons. It was short on tanks, artillery and soldiers. In order to restore the army's fighting strength Messe requested:
148 tanks, 20 scout cars, 28 armored cars.
590 trucks, 491 personnel carriers, 146 ambulances.
90 tractors, 475 motorcycles.

In addition he demanded 10 batteries of artillery with a total of 72 guns. According to General Messe's report the 10. PD was short 7,210 men and 100 tanks. The division had a total of 66 tanks available.

On the Razor's Edge

In the Mareth Position. From left: Generalmajor Graf Sponeck, commander of the 90th Light Division; Oberst Panzenhagen and Oberleutnant Diebold, the regimental adjutant.

Through the Faid Pass - Toward Tebessa

In the early morning hours of February 14, 1943 the Mareth Line was being held by the Italian Twentieth and Thirty-first Army Corps, reinforced by the 164. Light Division commanded by *Generalmajor* Freiherr von Liebenstein. The Sahara Group manned positions from Matmata as far as Toum-Tatahouine on the Schott el Djerid. Rommel had secured his rear in preparation for his own attack.

The two attack groups had assembled west of Sfax. The *"Centauro"* Division, reinforced by several German Panzer companies, stormed southwest toward Gafsa, while the second attack group under *Generalleutnant* Ziegler with the 10. and 21. Panzer Divisions set out toward Faid Pass. In the spearhead group were the companies of sPzAbt. 501, led by *Oberleutnant* Hartmann.

Ziegler split his force before reaching the pass. While the 21. PD veered south to outflank the pass and the tanks of the US 1st Armored Division on the heights there, *Generalmajor* von Broich led the 10. Panzer Division through the pass.

The first Sherman tanks to show themselves were knocked out by the Tigers. *Oberfeldwebel* Augustin managed to destroy a retreating Sherman from a range of 2,700 meters, proof of the effectiveness of the Tiger's gun. The breakthrough was achieved, and the tanks of PR 7 rolled past the Tigers before veering south to join up with the 21. PD which had radioed that it was in the area south of Sidi bou Zid. The 10. Panzer Division reached Sidi bou Zid and drove into the town.

There it was met by American tanks. The battle for Sidi bou Zid, in which both Panzer Divisions were involved, was a disaster for the US armored forces. They lost over 70 tanks. A major part of the success was due to the 21. PD's I./PR 8 led by *Hauptmann* Stotten. Although it began the raid with only 23 tanks the battalion accounted for a large proportion of the enemy tanks destroyed. The Second Battalion was still behind the Mareth Line regaining its strength.

The German tanks had scored a great success, but *Generalleutnant* Ziegler wanted more. He assembled his forces and early on the morning of February 15 set off along the aqueduct toward Sbeitla. The American Battle Groups A and C took on the German force a second time. Tank-versus-tank fighting broke out again. The 11th Company of the US 1st Armored Regiment under Colonel Alger was destroyed. The Colonel was taken prisoner by the Germans after his tank was disabled. Once again the Americans lost the majority of the tanks they had committed. US

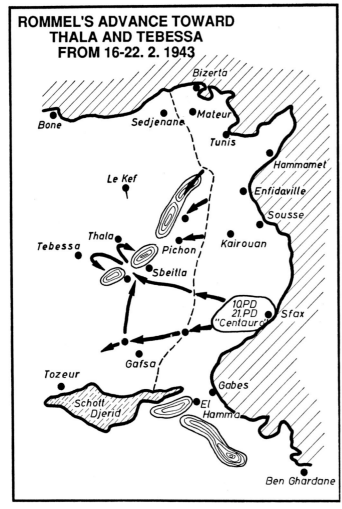

ROMMEL'S ADVANCE TOWARD THALA AND TEBESSA FROM 16-22. 2. 1943

losses in the two days were 165 tanks and armored cars. More than 2,000 American soldiers were taken prisoner.

In the White House, President Roosevelt turned to his military experts on receiving a report of the disaster and shouted accusingly:

"Don't our boys know how to fight?"

In the headquarters of the British First Army and at Allied Headquarters in Algiers it was believed that the main German thrust was yet to come. It was expected to be aimed at Fonduk. Allied troops carried out a fighting withdrawal toward the Kasserine Pass.

On February 16 the 10. Panzer Division turned north and advanced in the direction of Pichon, while the Tiger company received orders to eliminate the enemy forces at the crossroads 15 kilometers northwest of Sidi bou Zid. The attack was a success.

The powerful French battle group in Pichon, which *Generalmajor* von Broich wanted to eliminate, held out on February 16. Ziegler was sent IR 47 under *Oberstleutnant* Buhse. However, when the regiment arrived in position it was halted. Ziegler had received orders from army headquarters to halt the attack. The drive toward the Kasserine Pass by the 21. PD was also halted. Both Panzer divisions were now sent to *Feldmarschall* Rommel, while *Generalleutnant* Ziegler and *Oberst* Pomtow returned to Tunis-North. What had happened to stop this successful attack?

Feldmarschall Rommel had, as already mentioned, proposed an attack on February 5, which had been rejected. Nevertheless, the *Feldmarschall* gave orders for the 164. Light Division and the 15. Panzer Division to make preparations to attack.

When, on the morning of February 15, the US II Corps gave up Gafsa for fear of being hemmed in by Ziegler's advance, Rommel immediately sent *Oberst* Menton with the *Afrika* Panzer-Grenadier Regiment (the former Special Unit 288) toward Gafsa. Mentons's Panzer-Grenadiers occupied the town. A strong patrol was sent ahead toward Feriana. German troops were now due south of the Kasserine Pass. By February 17 elements of the DAK were occupying Feriana. Now Rommel's plan did not appear so audacious to the OKW. It might be possible to take Tebessa after all.

When Thelepte airfield was taken, the OKW placed both Panzer divisions of the 5. *Panzerarmee* under *Feldmarschall* Rommel's control and authorized the continuation of the battle in the direction of Tebessa. This meant the break-up of *kampfgruppe* Ziegler.

The 21. Panzer Division took Sbeitla. In the meantime Rommel had sent the 10. Panzer Division toward the Kasserine Pass. The pass was the gateway to the Tunisian mountain country. The attack began on February 19. At the same time German and Italian forces far to the south advanced on Tozeur and took the town. Reconnaissance units drove around the pass and rolled northwest along the road to Tebessa. They passed Garet en Naam, Djebel Dernaja and Djebel Chettabis. The objective of Tebessa lay within reach. Supported by artillery the 10. PD attacked late in the day on February 19. AA 3 reached the pass hill. After two hours of close-range fighting AA 3 was turned back. *Oberst* Menton attacked, but this attack, too, bogged down in the face of enemy artillery fire.

On the morning of February 20 the *Bersaglieri* of the *"Ariete"* Division attacked. They were turned back. The 10., 15. and 21. Panzer Divisions, the *"Centauro"* and elements of the *"Ariete"* Divisions began to bunch up in front of the pass.

Werferregiment 71, which had followed the attacking forces, now came into play. *Oberst* Andreas laid down destructive fire from the rocket launchers. Before the dust raised by the rocket salvoes had settled *Hauptmann* Hans-Günther Stotten led I./PR 8 into the pass and took out the anti-tank guns there. Stotten's attack smashed open the way. German motorized units, led by the Panzers, poured through to the west and north. Rommel had done it, and once more his watchword went down the line: "exploit!"

General Anderson ordered: "No one is to take one footstep back!"

On the evening of February 20 Rommel committed the 10. PD toward Thala. The 10. PD was sent around the foot of the mountain. This new attack cost the Anglo-Americans 169 tanks, 95 scout cars, 36 self-propelled guns and 50 artillery pieces.

IR 47 under *Oberstleutnant* Buhse stormed through Pichon toward the northwest in a move to support of the main attack and tie down the enemy in his present location. Buhse's forces reached Kessera.

On February 21 the main group captured another pass during its advance toward Tebessa. Now there remained only the pass over the Djebel el Hamra. The 10. PD captured Thala.

General Alexander, who had just assumed his duties as Commander-in-Chief, drove at once to Thala, assembling all the troops he could find along the way. The Sixth Armoured Division and the Guards reached the battlefield and halted the 10. PD. PR 7 lost ten tanks. Then the US 9th Infantry Battle joined the battle, mainly with its artillery. The 10. Panzer Division gave up Thala.

The second German column, which was advancing directly toward Tebessa, was stopped by Battle Group B, which had been ordered to protect tebessa and its airfield at Souk les Bains. At about midnight on February 21 Battle Group B was joined by Brigadier Nicholson of the British Sixth Armoured Division, who was to coordinate Allied operations. Nicholson gave Robinett the Twenty-sixth Armoured Brigade commanded by Brigadier McNabb as support. As a result, the 10. PD became involved with the Twenty-sixth Armoured Brigade while the DAK, which was being spearheaded by the *"Centauro"* Division, ran into Battle Group B.

Both sides suffered heavy losses in the ensuing fighting. Ten Stukas attacked at noon on February 21. Two were shot down. By the time it became dark and night fell, Battle Group B had halted the drive by the DAK.

Allied aircraft intervened in the battle for the last pass at first light. On this day — Washington's birthday — the DAK was again stopped by Battle Group B. *Feldmarschall* Rommel, who was with the DAK, was forced to run through a cactus grove to escape a surprise artillery barrage.

IR 47, which had advanced more than 20 kilometers past Pichon, waited in vain on 21. PD's northern wing. The division was stalled in front of dense minefield near Sbiba.

Feldmarschall Rommel, who at this critical moment had just received unfavorable reports from the Mareth Line, and realized that the attack toward Tebessa was not moving quickly enough, broke off the operation which had begun so well.

Opposite the Mareth Line the British Eighth Army had regrouped sooner than Rommel had anticipated. Following a situation briefing at the Kasserine Pass, which was attended by *Feldmarschall* Kesselring who had flown in from Frascati, Rommel called off the attack. During the briefing Kesselring sounded out Rommel to see if his state of health would allow him to take over the formation of an Army Group in Tunis and become its commander. Such a move would finally resolve the uncertain situation between Rommel, von Arnim and General Messe. The doctors had given Rommel only four weeks. Then he would have to resume his cure.

The divisions were withdrawn slowly toward their jumping-off positions. As they withdrew they blew up bridges and pass positions and laid mines.

On February 23 *Feldmarschall* Kesselring issued orders from Frascati for a new command structure. *Heeresgruppe Afrika* (Army Group Africa) was born. Under its command were all German Army, Luftwaffe anti-aircraft and Italian units. *Feldmarschall* Rommel was named Army Commander-in-Chief. His planned successor was *Generaloberst* von Arnim.

In the Mareth Line the defending Italian divisions, together with the Panzer-Grenadiers of the 90. Light Division and elements of the 15. Panzer Division, repelled Montgomery's first, tentative attacks. Nevertheless, the troops of the 15. PD were glad when First Battalion returned to the division following the Kasserine Pass raid, bringing with it a rich booty in captured trucks. *Hauptmann* Stotten was recommended for the Oak Leaves for his breakthrough. He received the decoration on May 10, 1943.

While preparations for a new offensive were under way in the Mareth Line, *Generaloberst* von Arnim was getting ready for another operation, code-named "*Ochsenkopf*." The attack was to capture the line of hills in the Tunis area and subsequently occupy the entire Medjez el Bab basin.

5. *Panzerarmee* was moved in; it consisted of IR 47, which had been relieved by the newly-arrived 999. ID, and the von Manteuffel Division. The latter had been raised from various units in January 1943 by *Generalmajor* von Manteuffel. The bulk of the division was formed from the "von Broich Division."

Hasso von Manteuffel and the division were to intervene in the northern sector near Djebel Abiod, where Witzig's Pionier were still in position.

Corps Group Weber and the Lang Brigade moved into position to the south. Also arriving were sPzAbt. 501, which now had 30 Tigers, and the main body of the 334. ID.

Operation "*Ochsenkopf*" began on the early morning of February 26. There was heavy fighting in every sector. German fighters and Stukas provided air support. The Tiger tanks, led by *Major* Lueder, rolled toward their objective of Beja, supported by 15 Panzer IVs of PR 7. It was raining hard and the Tigers soon bogged down. Nevertheless, the Allied strongpoint of Sidi en Sir was taken. The tanks had to turn back toward the road. Several were knocked out by anti-tank guns firing from the flank.

The attack continued the next day. After 10 kilometers heavy artillery fire began to come in and at 11.00 Allied fighter-bombers attacked. The attack force suffered heavy losses.

The advance was resumed on February 28. Twelve kilometers from Beja seven Tigers drove over mines one after another. *major* Lueder was wounded, as were *Oberleutnante* Hartmann, Kodar, Stockhammer, Loose and Pohl. Today a memorial stone erected by the Allies stands at this spot, marking the "Tiger graveyard at Beja." *Major* Seidensticker took command of the battalion.

The entire Corps Group Weber was stuck in the mud near Zebla. The soldiers of GJR 756 under *Oberst* Lang moved into positions on the hills northeast of Medjez el Bab. The Grenadiers of IR 47 were holding the Djebel el Ang and the nearby hills.

Advancing in the southern lane of attack were FJR 5 and the "*Hermann Göring*" Division. In the center was Jäger-Regiment 3. Bitter fighting broke out between Bou Arada and Goubellat. I./FJR 5 under *Hauptmann* Jungwirt was badly battered at Djebel Rihane by the paratroops of the British Sixth Commandos and elements of the Seventy-eighth Infantry Division's Eleventh Brigade.

III./FJR 5 under *Hauptmann* Schirmer took a British rest camp southeast of Kir el Briouigue in the first rush. 10./FJR 5 and ten tanks rolled up toward the top of the pass at Hir el Krima. At the top they came under concentrated fire. British machine-gun positions were taken out with hand grenades. The enemy pulled back and *Oberleutnant* Gasteyer, who was leading Tenth Company, pressed *Hauptmann* Hofbauer, who was commanding the escorting tank company, to continue the advance toward El Aroussa.

It was four hours before the advance was

resumed. The small battle group had meanwhile been joined by several anti-aircraft and anti-tank guns of the *"Hermann Göring"* Division.

Early in the afternoon of February 26, after covering two kilometers, the leading tank came under fire from anti-tank guns. Nine Panzer IIIs were quickly knocked out of action. The British ambush was fatal for the battle group. Enemy tanks appeared. The following 88mm Flak knocked out several before it was destroyed.

The group pulled back to the pass hill. Elements of 10./FJR 5 set up an all-round defensive position on Hill 351, to the right of the pass. The British attacked the hill on the 27th and were stopped. The German paratroops held onto the hill throughout February 28. The issue was decided on March 1. The positions had to be evacuated following a heavy British attack. The paratroops fell back, stopping to give battle to the pursuing British at Djebel Djaffa before rejoining their regiment on the plain of Goubellat.

It was not until now that it became known that 11./FJR 5 under *Oberleutnant* Kristufek had suffered very heavy losses at Lalla Manna. Kristufek and a few of his men had managed to fall back on March 1.

On March 1 *Hauptmann* Schirmer was awarded the german Cross in Gold and promoted to *Major*. In an address *Generalmajor* Schmid, commander of the *"Hermann Göring"* Division, revealed that, effective immediately, FJR 5 was renamed *Jäger-Regiment "Hermann Göring"* and was now a part of the division.

Stocktaking

The general situation of *Heeresgruppe Afrika* at the beginning of March had firmed despite the failed Operation *"Ochsenkopf."* The front was 455 kilometers long. In addition there was 400 kilometers of coastline which had to be guarded, as further Allied landings were a possibility.

A total of 34 German and 14 Italian battalions were available to the Axis defence. Each battalion had to man 10 kilometers of front. Ready to support the infantry were 49 batteries, mostly small caliber guns.

At the same time the British First Army possessed two infantry divisions, an armored division and two brigades with a total of 50,000 men. This force was supported by 240 artillery pieces, 400 anti-tank guns and 166 tanks. The US forces consisted of 40,000 men with 200 pieces of artillery, 200 anti-tank guns and 200 tanks. The units of the French Nineteenth Corps likewise consisted of 40,000 men in three divisions and one brigade.

Facing these forces was the 5. *Panzerarmee*.

Facing the Mareth Line General Montgomery's Eighth Army had 80,000 men, 400 guns, 550 anti-tank guns and 900 tanks, divided into eight divisions.

The entire *Heeresgruppe Afrika* consisted of 80,000 German and 40,000 Italian first-line troops. Rear echelon units included 230,000 men, 150,000 of them Italian. The Axis units were 50% below strength in tanks and heavy weapons.

With its weak forces *Heeresgruppe Afrika* tried to frustrate the enemy's build-up for his new year's offensive by launching sharp, local attacks. It was clear that the British offensive could not be prevented in the long run. It was just as clear that they would break through and cut off the 1. *Armee*.

In order to avoid this critical development the German command had to shorten the front *and* move the 1. *Armee* closer to the 5. *panzerarmee*. Therefore a stronger blow was planned by the armored forces from the Mareth position. The initial objective was Medenine.

The 90. Light Division was in positions in the Mareth area on both sides of the Medenine-Gabes road. To its left, and extending to the sea was the "Young Fascists" Division. To the right of the 90. Light were *"Trieste"* and *"Pistola."* The 164. Light Division was holding the mountain pass near Mareth. The deep flank west of El Kebilli and the mountain massif was guarded by Italian units and *Armee* reconnaissance units. As attack units Rommel had available the 15., 21. and 10. Panzer Divisions, the latter having been placed under his command for the operation. The *"Centauro"* Division and Brigade L under General Imperiali were covering the rear of the 1. *Armee*. Command of the DAK had been assumed by *General* Cramer, who had just returned to Africa.

Rommel had decided to carry out an attack from the west toward Medenine against the enemy forces in the southern Mareth Line. The plan's greatest disadvantage was the long approach march required, because the 10., 15. and 21. Panzer

March 1943. The Panzerführer Afrika, Oberst Irkens (without hat), gives orders to Hauptmann Stotten, commander of I./PR 8 (left), and Hauptmann Schnelle, commander of II./PR 8.

The commanders of PR 8. From left: Hauptmann Schnelle, Oberst Irkens and Hauptmann Stotten.

Divisions, as well as the 164. Light Division, were to "drive through Ksar el Hallouf Pass, going wide around the British left wing, and fall on the enemy's rear."

By March 3 the German units were in their assembly areas. PR 8 assembled during the night of March 5/6 with II./PR 8 in front, the Regimental Headquarters in the center and First Battalion in the rear.

The DAK's artillery opened the attack with a barrage on the Medenine-Métameur area. *Oberst* Irkens led the famous PR 8; PR 5 was under the command of *Panzerführer Afrika* . PR 7 attacked led by *Oberst* Gerhardt.

The tanks did not get far as they drove into a dense wall of fire from forty enemy batteries.

Oberst Irkens managed to reach the Allied front line, but his tank was then hit hard. Rolling into cover, the *Oberst* drove on. More and more of his tanks were knocked out. Their crews advanced on foot. The regiment, which had set out with 80 tanks, lost 55, only a few of which were repairable.

The other units also suffered heavy losses, and that afternoon at the command post of the 21. PD *General* Cramer proposed calling off the attack. Rommel agreed with a heavy heart.

Three days later Rommel handed over command in Africa to *Generaloberst* von Arnim and flew to *Führer* Headquarters to report to Hitler. The decision was reached in the FHQ on March 13. All non-motorized elements of 1. *Armee* were to be pulled out of the Mareth Line and sent to the Gabes Line. Only the fast units were to remain in the Mareth area. They were not to pull back until an enemy breakthrough was imminent or they were in danger of being outflanked. It was hoped they could hang on to the bridgehead until autumn.

Rommel requested that the southern front be pulled back 150 kilometers. The 300 Italian guns thus freed up could be employed in Bridgehead Tunisia. In his opinion this was the only way the bridgehead stood a realistic chance of holding out. Hitler rejected the idea. Rommel was ordered to resume his cure at once and regain his health as soon as possible.

There was a shake-up in the German command in Africa. *Generaloberst* von Arnim became the new Commander-in-Chief, while *General* Ziegler remained on as his deputy. *Generalmajor* Gause became Chief of Staff, while *Oberst* Pomtow was named Ia. *Generaloberst* Messe remained Commander-in-Chief of the 1. *Armee,* while General Mancinelli became his Italian Chief of Staff and *Oberst* Bayerlein his German Chief of Staff. The new Commander-in-Chief of 5. *Panzerarmee* was *General* von Vaerst, and his Chief of Staff *Generalmajor* von Quast. The DAK was commanded by *General* Cramer; his Chief of Staff was *Oberst* Nolte.

Briefing personnel of Kampfgruppe Irkens, March 1943.

Toward the End

Battles in the Northern Sector

At the beginning of March several Allied attacks against the Manteuffel Division in the northern sector were repulsed. On March 17 *Generalmajor* von Manteuffel attacked north of Djebel Abiod while his right wing remained stationary 12 kilometers south of Cap Serrat.

The attack pushed through to St. Temara; the second group attacking from the east reached a point due north of the pass and held there. The attack was resumed on the morning of March 19. Battle Group Witzig took Hill 199, northeast of Djebel Abiod. The other two battle groups and the *Bersaglierei* followed.

This line was held until March 28. Then the enemy broke through with powerful forces, including tanks and artillery. The Manteuffel Division was forced to pull back toward the east in driving rain, finally halting near Sedjenane where it set up defensive positions on both sides of the town.

The enemy forces managed to break through there on March 30. A counterattack regained some ground, but the Allies launched a new attack which led to a penetration of the division's lines. It was forced to withdraw into the area 20 kilometers east of Cap Serrat-St. Jefna-St. de Nair. The situation then firmed up. The division received supplies and replacements.

Operation Pugilist

While the battles were going on in the Northern Sector, on March 20 the British Eighth Army set out to capture the Mareth position. The British opened their offensive at 20.00 with a massed artillery barrage. Using assault ladders, the Fiftieth and Fifty-first Infantry Divisions negotiated the deep Zigzaghou wadi. However, as a result of the deep mud only six tanks managed to get forward.

Generalmajor
Willibald Borowietz.

The "Young Fascists" defended their positions and on March 21 *General* Borowietz decided to intervene with the 15. PD. Once again the attack was spearheaded by PR 8 under *Oberst* Irkens. Following two days of continuous fighting, the enemy was thrown back with heavy losses. The six British tanks were destroyed. General Montgomery called off the operation.

However, Battle Group Mannerini's front on Djebel Tabaga was pushed back. When *General-oberst* von Arnim arrived on the battlefield on March 23, he authorized *Generaloberst* Messe to pull back the non-mobile units of 1 *Armee* into the Akarit position.

The New Zealand Second Division attacked on the morning of March 26. The British First Armoured Division joined the attack. By evening they had achieved a deep penetration. If these forces succeeded in breaking through to the sea, 1 *Armee* would be lost.

Once again 15 Panzer Division was alerted. The Panzers rolled into the enemy's southern flank and halted the advance. This gained time for the remains of the 164 Light Division and 21 Panzer Division to establish a defensive line near El Hamma. Further British attacks on March 27 and 28 stalled in front of this line. These actions allowed 1 *Armee* to withdraw into the Akarit position.

Desperate fighting was also going on in other sectors. For example in the Guettar area the "*Centauro*" Division was defending against an enemy force twice its size.

The US II Corps had been instructed by General Alexander to support Montgomery's offensive from the Gafsa area. However, the US 34th Infantry Division did not get a chance to do so. At the same time the US 9th Armored Division tried to break through Sened into the coastal plain. It was stopped by small German battle groups and forced back. Battle group Medicus played a major role in the successful Axis defence. In the final stages it received support from Battle Group Lang. On April 18, 1943 *Major* Franz Medicus was awarded the Knight's Cross for his exploits. The Americans were thrown back sector by sector.

The supply situation of *Heeresgruppe Afrika* had become critical. No ships had got through since March 23. That in spite all these difficulties it managed to defend against the Eighth Army's advance toward Gabes with 7,000 vehicles was one of the miracles of the African Campaign.

To the Bitter End

On the late evening of April 4, 1943 the Eighth Army's Third Corps readied itself. At midnight the corps launched a frontal attack against the positions of the Italian Twentieth Corps with the Indian Fourth and the British Fiftieth and Fifty-first Infantry Divisions. The first three hill positions were overrun. Hill 167 and Hill 175 were lost. GR 200 of the 90 Light Division held its sector of the front and threw back the enemy. When an enemy breakthrough threatened, the tanks of 15 Panzer Division and a Panzer-Grenadier Battalion under the command of *Hauptmann* Pätzold carried out a counterattack.

Oberst Irkens described the action in his terse style:

"In the morning twilight we came upon a an assembly of enemy trucks with munitions and fuel, obviously meant for the enemy tanks which had broken through. They were destroyed or captured, not a single truck escaped.

We reached and secured the breach in the line, but a further advance was impossible, because at that moment 50 tanks which had broken through and then been cut off from their supplies came rolling back. They were engaged by the Ihde Company and then by the following tanks and anti-aircraft guns of the division. After suffering losses they turned away to the west. In the area of the breach in the line we found about twenty cut-off and stranded tanks of PR 5 and refuelled them.

The great success of the day was the preventing of the British outflanking of the Mareth position. We were able to withdraw the units still holding out there to the Schott position north of El Hamma-Gabes."

The next night PR 8 covered the withdrawal of the 90 Light Division and slowly fell back toward the Schott position. Enemy forces followed, but did not pursue vigorously.

Advancing hesitantly, the advance guards of the Eighth Army reached the Gabes-Gafsa road on the evening of April 7, where they met the US II Corps, now commanded by General Patton.

Battle groups from the DAK repeatedly turned and halted the following divisions of the Eighth Army which were attacking toward Sousse. Near Kairouan on April 11 the Americans established contact with the British Ninth Corps of the First Army which was advancing eastward toward Fonduk.

By this time the withdrawing 1 *Armee* had reached the Enfidaville mountain position.

Between Pichon and Fonduk the Fullriede Group, which had been formed from German and Italian units, was fighting against the US 6th Armored Division, which was supported by the US 34th Infantry Division and the British One-Hundred-and-Twenty-eighth Brigade. *Oberstleutnant* Fullriede held off the enemy for six days. Sixty enemy tanks were destroyed and the US 6th

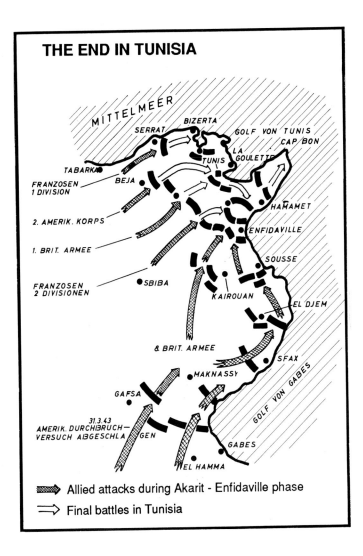

THE END IN TUNISIA

MITTELMEER

SERRAT · BIZERTA · GOLF VON TUNIS
CAP BON
LA GOULETTE
TUNIS
TABARKA
FRANZOSEN 1 DIVISION
BEJA
HAMAMET
2. AMERIK. KORPS
ENFIDAVILLE
1. BRIT. ARMEE
SOUSSE
FRANZOSEN 2 DIVISIONEN
· SBIBA
KAIROUAN
EL DJEM
8. BRIT. ARMEE
SFAX
· MAKNASSY
GAFSA
GOLF VON GABES
31.3.43 AMERIK. DURCHBRUCH-VERSUCH ABGESCHLAGEN
GABES
EL HAMMA

⟹ Allied attacks during Akarit - Enfidaville phase

⟹ Final battles in Tunisia

Armored Division brought to the brink of defeat. Fullriede's stand permitted a withdrawal to the Enfidaville position. In recognition of this defensive success *Oberstleutnant* Fullriede was awarded the Knight's Cross on April 18.

On April 10 the Eighth Army reached Sfax. On the evening of the 13th the spearheads of Tenth Corps reached the anti-tank ditches in front of the Enfidaville position.

As Commander-in-Chief of the Eighteenth Army Group, on April 12 General Alexander informed General Montgomery that the First Army was going to carry out the main attack in the final offensive toward Tunis. The Eighth Army's job was to tie down the enemy on the southern front.

Attack in the North

In the north, where the Allies had taken Cap Serrat on April 1, the French, Moroccans and Americans prepared to move. They attacked in the southern sector and achieved a penetration near Heidous. The Axis front line was restored by a counterattack led personally by *Generalmajor* von Manteuffel.

On April 7 the 78th Infantry Division and an attached armored brigade attempted to take Longstop Hill. The 334 ID under *Generalmajor* Krause gradually fell back, but still held Longstop.

The *"Hermann Göring"* Division had dug in on and around Hill 107 with FJR 5 in the central sector. *Oberstleutnant* Koch had been sent back to germany on account of illness. FJR 5 was now led by *Major* Schirmer. Everything appeared stable there.

In view of the prevailing situation and the combat strengths of its divisions, it was clear to *Heeresgruppe Afrika* that the battle in Bridgehead Tunisia was drawing to a close.

From the 14th to the 16th of April the newly-arrived British Fourth Infantry Division opened the attack near Sidi Nsir against the Lang Regiment of the 334 Infantry Division.

The general offensive toward the Enfidaville position by the Eighth Army began on the night of April 19/20. Enfidaville fell and Montgomery regrouped his forces on the 22nd. He shifted the main weight of his attack to the coastal zone. The hill positions near Enfidaville-Zaghouan were too difficult for him.

On April 24 the 78th Infantry Division captured Longstop Hill, opening the "gate to Tunis."

The Allies now launched the final battle. They advanced with all divisions. Near Sidi Nsir the US 34th Infantry Division tried for four days to take Djebel Tahent. Not until May 1 were the two battalions of IR 47 forced to retire.

The US 1st Infantry Division attacked the Manteuffel Division's Barenthin Regiment. In front of the 334 Infantry Division the attack columns of the US 9th Infantry Division assembled in the Tine Valley for an attack. When, on April 30 the enemy broke through the Manteuffel Division positions held by the *Bersaglieri* Regiment, *Generaloberst* von Arnim decided to pull the whole right wing back to a line west of Bizerta — Djebel Achkel (hills west of Mateur) — Edekila — Bordj Toum. The move was carried out during the night of May 1/2.

On Djebel Achkel Witzig's Pioniere dug in. The paratroops held there until May 6, 1943. When Djebel Berna was lost, Hasso von Manteuffel launched another counterattack. The hill was recovered, but the short, wiry officer collapsed on the battlefield. Sick for weeks, he had fought on until overcome by exhaustion.

On May 7 the defensive front west of Bizerta was broken. The harbor installations were blown up by the withdrawing Manteuffel Division. The division was still holding south of Lake Bizerta.

By May 4 the Allies were able to push their front ahead to a line Bordj Toum - French Ferme - Fourna - Ksartyr - Kamelberg hills near Pont du Fahs. Holding out on Hill 107 and a neighboring hill were the men of FJR 5. The "cactus farm," which was being held by a platoon under *Oberfeldwebel* Schäfer, had been under attack by strong British forces since April 28. Schäfer held out against heavy tank and air attacks for three days. His men destroyed 37 enemy tanks. Schäfer then fell back and rejoined his regiment. For this success he received the Knight's Cross on August 8, 1944 while a POW in Camp Harne, Texas.

Oberst Irkens had meanwhile been named *Panzerführer Afrika*. He commanded the remains of Panzer Regiments 5, 7 and 8, the two Tiger battalions and an Italian tank and assault gun battalion under Major Piscelli and was under the direct command of *Heeresgruppe Afrika*. With his last 70 tanks he was supposed to bring about a change in Axis fortunes and halt the Allied armored armada. His armored force saw action several times and halted the enemy for a time, but then came May 6, 1943.

On May 6 the British First Army launched the final offensive in the Medjez el Bab sector. An avalanche of more than 1,000 tanks rolled toward Tunis. Allied fighters and bombers droned overhead the steel phalanx.

Irkens' few tanks threw themselves against the wave of Allied armor. Just north of the point of penetration were 30 German tanks, mostly from PR 8, which was led by *Hauptmann* Schnelle. Irkens decided on his own to launch a counterattack against the northern wing and north flank of the enemy forces which had broken through. Once again the battle-tested tank commanders proved themselves, halting the enemy penetration for a short time. When the last 20 tanks broke contact with the enemy that afternoon they had destroyed 90 enemy tanks at a cost of 10 of their own.

During that night and the following day they drove back toward the airfield at El Alia. There, west of Tunis, the tanks fought several small battles until their ammunition and fuel was gone.

The last British prisoners, captured at the beginning of May 1943.

The last seven tanks were driven over the edge of a wadi and destroyed. For *Panzerkampfgruppe* Irkens the battle was over.

On the evening of the eventful 6th of May, 1943, FJR 5 prepared to fight its last battle at the Miliana, east of Pont du Fahs. It was supported by the 21. Panzer Division. The French attacked collapsed before these two units.

The Allies resumed their offensive at first light on May 7. Again there were heavy air and artillery bombardments. The battered German units pulled back toward Tunis. The British entered Tunis at 17.40, splitting the forces of *Heeresgruppe Afrika.*

Not until may 9 was the enemy able to break through east of lake Bizerta and capture Forte Farina. The last order from the Panzer-AOK 5 was issued at 15.24:

"Destroy all installations and equipment. Farewell! — Long live Germany!"

On the morning of May 8 the British occupied the rest of Tunis. During the night of May 7/8 *General* Frantz established a defensive line near Hammanlif and west of it behind the Miliane with the remains of the 19 Flak Division. What was left of 10 Panzer Division and the *"Hermann Göring"* Division assembled there. The British Sixth Armoured Division was unable to break through near Hammanlif until May 10. It was followed by the Indian Fourth Division which turned toward Cap Bone, occupying the peninsula by evening of May 12. The German soldiers there went into captivity.

The Sixth Armoured Division continued its southward advance into the rear of 1 *Armee,* which was still holding out against the Eighth Army. Elements of the 90 Light Division and the "Young Fascists" Division turned north and repelled the enemy on May 11 and 12.

On May 12 all the divisions of the German center group signed off with *Heeresgruppe Afrika,* which was in its final headquarters near Ste. Marie du Zit. *General* Cramer broke through to the headquarters with his last two tanks. On May 12 *Generaloberst* von Arnim reported to Rome that the headquarters was surrounded on two sides. The same day he offered the Allied High Command the surrender of *Heeresgruppe Afrika. General der Panzertruppe* Cramer sent the last radio message to the OKW:

"To the OKW: ammunition expended. Weapons and military equipment destroyed. As ordered, the *Afrika-Korps* has fought until it can fight no more."

The 90 Light Division surrendered on the evening of May 12. On the morning of May 13 the batteries of the 1 *Armee* fired off their last shells, some toward the north and some south. The 164 Light Division under *Generalmajor* Freiherr von Liebenstein fought on to the end.

At about midday *Generaloberst* Messe, who just before had received a promotion to *Feldmarschall* from the Duce, concluded a surrender with General Freyberg, commander of the New Zealand Second Division.

In Africa the guns fell silent. During the final few months the Italian and German forces had fought unbelievably well.

On May 13 General Alexander sent a message to Prime Minister Churchill. It said:

"Sir, it is my duty to report that the Tunisian Campaign is over. All enemy resistance has ceased. All of Africa is ours!"

For the Germans the end in Africa was as catastrophic as Stalingrad. In "Tunisgrad" 130,000 German soldiers went into captivity alongside 180,000 Italian troops.

The Tobruk Memorial.

100,000 soldiers of all nationalities lost their lives in this theater. German casualties were 18,594 dead and 3,400 missing.

The Italians lost 13,748 dead and 8,821 missing. On the British side 35,476 men were killed.

The USA, fighting exclusively in the Tunisia area, lost 16,500 men.

The number of French soldiers killed in Africa is unknown.

The last to die in the African war, however, was a young Arab named Achmed el Bedui. He came back from Africa with his commander, *Hauptmann* Kuhlmann, was captured and finally brought before a French court martial. He was sentenced to hang because he, as a "French citizen," had fought against France. He, too, died as a German soldier, even if his name appears on no grave stone.

Below left: Oberstleutnant Burkhard Hering following his harrowing escape across the Mediterranean in May 1943.

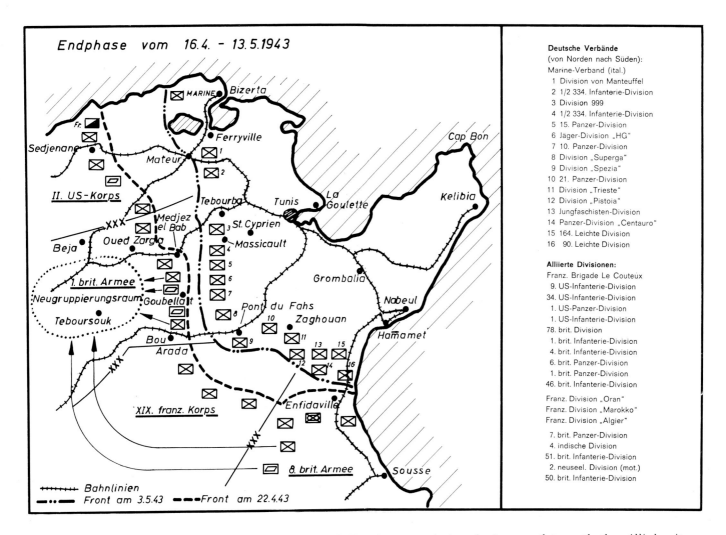

Endphase vom 16.4. – 13.5.1943

The final phase from 16.4 — 13.5 1943. The table on the right lists German units in order from north to south, then Allied units.

The High Command of the Wehrmacht Announces on May 13, 1943 that:

The heroic battle of the German and Italian African units has today reached its honorable conclusion. The last resisting groups in the Tunis area, without food or water for days, were forced to cease fighting after firing the last of their ammunition. They finally succumbed to lack of supplies, not to the assaults of the enemy, who often enough was forced to admit the superiority of our arms in this theater. Nevertheless, the Italian and German African fighters fully ac-

complished the tasks set them. Through their resistance, which made the enemy pay for every foot of ground during the months-long, bitter fighting, they tied down the enemy's most powerful forces and inflicted heavy losses on them in men and materiel. The relief provided to other fronts and the time won was of the greatest benefit to the command of the Axis powers. On May 10 the *Führer* sent the following radio message to *Generaloberst* von Arnim, who has been in command of the German-Italian forces for some time:

"I express my thanks and deepest appreciation to you and your heroically-fighting troops, who in true comradeship in arms with your Italian comrades defended every foot of African soil. It was with admiration that the entire German people watched with me the heroic battle of your soldiers in Tunisia. It has been of the greatest significance to the overall success of the war. The final action and conduct of your troops will be an example for the entire armed forces of the Greater German Reich and serve as an especially glorious page in the history of German warfare. Signed Adolf Hitler." (Archives of Contemporary History 1943, Page 5934 A)

Top: Retired General der Kavallerie Siegfried Westphal, representative of the Afrika-Korps veterans Association, lays a wreath on Anzac Day, April 25, 1971. He was the first German general to receive an invitation to Australia and New Zealand after the war.

Below: Frau Lucie-Maria Rommel, honorary member of the DAK Veterans Association, with retired General Westphal.

Sources

Alexander, Harold R., *D'El Alamein à Tunis à la Sicile*, Paris 1945

– *The Battle of Tunis*, 1957

Alman, Karl, *Ritter der Sieben Meere*, Rastatt 1963

– *Sprung in die Hölle*, Rastatt 1964

– *Graue Wölfe in blauer See*, Rastatt 1967

Altieri, James, *The Spearheaders*, New York 1960

Arcy-Dawson, John, de *Tunisian Battle*, London 1944

Arnim, Jürgen von, *Tunisien nach 14 Jahren*, ZS 1957

Audouin-Dubreuil, Louis, *La Guerre de Tunisie*, Paris 1945

Avallone, Enzo, *Riposta a Montgomery*, Rome 1959

Barré, G., *Tunisie 1942-43*, Paris 1950

Beil, Johannes, *II./PzAR 155 im Einsatz*, ZS and, in manuscript

Benz, Heinrich, *Unser Fallschirmjäger-Regiment 5*, In manuscript 1964

Bernig, Heinrich H., *Hölle Alamein*, Balve 1960

Bharucha, P.C., *The North African Campaign.*, London 1956

Bourgeon, Charles, *Les Carillons sans Joie*, Paris 1959

Bradley, Omar N., *A Soldier's Story*, New York 1964, 2nd Edition

Braddock, David W. , *The Campaigns in Egypt and Libya 1940-42*, Aldershot 1964

Briel, Georg, *Afrika-Einsätze der Kampfgruppe Briel*, In manuscript

Büschleb, H., *Feldherrn und Panzer im Wüstenkampf*, Neckargemünd 1964

Butcher, H.C., *My Three Years with Eisenhower*, New York 1946

Carell, Paul, *Die Wüstenfüchse.* Hamburg, 1961

Cramer, Hans, *Die letzte Panzerschlacht des DAK*, Magazine article 1962

Divine, Arthur Durham, *Road to Tunis*, 1944

Esebeck, Hans Gert von, *Afrikanische Schicksalsjahre*, Wiesbaden 1949

Fröhlich, Stefan, *Als Fliegerführer Afrika*, In manuscript 1968

Fullriede, Fritz, *Kampfgruppe Fullriede in Tunesien*, In manuscript 1968

Gause, Alfred, *Sonderunternehmen gegen Bizerta*, Magazine article 1957

Graziani, Rodolfo, *Africa settentrionale*, Rome 1948

Hambuch, Rudolf, *Einsätze in Tunesien*, In manuscript 1964-73

Harlinghausen, Martin, *Berichte und Kampfschilderungen*, In manuscript 1967

Hart, B.H.L., *Rommels letzter Schlag*, Magazine article 1953

Haupt, Werner, *Das Ende in Afrika*, Magazine article 1963

Heckstall-Smith, Anthony, Tobruk, London 1959

Herington, J., *Conquest of Tunisia*, 1954

Hissmann, Josef, *Insch Allah!*, Bochum 1967

Howe, Georg Frederick, *Northwest Africa*, Washington 1957

Huebner, Arnold, *Flak-Kanoniere in Afrika*, In manuscript 1967

Héraucourt, Ferry, *Im Kampf gewachsen*, Stettin 1942

Hartmann, Wilhelm, *Schwere Panzer-Abteilung (Tiger) 501*, Magazine article 1972

Irkens, Joseph Franz, *Panzerführer Afrika*, In manuscript 1974.

Jars, Robert, *Les Campagnes d'Afrique,* Paris 1957

Keiling, Wolf, *Das deutsche Heer 1939 bis 1945*, Bad Nauheim 1955

Kesselring, Albert, *Soldat bis zum letzten Tag,* Bonn 1953

Kirchheim, Heinrich, *Der Tod von General von Prittwitz*, In manuscript

Knoche, Wilhelm, *Beitrag zur Kriegsgeschichte des FJR 5*, In manuscript

Kollatz, Karl, *General der Fallschirmtruppe Ramcke.*

– Oberstleutnant Werner Marcks

– *Generalleutnant Fritz Bayerlein*

– *Generalleutnant Ernst-Günther Baade*

– *General der Panzertruppe von Manteuffel*

– *Oberleutnant Erich Schuster*

– *Handstreich vor Tunis*

– *Panzerschlacht bei Sidi Rezegh*, (all Rastatt in Baden 1958-1966)

Kurowski, Franz, *Panzer – Bomben – Wüstensand*, 1967

– *Der Kampf um Kreta*, Herford 1965

– *Das Tor zur Festung Europa*, Neckargemünd 1966

– *Brückenkopf Tunesien*, Herford 1967

– *Von Caserta nach Tunis, Der Kampf um Medjez el Bab.*

– *Der Durchbruch der Allierten bei Medjez el Bab.*

– *Entlastungsangriff am Djebel Djaffa.*

– *Nach 23 Jahren wieder in Tunesien.* (All magazine articles on German Paratroops 1966-1967)

– *Geschichte der Panzer-Regimentes 5.*

– *Mit Hans Cramer in Afrika.*

– *Der Löwe von Capuzzo*, (All in Die Oase 1970-1974)

Lange, Curt von, *Flakartillerie greift an*, Berlin 1941

Manteuffel, Hasso von, *Tunesien Einsatz – Auszüge aus den täglichen Meldungen des OKH an das OKW von 17. 3.–9. 5. 1943*, In manuscript

Maravigna, P., *Come abbiamo perduto la Guerra in Africa?*, Rome 1949

Marcks, Werner, *Soldatische Daten und Kampfberichte.*

Messe, Giovanni, *Come fini la Guerra in Africa*, 1949 1 + 2

Möller-Witten, Hans, *Männer und Taten*, Munich 1959

Montgomery, Bernard, *Von Alamein zum Sangro*, Bern 1949

– *Memoirs*, Munich 1958

Marwan-Schlosser, Hptm., *Flak-Regiment 135 in Afrika.* In manuscript

Moorehead, Alain, *Afrikanische Trilogie*, Hamburg 1958

Müller, Gerhard, *Panzer-Regiment 5 – Ritterkreuzträger*, In manuscript

Murphy, W.E., *Point 175. The Battle of Sunday of the Dead 1941*, Wellington N.Z. 1954

Nehring, Walther K., *Die erste Phase der Kämpfe in Tunesien bis zum 9. 12. 1942*, In manuscript

Ministero della difesa, *Operazion italo-tedesche in Tunisia*, Rome 1950-52

Pakenham-Walsh R.P., *North-West Africa*, 1948

Panzenhagen, Albert, *Mit der 90. Leichten vor Marsa Matruk*, Magazine article

Ramcke, B.H., *Vom Schiffsjungen zum Fallschirmjägergeneral*, Berlin 1943

– *Kampf in der Quattarasenke.* In manuscript

Reissmann, Werner, *Gefechtsbericht über die Eroberung des befestigten Werkes Got el Ualeb*, Magazine article 1970

Robinett, Paul-McDonald, *Armor Command*, Washington 1958

Roatta, Mario, *Otto milioni di Baionette.* Milan 1946

Rommel, Erwin, *Krieg ohne Hass*, Heidenheim 1950

Ryll, Edgar, *Das Afrika-Regiment 361*, In manuscript

Sauer, Paul, *Kampfgruppe Sauer in Tunesien,* In manuscript

Schmidt, Heinz Werner, *Mit Rommel in Afrika,* 1951

Schulz, Johannes, *Die verlorene Armee*, Balve 1960

– *Der Weg nach Tobruk*, Balve 1959

– *Kampf am Pont du Fahs*

– *In Gambut war der Teufel los.*

– *Endrunde Tunis*

– *Duell in der Nacht*

– *So fiel Bir Hacheim* (all Munich 1957-1961)

Schuster, Erich, *Von der Versuchsabteilung zum Sturmregiment und zum Fallschirmjäger-Regiment 5*, In manuscript

Scoullar, J.L., *Battle for Egypt*, Wellington N.Z. 1955

Seemen, Gerhard von, *Die Ritterkreuzträger 1939 bis 1945*, Bad Nauheim 1955

Seventh Army, *Report of Operations of the United States Seventh Army*, New York 1945

Stahlschmidt, Hilde, *Mein Sohn Hans-Arnold Stahlschmidt*, In manuscript

Streich, Johannes, *Mit der 5. Leichten Division in Afrika*, In manuscript

Strunz, Bruno, *Die 334. ID*, In manuscript

Suire, *Tankers in Tunisia*, Fort Knox 1943

Vaerst, Gustav von, *Kampfberichte aus Afrika.* In manuscript

Warlimont, Walter, *Im Hauptquartier der deutschen Wehrmacht 1939-1945*, Frankfurt Main 1962

Wahl, Wolfgang, *Das Panzer-regiment 8 in Afrika*, In manuscript

Weber, Friedrich, *Der Einsatz der 334. ID in Afrika*, Magazine article 1972

Wechmar, Irnfried, *Herren des Vorfeldes*, Berlin 1942

Westphal, Siegfried, *Heer in Fesseln*, Bonn 1950

– *Schicksal Nordafrika*, 1954

– *Persönliche Daten und Berichte*, In manuscript

Wolz, Alwin, *Rommelnde Luftwaffenflak in Afrika*, In manuscript

Yindrich, Jan, *Fortress Tobruk*, London 1951

Young, Desmond, *Rommel*, Wiesbaden

Zimmermann, Horst, *Einsatz des II./FJR 5 in Tunesien*, In manuscript

Periodicals

Der Adler, 1941-1943
Der deutsche Fallschirmjäger, 1952-1967
Alte Kamaraden, sporadic
Die OASE, 1952-1974
Panzer-Kampftruppen, 1961-1967
Das Ritterkreuz, 1964-1974
Sie Wehrmacht, 1941-1943
Der Windhund, 1966-1968

The author thanks all persons and institutions who contributed to this work.

Special thanks go to:
The Bundesarchiv Central records Office in Kornelimünster,
Herr R. Absolon,
The Central Library of the Bundeswehr,
Library Director Dr. Sack,
The Registered Society of the Units of the *Deutsche Afrika-Korps*,
Retired *General der Kavallerie* Siegfried Westphal,
Retired *General der Panzertruppen* Walther K. Nehring, who scrutinized the chapter on operations in Tunisia,
Retired *Oberst* Georg Briel,
Retired *Oberst* E.H. Brix, who made available the orders of battle,
Herr Heinrich Benz, caretaker missing personnel of FJR 5,
Herr Rudolf Hambuch, Chairman of the Veterans Association of FJR 5,
Special thanks go to all those former soldiers, from General to Grenadier, whose contributions helped create this book.

Appendix
Order of Battle of the Deutsche Afrika-Korps
(until 18. 2. "Commander-in-Chief of German troops in Libya")

Commanding General	Generalleutnant Rommel
Ia:	Oberstleutnant von dem Borne
Ic:	Hauptmann von Plehwe
Pi. Officer	Oberstleutnant Hundt
Luftwaffe Liaison Officer	General Staff Major Grunow
Headquarters Commandant	Oberleutnant Behrendt

Commanding Generals:

15. 8. – 8. 3. 1942	Generalleutnant Crüwell
9. 3. – 31. 8. 1942	Generalleutnant Nehring
31. 8. – 31. 8. 1942	General Staff Oberst Bayerlein
31. 8. – 17. 9. 1942	Generalmajor von Vaerst
17. 9. – 4. 11. 1942	General der Panzertruppe Ritter von Thoma
4. 11. – 19. 11. 1942	Oberst Fritz Bayerlein
19. 11. – 16. 1. 1943	General der Panzertruppe Fehn
16. 1. – 17. 2. 1943	Generalmajor von Liebenstein
17. 2. – 5. 3. 1943	Generalleutnant Ziegler
5. 3. – 12. 5. 1943	General der Panzertruppe Cramer

Divisions and Corps Units

5th Light Division (21st Panzer Division)

Division Commander:	Generalmajor Streich (until 1. 10. 1941)
	Generalmajor von Ravenstein (until 29. 11.)
	Oberstleutnant Knabe (until 30. 11. 41)
	Generalleutnant Böttcher (until 30. 1. 42)
	Generalmajor v. Bismarck (until 30. 8. 42)
	Oberst Lungershausen (until 18. 9. 42)
	Generalmajor v. Randow (until 21. 12. 42)
	Oberst Hillebrandt (until 25. 4. 1943)
	Generalmajor von Hülsen (until 13. 5. 43)
Ia:	General Staff Major Hauser
	General Staff Major Frhr. von Susskind und Schwendi
	General Staff Major Heuduck
	Oberst Stempel
Ib:	Hauptmann Böhles
Ic:	Oberleutnant Rickert
IIa:	Hauptmann Garke
Division Medical Officer:	Oberfeldarzt Dr. Pott

5th Panzer Regiment	Oberst Olbrich
	Oberst Stephan
	Oberstleutnant Mildebrath
	Oberst Müller
104th Motorized Inf. Rgt. (104th Panzer Grenadier Rgt.)	Oberst von Holtzendorff
	Oberst Ewert
	Oberstleutnant Knabe
	Oberstleutnant Pfeiffer
155th Armored Artillery Rgt.	Oberst Bruer
AA 3	Major (Oberstleutnant) von Wechmar
PzJägAbt.200	Hauptmann Deitelmann
PzJägAbt.39	Major Jansa

200th Motorized Signals Btl.	Major Richter
200th Armored Supply Btl.	Major Dassler
200th Armored Engineers Btl.	Major Streitz
609th Flak Battalion	Major Hissmann
2nd MG Battalion	Major Warrelmann
8th MG Battalion	Oberstleutnant Ponath
Repair Battalion	Oberstleutnant Johannes
200th Map Section	
200th Replacement Training Battalion	
200th Supply Column	
200th Bakery Company	
200th Butchery Company	
200th Ration Supply Office	

15th Panzer Division

Division Commander:	Generalmajor von Prittwitz (until 10. 4. 41)
	Generalmajor von Esebeck (until 25. 7. 41)
	Generalmajor Neumann-Silkow (until 7. 12. 41)
	Oberst Menny (until 8.12.41)
	Generalleutnant von Vaerst (until 26. 5. 42)
	Oberst Crasemann (until 8. 7. 42)
	Generalleutnant von Vaerst (until 31. 8. 42)
	Generalmajor von Randow (until 17. 9. 42)
	Generalleutnant von Vaerst (until 11. 11. 42)
	Oberst Crasemann (until 11. 11. 42)
	Generalleutnant von Vaerst (until12. 12. 42)
	Generalmajor Borowietz (until 13. 5. 43)
Ia:	Major Kriebel
	General Staff Oberst Müller
Ib:	General Staff Major Frey
	Oberleutnant Dittmann
IIa:	Major Riese
	Major Stollbrock
Division Medical Officer:	Oberfeldarzt Dr. Pelizaeus
8th Panzer Regiment:	Oberstleutnant Cramer
	Oberst Teege
	Oberst Irkens
115th Panzer Grenadier Rgt.:	Oberst von Herff
	Oberst Geissler
	Oberstleutnant Zindel
	Oberst Baade
33rd Armored Artillery Rgt.:	Oberstleutnant Crasemann
AA 33:	Oberstleutnant Beil
	Hauptmann Linau
	Hauptmann Héraucourt
33rd Anti-tank Battalion:	Oberstleutnant Beil
15th Motorcycle Battalion:	Oberstleutnant Knabe
	Major von Debschitz
	Major Ehle
78th Armored Signals Battalion	
33rd Supply Column	
33rd Armored Engineer Battalion	
33rd Flak Battalion	
Repair Battalion	
200th Motorized Rifle Regiment	Oberstleutnant Eschenlohr
33rd Field Post Office	

33rd Cartography Section
33rd Replacement Training Battalion
36th Field Hospital

DAK Corps Units:
DAK Corps Headquarters
Corps Cartography Section
300th Special Purpose Oasis Battalion
I Battalion, 18th Flak Regiment
576th Anti-tank Regiment
I Battalion, 33rd Flak Regiment
475th Motorized Signals Battalion
572nd Motorized Supply Battalion
580th Motorized Water Supply Battalion
580th Motorized Reconnaissance Company
598th and 599th Training and Replacement Battalions
Corps Supply Dump (motorized)
Field Post Office (motorized)
554th Bakery Company (motorized)
498th Military Police Squad

Panzergruppe Afrika
(from 30. 1. 1942 Panzerarmee Afrika)
Commander-in-Chief:

15. 8. 1941 – 9. 3. 1942:	General der Panzertruppe Rommel
9. 3. 1942 – 19. 3. 1942:	Generalleutnant Crüwell
19. 3. 1942 – 22. 9. 1942:	Generaloberst Rommel
22. 9. 1942 – 24. 10. 1942:	General der Kavallerie Stumme
24. 10. 1942 – 25. 10. 1942:	Generalleutnant Ritter von Thoma
25. 10. 1942 – 23. 3. 1943:	Generalfeldmarschall Rommel
23. 2. 1943 – 13. 5. 1943:	Italian Army General Messe

Chief of Staff:	Generalmajor Gause
	Oberst Bayerlein
	Oberst Westphal
	Oberst Bayerlein
	Oberst Westphal
Ia:	General Staff Major von Mellenthin
	General Staff Major Feige
OQu:	Major Otto
	General Staff Major Schleusener
Ic:	General Staff Major von Mellenthin
	General Staff Major Zolling
	Major Liebl
IIa:	Major Schräpler
IVb:	Oberstarzt (Generalarzt) Dr. Asal
Liaison Officer to the	
Reich Press Chief and to	
Hitler:	Oberleutnant (Hauptmann) Berndt
Army Signals Officer:	Oberst Büchting
Engineer Officer:	Oberst Hecker
	Oberst Bülowius

Units of Panzerarmee Afrika
as of 15. 8. 1942:

Army Headquarters
Deutsche Afrika-Korps with:

15th Panzer Division:	Generalleutnant von Vaerst
21st Panzer Division:	Generalmajor von Bismarck
90th Light Division:	Generalmajor Kleemann
164th Light Division:	Oberst Lungershausen
Ramcke Parachute Brigade:	Generalmajor Ramcke
Tenth Italian Army Corps:	General Gioda
"Brescia" Infantry Division:	General Predieri
"Pavia" Infantry Division:	General Lombardi

Twentieth Italian Army Corps:	General Zingales (Baldassare) De Stefanis
"Trieste" Motorized Infantry Division:	General La Ferla

"Ariete" Armored Division:	General Baldassare
"Littorio" Armored Division:	Generals Azzi, Bitossi, Becuzzi
"Folgore" Parachute Division:	General Frattini

Twenty-first Army Corps:	General Navarrini, General Berardi
"Trento" Infantry Division:	General de Stefanis
"Bologna" Infantry Division:	General Gloria

Independent Units and Detachments:
15th Special Purpose Brigade Headquarters
DAK Combat Echelon (motorized)
575th Cartography Section (motorized)
288th Special Unit (motorized), Menton
2nd Reconnaissance Headquarters (Army)
HQ of the Commander of the Luftwaffe, Libya
605th Motorized Anti-tank Battalion
104th Artillery Detachment
721st to 730th Motorized Artillery Survey Detachments
11th Motorized Observation Battalion
606th, 612th, 617th Motorized Flak Battalions
135th Motorized Flak Regiment
10th Motorized Signals Regiment
73rd Motorized Army Construction Battalion
585th Motorized Supply Regiment
148th, 149th, 529th, 532nd, 533rd, 902nd, 909th Motorized Supply Battalions
548th Motorized Vehicle Repair Battalion
317th and 445th Motorized Rations Supply Offices
"Afrika" Motorized Rations Supply Office
542nd and 667th Motorized Military Hospitals
"Afrika" Guard Battalion
Local Commandants in:
Misurata-615, Barce-619, Tripoli-958, Benghazi-959 and Derna
Prisoner-of-War Processing Camp 782
659th and 762nd Special Post Offices (motorized)

Order of Battle of XC Armeekorps (Tunisia):

Commanding General:	General der Panzertruppe Nehring
Chief of Staff:	Oberst Pomtow
Ia:	General Staff Major Moll
	Leutnant Junker (assistant)
Ib:	Hauptmann Kirsten
IIa:	Major von Seubert
Corps Medical Officer:	Stabsarzt Dr. Herzberger

Order of Battle 5. Panzerarmee:
Commander-in-Chief:

8. 12. – 9. 12. 1942:	General der Panzertruppe Nehring
9. 12. – 9. 3. 1943:	Generaloberst von Arnim
9. 3. – 9. 5. 1943:	General der Panzertruppe von Vaerst
Chief of Staff:	Generalleutnant Ziegler
	Generalmajor von Quast
Ia:	General Staff Oberst Pomtow
	General Staff Markert
Ib:	General Staff Major Moll
Ic:	Hauptmann Kirsten
IIa:	Major Seubert
IIb:	Major Halser
IVb:	Oberstarzt Dr. Schulz
Defence officer:	Oberleutnant Fiedler
Propaganda Officer:	Oberleutnant Haupt

Divisions and Combat Units:

10th Panzer Division:	Generalmajor Fischer
von Broich Division:	Oberst (Generalmajor) von Broich
20th Flak Division:	Generalmajor Neuffer
334th Infantry Division	Oberst Weber

I and II Battalions, 54th Flak Regiment	
5th Parachute Regiment:	Oberstleutnant Koch
501st Heavy Panzer Battalion (Tiger):	Major Lueder
190th Panzer Battalion	
190th Armored Recon. Battalion	
"Superga" Infantry Division:	General Imperiali
von Manteuffel Division:	Generalmajor von Manteuffel
"Hermann Göring" Jäger Division:	Generalmajor Schmid

from 1. 3. 1943:

21st Panzer Division:	Oberst Hildebrandt
19th Flak Division:	Generalleutnant Frantz
47th Grenadier Regiment:	Oberstleutnant Buhse
999th Afrika Division:	Generalleutnant Thomas
	Oberst Baade
"Centauro" Armored Division:	General Conte Calvi
	General Costa
"Superga" Infantry Division:	General Conte Gelich
	General Benigni

Heeresgruppe Afrika:	
Commander-in-Chief:	Generalfeldmarschall Rommel
	(until 9. 3. 1943)
	Generaloberst von Arnim
Chief of Staff:	Oberst Bayerlein
	Generalleutnant Ziegler
Ia:	General Staff Oberst Pomtow
	General Staff Oberst Markert
Ic:	Major Moll
5. Panzerarmee:	General der Panzertruppe von Vaerst
"Manteuffel" Division:	Generalmajor von Manteuffel
334th Infantry Division:	Generalmajor Krause
999th Division:	Oberst Wolff
"Herman Göring" Jäger Division:	Generalmajor Schmid
10th Panzer Division:	Generalleutnant Fischer
	Generalmajor Frhr. von Broich
20th Flak Division:	Generalmajor Neuffer
Air Forces:	Oberst Harlinghausen
(Fliegerführer Tunesien)	General der Flieger Seidemann
5th Parachute Regiment:	Oberstleutnant Koch
501st Heavy Panzer Battalion (Tiger):	Major Seidensticker
1. Armee:	General Messe
"Young Fascists" Division:	General Sozzani
	Generals Tannucci, Boselli
"Trieste" Motorized Infantry Division:	General La Ferla
90th Light Division:	General Graf Sponeck
"Pistoia" Infantry Division:	General Falugi
	General D'Antoni
"Spezia" Airborne Infantry Division:	General Pizzolato
	General Scattini
164th Light Division:	Generalleutnant von Liebenstein
"Centauro" Armored Division:	General Calvi di Bergolo
Gruppe Sahara:	Oberst (Generalmajor) Mannerini
15th Panzer Division:	Generalmajor Borowietz
Panzerführer Afrika:	Oberst Irkens
21st Panzer Division:	Generalmajor Hildebrandt
19th Flak Division:	Generalleutnant Frantz
Panzer Grenadier Regiment "Afrika":	Oberstleutnant Rangerhagen
	Oberst Menton
Sfax Sector:	34th Infantry Regiment (Italian)
Gabes Sector:	280th Infantry Regiment (Italian)

German-Italian Units

on 18. 11. 1941	
Panzergruppe Afrika:	General Rommel
with:	

(Generalmajor as of 1. 1. 1943)

Deutsches Afrika-Korps:	General Crüwell
21st Panzer Division (5th Light):	General von Ravenstein
15th Panzer Division:	General Neumann-Silkow
90th Light Division:	General Sümmermann
Area of Operations:	Tobruk Front
Corps Units:	
475th Signals Battalion	
Rear Echelon Services	
Water Services	
Area of Operations:	Sollum Front
"Savona" Division:	General de Giorgis
XXI Army Corps:	General Navarrini
"Brescia" Division:	General Zambon
"Trento" Motorized Infantry Division:	General de Stefanis
"Pavia" Division:	General Franceschini
"Bologna" Division	General Gloria

Army Units:
Arko 104, Flak Battalion I./18, Pi.Btl. 900, Flak Btl. I./33, PzJägAbt.605, Flak Btl. 606, 580th Recon. Company, Flak Btl. 612, Special Purpose Btl. 300, 11th Observation Battalion.

Reserves:	
XX. Army Corps	General Gambarra
"Ariete" Armored Division	General Balotta
"Trieste" Armored Division	General Piazzoni

British Units on 18. 11. 1941

Commander-in-Chief Middle East	
Headquarters in Cairo:	General Auchinleck
British Eighth Army:	General Cunningham
(from 27. 11. 1941):	General Ritchie
Tobruk Garrison:	General Morshead
Seventieth Infantry Division:	General Scobie
Thirty-second Armoured Brigade:	Brigadier Willison
Polish Brigade Group:	General Kopenski
Attack Forces on Right Wing:	
Thirteenth Corps:	General Godwin-Austen
Second New Zealand Division:	General Freyberg
Fourth Indian Division:	General Messervy
First Armoured Brigade:	Brigadier Watkins
Attack Forces on Left Wing:	
Thirtieth Corps:	General Norrie
Seventh Armoured Division:	General Gott
First South African Division:	General Brink
Twenty-second Guards Brigade:	Brigadier Marriott
Reserves:	
Second South African Division:	General de Villiers
Oasis Group (Force E):	Brigadier Reid

Battle Order of the British Seventh Armoured Division:

Fourth Armoured Brigade:	Brigadier Gathouse with:
Third Royal Tank Regiment	
Fifth Royal Tank Regiment	
Eighth Hussars Regiment	
Seventh Armoured Brigade:	Brigadier Davy

Second Royal Tank Regiment
Sixth Royal Tank Regiment
Seventh Hussars Regiment

Twenty-second Armoured Brigade: Brigadier Scott-Cockburn
Second Hussars Regiment
Third Yeomanry Regiment
Fourth Yeomanry Regiment

Division Support Group: Brigadier Campbell
Infantry, artillery,
anti-tank and anti-aircraft guns

Eleventh Hussars (reconnaissance battalion)
Total troop strength: 14,000 men
Tank strength: 500

(Each of the three Armoured Brigades possessed more tanks than a German Panzer Division.)

The 90th Light Division:

Division Commander:	Generalmajor Sümmermann (until 10. 12. 41)
	Oberst Mickl (until 27. 12. 41)
	Generalmajor Veith (until 28. 4. 42)
	Generalmajor Kleemann (until 14. 6. 42)
	Oberst Marcks (until 18. 6. 42)
	Oberst Menny (until 19. 6. 42)
	Oberst Marcks (until 21. 6. 42)
	Generalmajor Kleemann (until 8. 9. 42)
	Generalmajor Ramcke (acting until 17. 9. 42)
	Oberst Schulte-Heuthaus (until 22. 9. 42)
	Generalleutnant Graf Sponeck (until 12. 4. 43)
Ia:	General Staff Major Ziegler und Klipphausen
	General Staff Major Schumann
Ib:	Major Lippmann
	Major Übigau
Ic:	Leutnant Wiese
	Oberleutnant Hiltmann
	Hauptmann Kirchner
IIa:	Major Kolbeck
IIb:	Oberleutnant Rauert
Division Medical Officer:	Oberfeldarzt Dr. Werlemann
155th Panzer Grenadier Rgt.:	Oberst Mickl
	Oberst Marcks
200th Panzer Grenadier Rgt.:	Oberst Köster
	Oberst Geissler
361st Afrika Regiment:	Oberstleutnant von Barby
	Oberstleutnant Panzenhagen
190th Artillery Regiment:	Oberstleutnant Seiderer
190th Artillery Battalion:	Hauptmann Kaul
	Hauptmann von Schrimpf
190th Anti-tank Battalion:	Hauptmann Kahle
580th Motorized Artillery Battalion:	Rittmeister von Homeyer
	Hauptmann Voss
605th Anti-tank Battalion:	Major Schulze
	Hauptmann Koberg
190th Motorized Signals Battalion:	Hauptmann (Major) Ploch
900th Pionier Battalion:	Major Melzer
	Major Kube
606th Flak Battalion:	Major Briel
190th Medical Battalion,	
First and Second Companies:	Stabsarzt Dr. Scheringer
361st Artillery Battalion:	Hauptmann Kaul
190th Training and Replacement Battalion:	Major Rotschuh
Cartography Section (motorized) 259 D	
190th Bakery and Butchery Company	
190th Ration Supply Office	

The 164th Light Division:

Division Commander:	Oberst Lungershausen (until 30. 11. 42)
	Oberst Westphal (until 30. 12. 42)
	Generalmajor von Liebenstein (until 16. 1. 43)
	Generalmajor Krause (until 13. 3. 43)
	Generalmajor von Liebenstein (until 13. 5. 43)
Ia:	Oberst Markert
	General Staff Major Feige
Ib:	General Staff Hauptmann Meinicke
	General Staff Hauptmann von Treskow
	General Staff Major Gerhardt
Ic:	General Staff Hauptmann Gerhardt
	Oberleutnant Gruhl
IIa:	Major Elterich
	Major Werner
	Hauptmann Münchmeyer
HQ:	Hauptmann Dr. Schulz
Division Medical Officer:	Oberstarzt Dr. Ziegler
125th Panzer Grenadier Regiment:	Oberst Petersen
	Oberst Almers
382nd Panzer Grenadier Regiment:	Oberstleutnant Hirsch
	Oberst Beukemann
	Oberstleutnant von Lewinski
433rd Panzer Grenadier Regiment:	Oberstleutnant von Neindorf (Oberst)
	Oberstleutnant Stiefvater
220th Artillery Regiment:	Oberst Schieb
	Oberst Becker
AA 220 (motorized)	
220th Signals Battalion:	Hauptmann Kulle
	Hauptmann Fuhrmann
	Hauptmann Rentsch
220th Supply Column:	Major Oberländer
220th Motorized Pionier Battalion:	Oberstleutnant Springorum
	Major Endress
220th Cartography Section (motorized)	

334th Infantry Division	
Division Commander:	Oberst (Generalmajor) Weber (until 15. 4. 43)
	Generalmajor Krause (until 8. 5. 43)
Ia:	General Staff Major Strzeiczny
	Hauptmann Lerche
Ib:	Hauptmann Lerche
Ic:	Oberleutnant Dr. Rietschel
IIa:	Hauptmann Reinhardt
754th Grenadier Regiment:	Oberst lang
755th Grenadier Regiment:	Oberstleutnant Eder
756th Mountain Infantry Regiment:	Oberstleutnant Hansel
334th Anti-tank Battalion	
334th Artillery Regiment	
334th Pionier Battalion	
334th Signals Battalion	

The Allied Expeditionary Forces

Western Task Force:

Naval Commander:	Rear Admiral H.K. Hewitt
Land Commander:	Major General George S. Patton
Forces:	
3rd US Infantry Division	Major General Truscott
Battle Group A	
9th US Infantry Division	Major General S. Eddy

Total Strength: 35,000 men

Center Task Force:
Naval Commander: Captain T.H. Troubridge
Land Commander: Major General Fredenhall

Forces:
1st US Infantry Division — Major General Terry M. Allen
Battle Group B: — Major General Robinett
1st Ranger Battalion
Corps Units II US Corps

Total Strength: 39,000 men

Eastern Task Force:
Naval Commander: Vice Admiral H.M. Burrough
Land Commander: Major General Ryder

Forces:
9th US Infantry Division — Major General Ryder
34th US Infantry Division — Major General Ryder
Seventy-eighth British Infantry Division — Major General Evelegh

Total Strength: 33,000 men

Total Allied Forces: 107,000 men

The Allied Forces in March 1943

Allied Force Headquarters – Algiers

Commander-in-Chief: General Eisenhower
Chief of Staff: Brigadier General Walter B. Smith

Eighteenth Army Group: General Harold Alexander

Units (from north to south):
French Le Couteux Brigade — General Le Couteux de Chaumont
9th US Infantry Division — General Manton S. Eddy
34th US Infantry Division: — Major General Ryder
1st US Armored Division — Major generals Harmon, Ward
1st US Infantry Division — Major General Terry M. Allen
Seventy-eighth British Infantry Division — Major General Evelegh
Sixth British Armoured Division — Major General C. Keightley
First British Armoured Division — Major General Briggs
Forty-sixth British Infantry Division — Major General Atwood
French "Oran" Infantry Division — General Boissau
French "Morrocco" Infantry Division — General Mathenet
French "Algiers" Infantry Division — General Conne
Seventh British Armoured Division — Major General Horrocks
Fourth Indian Infantry Division — Major General Tucker
Second New Zealand Motorized Infantry Division — Major General Freyberg
Fiftieth British Infantry Division — Major General Kirkman

Reserves:
First British Infantry Division — Major General Penney
Fourth British Infantry Division — Major General Ward
Fifty-first British Infantry Division — Major General Wimberley

The Knight's Cross Wearers of the Afrika-Korps

(The numbers in brackets indicate the number in the sequence of the awarding of the decoration.)

Oak Leaves with Swords and Diamonds

Hauptmann Hans-Joachim Marseille (4)	2. 9. 1942 (*)
Generalfeldmarschall Erwin Rommel (6)	11. 3. 1943 (*)
Generalfeldmarschall Albert Kesselring (14)	19. 7. 1944
General der Fallschirmtruppe B.H. Ramcke (20)	20. 9. 1944

Oak Leaves with Swords

General der Panzertruppe Erwin Rommel (6)	20. 1. 1942 (*)
Oberleutnant Hans-Joachim Marseille (12)	18. 6. 1942 (*)
Generalfeldmarschall Albert Kesselring (15)	18. 7. 1942
Hauptmann Joachim Müncheberg (19)	9. 9. 1942 (*)
Generalleutnant Fritz Bayerlein (81)	20. 7. 1944
General der Fallschirmtruppe B.H. Ramcke (99)	19. 9. 1944
Generalleutnant Ernst-Günther Baade (111)	16. 11. 1944 (*)
General der Panzertruppe Walther K. Nehring (124)	22. 1. 1945

Knight's Cross with Oak Leaves:

General Staff Oberstleutnant Martin Harlinghausen (8)	30. 1. 1941
Generalleutnant Erwin Rommel (10)	20. 3. 1941 (*)
Oberleutnant Joachim Müncheberg (12)	7. 5. 1941 (*)
Generalleutnant Ludwig Crüwell (34)	1. 9. 1941
Generalfeldmarschall Albert Kesselring (78)	25. 2. 1942
Oberleutnant Hans-Joachim Marseille (97)	6. 6. 1942 (*)
Oberstleutnant Walter Sigl (116)	3. 9. 1942 (*)
Generalmajor B.H. Ramcke (145)	15. 11. 1942
Generalleutnant Wolfgang Fischer (152)	9. 12. 1942 (*)
Hauptmann Dr. Eberhard Zahn (204)	6. 3. 1943
Generalmajor Willibald Borowietz (235)	10. 5. 1943 (*)
Hauptmann Hans-Güther Stotten (236)	10. 5. 1943 (*)
Major Gustav Rödel (255)	20. 6. 1943
Generalmajor Fritz Bayerlein (258)	6. 7. 1943
Hauptmann Werner Schroer (268)	2. 8. 1943

Generalleutnant Ulrich Kleemann (304)	16. 9. 1943
Hauptmann Rolf Rocholl (287)	31. 8. 1943
Oberst Heinrich Voigtsberger (351)	9. 12. 1943 (*)
Leutnant Hans-Arnold Stahlschmidt (365)	3. 1. 1944 (*)
General der Panzertruppe Walther K. Nehring (402)	22. 2. 1944 (*)
Generalmajor Ernst-Günther Baase (402)	22. 2. 1944 (*)
Hauptmann Josef Rettemeier (425)	13. 3. 1944
Oberst Hinrich Warrelmann (555)	19. 8. 1944
Generalmajor Werner Marcks (593)	21. 9. 1944
Major Curt Ehle (673)	29. 11. 1944
Generalmajor Eduard Crasemann (683)	18. 12. 1944
Oberst Fritz Fullriede (803)	23. 3. 1945

Knight's Cross of the Iron Cross
(in alphabetical order)

Hauptmann Hans-Wilhelm Albers	10. 5. 1943
Oberfeldwebel Peter Arent	4. 12. 1942 (*)
Generalleutnant Jürgen von Arnim	4. 9. 1941
Oberstleutnant Paul Audorff	27. 6. 1943
Oberst Ernst-Güther Baade	6. 7. 1942 (*)
Hauptmann Wilhelm Bach	9. 7. 1941 (*)
Oberstleutnant Hans-Levin von Barby	13. 12. 1941 (*)
Oberstleutnant Fritz Bayerlein	26. 12. 1941
Oberleutnant Winrich Behr	14. 5. 1941
Hauptmann Helmut Belser	6. 9. 1942
Oberfeldwebel Karl-Heinz Bendert	30. 12. 1942
Oberst helmut Beukemann	14. 5. 1941
Oberst Georg von Bismarck	18. 10. 1940 (*)
Major Rudolf Boeckmann	6. 8. 1942
Major Ernst Bolbrinker	15. 5. 1941
Oberstleutnant Willibald Borowietz	24. 7. 1941
Major Georg Briel	28. 7. 1942
Oberst Fritz Frhr. von Broich	1. 9. 1942
Oberst Alfred Bruer	4. 8. 1942
General Staff Oberstleutnant Ulrich Bürker	26. 1. 1943
Oberstleutnant Rudolf Buhse	17. 8. 1942

Major Friedrich Buschhausen	10. 5. 1943	Unteroffizier Reinhard Melzer	30. 6. 1941
Oberstleutnant Eduard Crasemann	10. 1. 1942	Oberst Erwin Menny	26. 12. 1941
Hauptmann Georg Christl	18. 3. 1942	Oberst Johann Mickl	13. 12. 1941
Generalmajor Ludwig Crüwell	14. 5. 1941	Oberstleutnant Werner Mildebrath	14. 8. 1942
Hauptmann Curt Ehle	22. 7. 1941	Oberst Gerhard Müller	15. 9. 1942
Hauptmann Wolfgang Everth	11. 7. 1942	Generalmajor Gottlob Müller	1. 6. 1943
Oberst Herbert Ewert	22. 8. 1942	Hauptmann Klaus Müller	14. 10. 1942 (*)
Major Günther Fenski	31. 12. 1941	Oberleutnant Joachim Müncheberg	14. 9. 1940 (*)
Oberst Wolfgang Fischer	3. 6. 1940	Major Friedrich-Heinrich Musculus	26. 2. 1943
Generalleutnant Gotthard Frantz	25. 5. 1943	Generalmajor Walther K. Nehring	24. 7. 1941
Oberleutnant Ludwig Franzisket	23. 7. 1941	Generalmajor Georg Neuffer	8. 8. 1943
Generalmajor Stephan Frölich	4. 7. 1940	Oberst Walter Neumann-Silkow	5. 8. 1940 (*)
Hauptmann Walter Fromm	5. 7. 1941	Oberstleutnant Albert Panzenhagen	7. 10. 1942
Oberstleutnant Fritz Fullriede	18. 4. 1943	Oberleutnant Peter-Paul Plinzner	20. 10. 1941 (*)
Generalmajor Alfred Gause	13. 12. 1941	Oberstleutnant Gustav Ponath	13. 4. 1941 (*)
Oberst Erich Geissler	3. 8. 1942	Generalmajor Bernhard Hermann Ramcke	21. 8. 1941
Hauptmann Kurt Gierga	27. 6. 1941	Oberleutnant Karl-Wolfgang Redlich	9. 7. 1941 (*)
Oberleutnant Franz Götz	4. 9. 1942	Hauptmann Werner Reissmann	1. 8. 1942
Hauptmann Werner Grün	8. 2. 1943	Hauptmann Josef Riepold	3. 8. 1942 (*)
Major Ernst Gürke	12. 11. 1942	Oberleutnant Rolf Rocholl	3. 8. 1942 (*)
Grenadier Günther Halm	7. 8. 1942	Oberleutnant Gustav Rödel	22. 6. 1941
General Staff Major Martin Harlinghausen	4. 5. 1940	Generalmajor Erwin Rommel	26. 5. 1940 (*)
Oberfeldwebel Werner Haugk	21. 12. 1942 (*)	Major August Seidensticker	17. 7. 1943
Major Erich Haut	10. 5. 1943	Oberleutnant Ott-Friedrich Senfft von Pilsach	27. 6. 1941
Major Max Hecht	4. 2. 1942	Leutnant Werner Schroer	5. 11. 1942
Unteroffizier Erich Heintze	7. 3. 1942	Oberfeldwebel Otto Schulz	22. 2. 1942
Oberfeldwebel Richard Heller	21. 8. 1941	Oberleutnant Fritz Schulze-Dickow	7. 3. 1942
Oberst Maximilian von Herff	13. 6. 1942	Oberleutnant Theodor Schwabach	30. 6. 1940
Major Otto Heymer	13. 4. 1941 (*)	Oberleutnant Franz Schweiger	16. 2. 1942 (*)
Major Josef Hissmann	13. 5. 1943	Hauptmann Walter Sigl	21. 7. 1940
Hauptmann Richard von Hösslin	28. 7. 1942	Oberleutnant Otto Stiefelmayer	24. 7. 1942 (*)
Generalleutnant Otto Hoffmann von Homeyer		Oberleutnant Rudolf Struckmann	30. 1. 1942
	28. 6. 1942 (*)	Leutnant Hans-Günther Stotten	4. 7. 1940 (*)
Rittmeister Friedrich von Homeyer	10. 7. 1942 (*)	Oberst Johannes Streich	31. 3. 1941
Oberleutnant Gerhard Homuth	14. 6. 1941	Leutnant Hans-Arnold Stahlschmidt	28. 8. 1942 (*)
Gefreiter Arnold Huebner	7. 3. 1942	Oberfeldwebel Werner Stumpf	18. 8. 1942 (*)
Leutnant Erhard Jähnert	6. 1943	Oberst Gustav von Vaerst	30. 7. 1941
General der Flieger Albert Kesselring	30. 9. 1939 (*)	Major Heinrich Voigtsberger	9. 7. 1941
Hauptmann Rudolf Kiehl	11. 7. 1942	Hauptmann Wolfgang Wahl	15. 1. 1942
Generalmajor Heinrich Kirchheim	14. 5. 1941	Oberstleutnant Irnfried Frhr. von Wechmar	13. 4. 1941
Hauptmann Hans Klärmann	18. 9. 1942	General Staff Oberst Siegfried Westphal	30. 11. 1942
Oberst Ulrich Kleemann	13. 10. 1941	Oberleutnant Alfred Wehmeyer	4. 9. 1942 (*)
Oberstleutnant Gustav-Georg Knabe	1. 6. 1941	Hauptfeldwebel Wilhelm Wendt	30. 6. 1941
Hauptmann Friedrich von Koenen	17. 9. 1943	Major Bernhard Woldenga	5. 7. 1941
Leutnant Friedrich Körner	6. 9. 1942	Oberst Alwin Wolz	17. 6. 1943
Hauptmann Heinz Kroseberg	19. 6. 1942	Leutnant Dr. Eberhard Zahn	27. 6. 1941
Oberleutnant Johannes Kümmel	9. 7. 1941	Leutnant Konrad Zecherle	10. 5. 1943
Generalmajor Kurt von Liebenstein	10. 5. 1943	Generalleutnant Heinz Ziegler	18. 4. 1943
Hauptmann Detlef Lienau	9. 5. 1943 (*)		
Hauptmann Helmut Mahlke	16. 7. 1941		
Oberstleutnant Werner Marcks	5. 2. 1942	(Most of the dates given for the award of the Knight's Cross	
Leutnant Hans-Joachim Marseille	22. 2. 1942 (*)	and other grades are the dates the awards were published.)	

Terms and Abbreviations

Arko	Artilleriekommandeur	Corps Artillery Commander
AA	Aufklärungsabteilung	Reconnaissance Battalion
AR	Artillerieregiment	Artillery Regiment
AK	Armeekorps	Army Corps
DAK	Deutsches-Afrika-Korps	German Africa Corps
FHQ	Führerhauptquartier	Führer Headquarters
FJR	Fallschirmjäger-Regiment	Parachute Regiment
Flak	Flugabwehrkanone	Anti-aircraft Gun
FlaRgt.	Flak-Regiment	Anti-aircraft Regiment
FlaBtl.	Flak-Bataillon	Anti-aircraft Battalion
FlK.	Fliegerkorps	Air Corps
GJR	Gebirgsjäger-Regiment	Mountain Infantry Regiment
IR	Infanterie-Regiment	Infantry Regiment
KB	Kradschützen-Bataillon	Motorcycle Battalion
O1	Staff Officer to Ia	
OB-Süd	Oberbefehlshaber-Süd	Commander-in-Chief South
OBdL	Oberbefehlshaber der Luftwaffe	Commander-in-Chief of the Air Force
OKH	Oberkommando des Heeres	Army High Command
OKW	Oberkommando der Wehrmacht	Armed Forces High Command
Pi.	Pionier	Combat Engineer
PiBtl.	Pionier-Bataillon	Combat Engineer Battalion
PGR	Panzergrenadier-Regiment	Armored Infantry Regiment
PR	Panzer-Regiment	Armored regiment
PzAbt.	Panzerabteilung	Armored Battalion
PzJägAbt.	Panzerjägerabteilung	Anti-tank Battalion
PzAR.	Panzerartillerieregiment	Armored Artillery Regiment
SR	Schützen-Regiment	Rifle Regiment
Ia	General Staff Officer (Command)	
Ib	General Staff Officer (Supply)	

Examples of unit designations:

AA 33 – 33rd Reconnaissance Battalion
1./Fla 617 – First Company, 617th Anti-aircraft Battalion
2./MG 8 – Second Company, 8th Machine-gun Battalion
11./IR 361 – Eleventh Company, 361st Infantry Regiment

1./PR 8 – First Company, 8th Armored Regiment
II./AR 33 – Second Battalion, 33rd Artillery Regiment
I./PR 8 – First Battalion, 8th Armored Regiment

I wish to express my heartfelt thanks to the following gentlemen who provided the necessary corrections and additions for subsequent editions:

Retired Oberstleutnant Johannes Beil,
Retired Oberstleutnant Curt Ehle,
Manfred Lichtenfeld,

Retired Generalmajor Gerhard Müller and
Retired General der Kavallerie Siegfried Westphal.

Volkmar Kühn, Author

Afterword: ROMMEL 1891-1991

From military history and the lives of highly decorated soldiers we know that great soldiers and field marshals do not arise from the common people. Nor do they come exclusively from the realm of the professional soldier and climb the usual ladder; instead they come from the most varied types of backgrounds.

The path that leads through the war college or the general staff is likewise no guarantee of making one a field marshal. Programming a military career in advance, with the goal of becoming a field marshal, is just as unsure.

What is vital in attaining this highest rank in any military force, any army, is that the right officer is in the right place at the right time and, in this theater of war, applies his life to leading the decisive attack by his troops and assuring its success.

Rommel Before Africa

Erwin Johannes Eugen Rommel, born in Heidenheim, near Ulm, on November 15, 1891, was one of those men who become soldiers because it is their calling. Characterized by unshakable self-confidence that enabled him to seize the initiative again and again, even after defeats and retreats, and achieve victories, he was given command of that arm of the army that determined the outcome of battles in World War II: the Panzer troops.

Thus Erwin Rommel was a man who, in his military career, was a member of neither the Prussian nobility nor the general staff, from whose ranks the highest officers of the Imperial and Reich armies came. It is well known that, for this reason, he was regarded in certain quarters of the OKH and the OKW as an "inexperienced parvenu", and that this opinion also led to problems for the *Afrika-Korps*.

In the 1930s Rommel had the opportunity to be assigned to the War College. He declined. He was and remained what he always was: a man who owed his success only to himself, his bravery and his ability to command, and not to any promoters or institutions.

Rommel's father and grandfather were schoolteachers. In 1898 his father became the principal of the Realgymnasium at Aalen. There Erwin Rommel spent his childhood.

After he graduated, he joined the King Wilhelm I Infantry Regiment (6th Württemberg) No. 124 as a *Fahnenjunker*.

When World War I broke out, Rommel stood out from the start as a tough fighter and decisive leader. On August 22, 1914 — despite illness — he led a shock troop toward Bleid, near Longwy. He and three of his men penetrated the village and captured the houses, which were occupied by the enemy. For this achievement he was decorated with the Iron Cross First Class.

At the end of September, Rommel was wounded; he returned to the front only on January of 1915 and immediately began to lead scouting and shock troops again. *Leutnant* Rommel volunteered for these tasks, and his platoon likewise volunteered.

His officers took notice and transferred him to a newly established elite unit: the Württemberg Mountain Battalion, and were used as "firemen" wherever there was trouble.

Here Erwin Rommel found his home as a soldier. Here he could fully develop his special gifts as an independent battle-group leader.

In 1917 this battalion was subordinated to the Alpine Corps, which was on the Rumanian front. In the attack on the village of Gastegi, still in January of 1917, the Rommel battle group used a tactic developed by him: binding the enemy before the front with part of his forces, surrounding them with the main body and attacking them from the rear. At Gastegi the Rommel battle group took 400 prisoners.

Only after his transfer to Italy, after Karl I. of Austria had called on Wilhelm II for help on August 26, 1917, did the fame of the young officer Rommel grow and glow. On October 24 the 12th battle of Isonzo began. The German Alpine Corps saw its first full-scale action in Italy. By October 22, Rommel's battalion had already reached the assembly area. "Here we had a well-equipped and equally well-prepared enemy before us," Rommel recorded.

When the attack began on October 24, the Alpine Corps was on the right wing. The Sprösser Battalion had the task of covering the right flank of the Bavarian Guards. The target was a long range of hills with three peaks: the Kuk, the Hum, and Monte Matajur. There three Italian lines of defense had been spotted.

Rommel's company in the Sprösser Battalion reached the first of these three defense lines and overwhelmed it in its first advance. Shortly thereafter, Rommel led the spearhead of his men into the second line of defense. Here they disguised themselves as Italians and made their way along a narrow path to the Italian reserve position.

The third line of defense on Monte Matajur now lay before them. Since the Bavarian Guards had come to a stop under the massed Italian artillery fire, their commander, Major Count Bothmer, ordered Rommel, who was subordinate to him, not to push forward. Rommel replied: "I would like to mention that I receive my commands exclusively from Major Sprösser."

And on the morning of October 25, Major Sprösser was agreeable to the continuation of Rommel's attack and subordinated another mountain company of his battalion to *Oberleutnant* Rommel. In addition, he added part of his machine-gun company to this ad-hoc battle group.

The attack was continued. Rommel's battle group proceeded to capture twelve officers and 200 men. By evening, though, he had not yet reached Monte Matajur.

In the first light of dawn on October 26, Major Sprösser sent the whole battalion through the breach. Rommel was already moving forward again and had passed through the open country even before daylight. A little later, his men encountered the Salerno Brigade. Their first opposition was broken, 43 officers and 1500 men were taken prisoner. The breakthrough had succeeded. But Rommel commanded: "Push ahead. Take the whole range. Roll up the positions all the way to the lowlands."

On the evening of October 26, Monte Matajur was firmly in German hands. 150 officers and 9000 men had surrendered to the Rommel battle group. The British historian Cyril Falls commented: "The fact of this attack, as Rommel describes it, is an extraordinary example of a capable and venturesome undertaking, such as one very seldom finds in the annals of modern war."

For the conquest of Monte Matajur, *Oberleutnant* Rommel was awarded the *Pour le Mérite* medal on December 10, 1917, the youngest officer in the army to receive it.

At Longarone on the Piave front, Rommel achieved the greatest of his series of successes with another Hussar trick. With just one strengthened company, his troops — far out in front again — pushed into the city, through which an Italian division was just marching. Rommel blocked this long column's line of march, had his soldiers move forward on the flanks and made the enemy believe he had a large body of troops. The enemy surrendered; ten thousand Italians marched off as prisoners.

In all of this action, Rommel developed the freedom of thinking that was to stand him in good stead later as Commander of the 7th Panzer Division in France and then as Commanding General of the *Afrika-Korps* and Commander of the *Panzerarmee Afrika*.

Rommel had made his own observations of mobile infantry combat. Later he applied them capably to the leadership of armored units.

Between Two World Wars

In the staff of General Command 64, Rommel was promoted to *Hauptmann* and experienced in this unit the depressing events of the ending stages and final defeat. Yet he remained a soldier. At that time his Fatherland already meant more to him than any other confession of faith. He was one of those 4000 officers who remained in active army service. His old 124th Regiment took him back. After it was disbanded in 1921, Rommel joined Infantry Regiment 13 in Stuttgart. On November 27, 1916 he had married Lucie-Maria Mollin. On Christmas Eve of 1928 their only child, a son named Manfred, was born. Rommel stayed in Stuttgart until September of 1929.

In October of that year he was ordered to the Infantry School in Dresden. His promotion to Major and a troop command, as commander of a mountain battalion, followed in 1933. With that Erwin Rommel saw the goal he had wanted: a front command with a troop that was meant to fight in the mountains.

In Goslar, the garrison of his Jäger battalion, Rommel took everything he had experienced and put into the book *Infanterie greift an* (*Infantry Attacks*) and used it to train his troops. His battalion became one of the best in the army.

In 1935 Erwin Rommel, who had been promoted to *Oberstleutnant* on March 1, met Hitler, who visited his battalion. Himmler and Goebbels accompanied Hitler, so that Rommel could also get a first impression of them. It was Dr. Goebbels who drew Hitler's attention to Rommel. As a result, *Oberstleutnant* Rommel was ordered to the Potsdam War College at the end of 1935. Here he was soon informed that he was to function as the Wehrmacht's liaison officer to the staff of the Hitler Youth leader, Baldur von Schirach. In this position it was his duty to oversee the pre-military training of the Hitler Youth.

At this time Hitler had just read Rommel's book *Infanterie greift an* and was fascinated by it. He appointed the officer, who had been promoted to *Oberst* on August 1, 1937, to be the Commander of the newly formed Führer Escort Battalion. With this battalion, Erwin Rommel took on the task of protecting Hitler during his visits to Wehrmacht areas.

In November Rommel was briefly the Commander of the War College at Wiener-Neustadt, where he stayed until March of 1939. After that he returned to his former position.

In the Polish campaign too, Rommel and his battalion accompanied Hitler on his visits to the front and was present at almost all the Führer's conferences and camp speeches. Thus he had the opportunity of experiencing all phases of this first "Blitz" campaign at the control center.

He used this experience at once to complete his personal knowledge of the leadership of a fast attack, carried by panzer units, deep into the field: the prerequisite for successful Blitzkrieg action.

With the "Gespenster" Division in France

On August 1, 1939 Erwin Rommel was promoted to *Generalmajor*. When he asked for a new command, Hitler agreed and left the choice of which unit he wanted to command to Rommel. Rommel requested a Panzer division.

At Bad Godesberg he took command of the 7th Panzer Division, newly formed of the 2nd Light Division, on February 15, 1940.

Rommel had reached the goal he had wanted. Now he had a new fast-moving unit at his command, with which it was possible for him to test out the principles he had worked out. These were: Always stay in motion! Give the enemy no time! Utilize every chance that is available and every backward movement of the enemy! He trained the 7th Panzer Division according to these principles. He was aggressive and dynamic, surprising and always commanding from the front. His commanders also had to lead from the front whenever it was possible.

When the western campaign began, the 7th Panzer Division stormed forward. Rommel's task was to protect the right flank of Army Group A, under *Generaloberst* von Rundstedt, and break the enemy front between Liege and Sedan. The AOK had given his units the following command:

"The success of the operation depends on the fast advance of the Panzer divisions . . . The fastest advance of the 7th Panzer Division is especially important."

By the evening of May 10, when the western campaign began, the 7th Panzer Division had gained 20 kilometers of ground. At daybreak on May 13, the first parts of the division crossed the Meuse, reaching Avesnes on May 17. At the heights of La Cateau, Rommel assembled his commanders and gave his classic command:

"Further line of march Le Cateau - Arras - Amiens - Rouen -Le Havre."

"Here the 'Rommel Road' began," reported General of the Panzer Troops Hasso von Manteuffel in his *History of the 7th PD*. From now on the movement, that has been called "Rommeling" since that day, began. In a tank battle at Flavion, 33 enemy tanks were destroyed. Rommel saw Philippeville in the Panzer company under *Hauptmann* Adalbert Schulz. The enemy, who stopped here, was defeated, and in the further advance to Vodecée, 13 enemy tanks were shot down by Schulz's tanks.

For the success of May 16 and 17, *Generalmajor* Rommel was decorated with the Knight's Cross of the Iron Cross.

After the first part of the French campaign ended, the 7th Panzer Division was given a few days' rest. When the second phase began, they stormed out of the L'Etoile-Bourdon sector, west of Amiens, and across the Somme to the south. *Generaloberst* Hermann Hoth reported on this advance:

"The 7th PD, on the first day of the attack, created the prerequisites that allowed the XV. Panzer Corps, coming across country in the next few days and breaking all opposition, to advance to the Seine."

They were "Rommeling" as never before. Rommel's radio reports drove the division on to "faster", then "fastest" and finally "fastest, highest speed forward!"

A little later the division stormed to the ocean at Fécamp, 200 kilometers ahead of the corps. The artillery had to fight at St. Valéry, and Rommel wished the troops a "first good bath in the sea" after the city surrendered.

Along the way a parody came into existence, its seventh verse making clear who was the driving force of this incredible Panzer raid:
"Auf der Rommelbahn nachts um Halb Drei
jagen Geister mit Achtzig vorbei!
Rommel selbst voran, jeder hält sich dran,
auf der Rommelbahn nachts um Halb Drei."

When all the guns in France fell silent on June 25, *Generaloberst* von Kluge wrote of the commander and his "ghost division":
"Among the deeds of the German Army, the 7th PD holds a special place. Boldly and at the same time sensibly led by their commander, who had already proved himself particularly in the World War, they hurried from victory to victory . . . Major General Rommel became a model of German troop leadership for all time."

Rommel After Africa

Field Marshal Rommel had no particular assignments until July of 1943. Only on July 27 did he receive orders from Hitler to go to Saloniki to observe the situation there. After Mussolini's fall in Italy, Hitler called Rommel back again. In Rastenburg he said to him after his report: "Marshal Rommel, I expect to have to march into Italy. You will then lead Army Group H in northern Italy."

On August 17, Field Marshal Rommel moved into his new staff quarters in Italy. He had the Goth Line set up between Pisa and Rimini. Now there were two commanders in Italy: Field Marshal Rommel in the north and Field Marshal Kesselring in the south. Only in October did Hitler place all of Italy under the command of

Field Marshal Kesselring. After an intermezzo of examining the defense lines of the Atlantic Wall, Rommel was named Commander of Army Group B, which was subordinated to the commander in the west, Field Marshal von Rundstedt, on December 31, 1943.

Rommel inspected the defense lines and saw to it that a new spirit arose in this "Etappe." Vice-Admiral Ruge commented on this: "Rommel changed the situation from the ground up. Into an atmosphere of absolute indifference he injected hard work and clear plans. With that he raised the troops' morale. This ability of raising the morale of a fighting force is one of the many qualities that made Rommel a great troop leader in World War II."

On June 5 Rommel went home — the situation was described as completely quiet. The weather forecasters had said that no invasion could take place in the next two weeks.

On the next morning, the invasion began in Normandy. On the morning of this day, General Speidel, Chief of Staff of Army Group B, called his commander, who ordered him to have the 21st Panzer Division ready for a counterattack immediately.

But here Rommel lacked the Panzer Lehr Division, which for very obscure reasons was held 150 kilometers away from the place where it should have pushed the enemy back into the ocean.

It was already clear to Rommel on June 11 that Normandy could no longer be held, and that it was necessary to withdraw to a favorable defense line and fight off the enemy attack there. This was reported to Hitler, who appeared at Margival, near Soissons, on June 17. Rommel suggested a risky but very promising military strategy:

"We should hold the British front in the Orne area with the infantry divisions, draw the German Panzer units together on the flanks, and then draw the enemy into this tank trap by a step-by-step withdrawal of the infantry."

Hitler did not agree with this suggestion, which could have changed the situation one last time, but ordered that Normandy must be held. Rommel had one last talk with Hitler on June 29. His attempt to change Hitler's mind failed.

On July 17, Rommel went to the front and visited the position of the I. SS Panzer Corps to discuss the situation with *Oberst-gruppenführer* Dietrich. From there he began the withdrawal at 4:00 P.M. Along the way, his car was attacked by enemy low-level aircraft with bombs and guns, as well as machine-gun salvos. Rommel's head was dashed against the windshield of the car. He fell heavily onto the road and lay there unconscious. His driver, *Unteroffizier* Daniel, had been shot in the shoulder, which had caused him to lose control of the car.

Rommel had a skull fracture, two fractures on the temples, and other injuries. But the Desert Fox survived. The great tragedy of his life was still before him.

Death of a Field Marshal

In February of 1944, Erwin Rommel had received Dr. Karl Strölin at his home in Ulm. Strölin had told him that he was the only one who could prevent a civil war, and that it was his duty to give his support to the resistance movement and thus save Germany.

But Rommel, who had not been informed of the plans to assassinate Hitler because he never would have approved of it, advocated bringing Hitler into open court and accusing him. After that he would be ready to take command of the army.

After the attempt on Hitler's life on June 20, 1944, the great officer "cleanup" began. Rommel, who had returned to his home in Ulm after his recovery, received an invitation from Field Marshal Keitel, after much negotiation, to come to a conference in Berlin. Rommel suspected what this would amount to and declined. Rommel said to Vice-Admiral Ruge, who was his guest on October 11, that he probably would not have come through that trip alive.

On October 13, Field Marshal Rommel was informed that two generals from Berlin had made an appointment to see him on the 14th.

On his last day of life, Erwin Rommel put on his *Afrika-Korps* uniform. Hitler's henchmen, Generals Burgsdorf and Maisel, were on time. They revealed to the Field Marshal that he would either be tried by a People's Court or given a small pill to take. In the first case, he would be condemned to death and his wife would not receive a pension. In the second case, he would be given a state funeral and his wife and son would be supported in the future.

Field Marshal Erwin Rommel decided on the second course and thus assured his family's future. In the executioners' car he took the capsule of poison, bit into it and fell to the side. The Desert Fox was dead.

Erwin Rommel received a state funeral. The German radio broadcast that he had died of the wounds that he had sustained in Normandy. The telegram that the Führer sent to Mrs. Rommel and Rommel's son Manfred was the epitome of hypocrisy. Hitler had foreseen only one thing correctly: "The name of Field Marshal Rommel will be linked forever with the heroic fighting in North Africa."

Field Marshal Rommel, the military commander who had risked his life more than once on the front lines, is still honored today by friend and foe. African fighting men from Germany, Britain, South Africa, New Zealand and Australia come to the meetings of the *Afrika-Korps* Society. For all who knew him, he is and will always remain a shining example who banned inhumanity from his area of command and blazed a trail for humanity in the world through his courage and his love for Germany. Friends and foes alike will always cherish his memory.

Erwin Rommel, born in Heidenheim: November 15, 1891.
Last rank: Generalfeldmarschall.
Pour le Mèrite: December 10, 1917.
Knight's Cross of the Iron Cross: May 27, 1940.
Oak Leaves to the Knight's Cross: March 30, 1941.
Swords to the Knight's Cross with Oak Leaves: January 20, 1942.
Diamonds to the Knight's Cross with Oak Leaves and Swords: March 11, 1943.
Death: October 14, 1944.

US $49.99

9 780887 402920   54999

ISBN: 978-0-88740-292-0

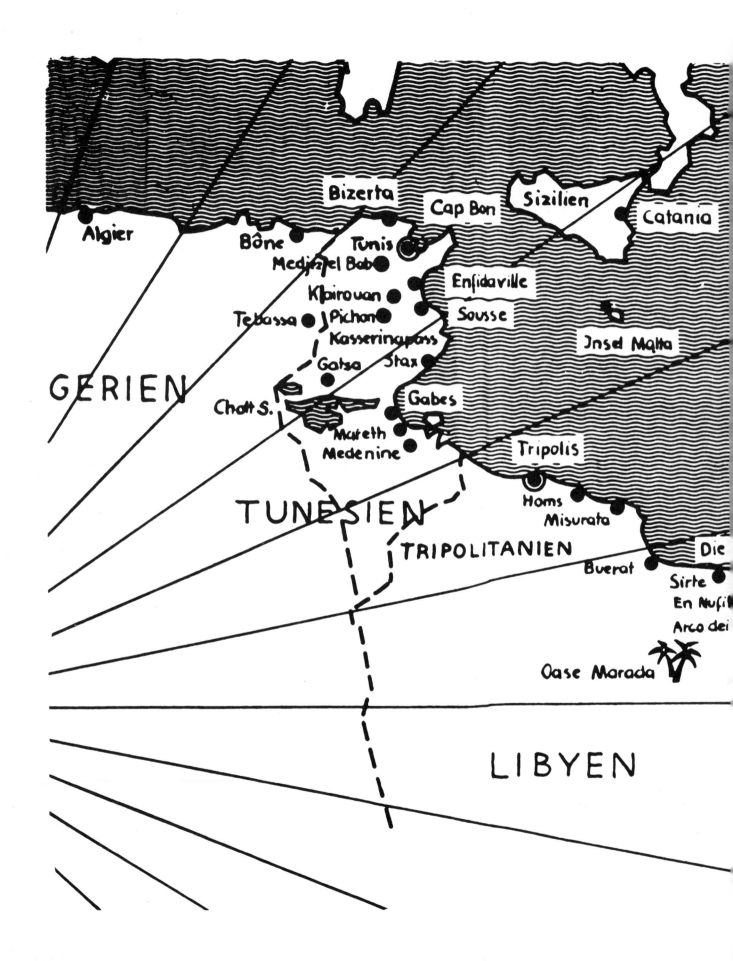